SAI BABA

SAI BABA

THE
ULTIMATE
EXPERIENCE

Phyllis Krystal

SAMUEL WEISER, INC.

York Beach, Maine

First published in 1994 by
Samuel Weiser, Inc.
Box 612
York Beach, Maine 03910-0612

99 98 97 96
9 8 7 6 5 4 3 2

Library of Congress Cataloging-in-Publication Data

Krystal, Phyllis
    Sai Baba : the ultimate experience / by Phyllis Krystal.
        p.   cm.
    Originally published: Los Angeles, Calif. : Aura books, 1985.
    1. Sathya Sai Baba, 1926-   .   2. Spiritual life--Hinduism.
    I. Title.
    BL1175.S385K79   1994
    294.5'092--dc20   93-44598
                                                          CIP
ISBN 0-87728-794-5
MV

Cover photograph was taken by the author.

Typeset in 10 point Palatino

Printed in the United States of America

The paper used in this publication meets the minimum requirements of the American National Standard for Permanence of Paper
for Printed Library Materials Z39.48-1984.

Dedicated to
Sri Sathya Sai Baba

CONTENTS

PREFACE

WHY HAVE I undertaken the formidable task of writing a book about Sai Baba? It is indeed a challenge, and one I would never have dreamed of undertaking on my own initiative. How could an ordinary human being do justice to such a multi-faceted personality who is reputed to be a divine *Avatar*? I most certainly did not feel competent to do so.

For the past twenty-five years or more I have been involved in an inner search for meaning to life, using a meditation technique which can be likened to a waking dream, or reverie. The result of this quest is a method consisting of a series of visualization exercises and symbols. These can be used in counseling sessions, and can also be given to individuals to practice independently in the privacy of their own homes.

Many people with whom I have worked in this way urged me to write a book about this method. I was, however, far too busy using it, in addition to my roles of wife and mother, to find time to devote to such a task. Moreover, I have never entertained the slightest aspiration to be a writer. I firmly believed that I had found the work I enjoyed, and craved no other. However, the pressure from those who had benefited from the work to make it available in book form, to reach a wider audience, increased to the point where I finally agreed to attempt it.

When I took the finished manuscript to Sai Baba to ask for his blessing, I also asked his permission to add a chapter at the end about him. Instead, to my surprise, he directed me to write a separate book about him.

Many books have been written by far more experienced writers about Baba and his teachings, miracles, and healing. I have therefore decided to limit my own account as much as possible to my personal experiences, impressions, and learning. I have tried to show how Baba has led me, by one barely indicated step at a time, along the path which he is able to ascertain as being the correct one for me. In this way he has been the supreme Zen Master. There are many different paths from which a master selects the appropriate one according to the individual requirements of each aspirant. Even though many thousands of people throng to visit Baba to obtain his blessing, he can not only tell exactly which ones are ready to tread the inner path back to union with the God within, but just which path is best suited to each one for the attainment of that goal. He recommends the path of *bhakti*, or devotion, for the majority of people living in this present *yuga*, or age, as it is the safest method for everyone. However, even when many people happen to be taking a similar path, the actual steps along the way are very different, as are the various tests which determine the progress and understanding of each individual devotee.

Baba says himself that he is a divine *Avatar* who has incarnated in the world at this present time of great stress to help humanity to rediscover the ancient wisdom with which to avert disaster. Other divine *Avatars*, such as Rama and Krishna, have likewise taken human form in past periods of extreme crisis to help and guide people in a similar way. Baba's primary and self-assumed task is first to teach the people of his native India, and reconnect that country and its people to their ancient heritage of Vedic teachings, which have been neglected in favor of the materialistic aspects of Western culture and customs. He also graciously extends his love and attention to people from all over the world who have found their way to him.

In this microcosmic account of my own very personal experiences with Baba I have presented his many diverse roles as wise teacher and spiritual *guru*, loving parent, both mother and father, friend and comforter, healer and psychologist. In addition, I have attempted to show his vaster, macrocosmic aspects as diplomat and administrator, advisor and educator, and above all, world leader.

There are many people who are far better qualified to present his many-faceted personality and full active life, because they have lived daily in his immediate presence for long periods at a time. Such close proximity has enabled them to observe him under all kinds of circumstances and with thousands of different people. Many have known him since he was a child and have watched his development over the years.

I have visited him for only short periods at a time, at yearly intervals. However, as I look back over those brief visits, I can see a pattern beginning to emerge, revealing the method he has been using to teach me. This pattern is also reflected in the vaster plan he has used to initiate his world mission at this turbulent time in the world's history and evolution. As the world is peopled with individuals, both approaches are necessary for the whole plan to become visible and active.

This account, to be meaningful, must necessarily be about my own personal experiences since they form the basis of all I have become to know about him. However, I wish to stress that my firm intention has been, first and foremost, to present him and his teachings with references to myself only because through his effect on my life can be glimpsed, as in a window or mirror, the effect he can have on the lives of all who seek his help.

My hope is that many people who read this book will feel drawn to Baba and his message and wish to join his devotees in helping to bring his mission to fruition in this troubled world. However, it is not necessary to be with his physical form in India, nor will he always be easily accessible, as he has announced that he will be withdrawing from public appearances. In line with this decision is one of his latest messages, "Inner view not interview." In other words, everyone who is ready and willing to make the attempt can directly contact within themselves that spark of the Divine inherent in everyone and every living thing. I hope to show how this is possible.

ACKNOWLEDGMENTS

First and foremost, I offer my heartfelt thanks to Sai Baba for his physical presence in the world and for the opportunity it presents to all who so desire to allow him to ignite the spark of the Divine within each one.

I also honor and thank this same spark within the countless people who have in so many ways, and with such love, helped me in the writing of this book.

I wish to express my deep appreciation to my husband, Sidney, our daughter, Sheila, and our deceased daughter, Lorna, for all they have taught me.

In particular I thank Sidney for his support throughout the years and during the preparation of this book; and Sheila for her invaluable assistance in thoughtful and careful editing of the manuscript.

CHAPTER ONE

"WHO IS SAI BABA? He is love, love, love." I can still hear Baba's lilting voice singing this little refrain as he entered the interview room at his *ashram* one day. Repeating it softly, he moved with a light skipping step to welcome the assembled devotees whom he had invited to a group interview. Thus, in his inimitable way, he answered the question which is always uppermost in everyone's mind. His own seemingly simple statement is actually the truth. However, he himself is by no means simple.

I first heard about Baba in April of 1972, a few days before my husband, Sidney, and I left on a trip to northern India, my second visit to that country. A few days before our departure we visited a local bookshop to purchase reading material for the long plane flight ahead of us. As I reached up to a high shelf to pull down a book, another book fell down at the same time, barely missing my head. I picked it up and was immediately impressed by the picture of a most striking looking man on the cover beneath the title *Baba*, by Arnold Schulman. I remember my surprise that here was a holy man I had never seen or heard of before. I wondered how I could have missed him since I had read all I could find about Eastern teachers and their methods. Besides, this one was so unusual looking that I was certain that once seen, I could not easily have forgotten him. His was not a typically Indian face, though I scarcely noticed the rest of his features as my attention was riveted on his eyes, which seemed to penetrate clear through to my very core.

I have learned through my work to watch for what I have come to call "signs" to help to guide me in my daily life, so I took this particular incident as a sign to look more closely at this book which had fallen not into my lap, but almost on top of my head. As I leafed through it, hoping to discover what the message for me might be, I paused to study more carefully several other pictures of Baba. They showed him with a wide variety of different expressions and attitudes, but always clad in the same simple long straight orange or reddish robe. His dark hair looked like a halo around his head, and those extraordinary eyes seemed to dominate everything. As I studied each picture I began to feel very strongly drawn to him and wanted to know more about him. So I added this book to the others I had already selected to read on our approaching journey. However, the attraction was so compelling that I started to read it as soon as I reached home. Once started I found it impossible to put down and finished it before we left home. I was fascinated by the concept of Sai Baba, but even more by the strange way he seemed to speak to me from the pages of the book. I soon found that I was developing an extremely strong desire to meet him in person, and as soon as possible! I looked at the schedule we had outlined and realized to my dismay that it would not be at all practical to try to arrange to visit him while we were in northern India. We would be far from either his house in Whitefield, on the outskirts of Bangalore, or his *ashram* at Puttaparthi, in Andhra Pradesh, both in southern India. Our itinerary had been planned in advance with all the flights and hotel reservations confirmed. We were to leave in a few days, which left no time to try to make any changes. However hard I tried to rearrange it in my mind, I could find no space for even a flying visit to him, which caused me great frustration.

Since then I have heard Baba say on many occasions that no one ever visits him unless and until he so wishes, as the timing is very significant in a person's life. Several years later we were to observe how true that statement could be, when several friends who planned to accompany us to see Baba were all prevented from leaving at the last minute for various reasons. One by one, they were obliged to cancel their plans due to unexpected situations arising in their lives stopping them from leaving home at the appointed time. For example, one young woman planned to board a plane to India from Paris. She went to the airport on three successive days, only to discover that, for various reasons, the plane would not be leaving. She finally got the point and canceled her flight. Some time later, as each one looked back, it was very clear that it would not have been appropriate for any of them to be away from home at that time.

But none of this did I know at the time of my first exposure to Baba through the book I had just read, and I was increasingly beset with feelings of frustration at the prospect of going to India, yet not being able to meet him. It was on this wistful note that I started that trip.

Our first stop was Rangoon, Burma, where we had gone for the first time eleven years earlier, in January 1961, before the present military government came to power. At that time I had fallen in love with both the country and the people. We had been given letters of introduction to several families living in Rangoon, and had made some wonderful friends with whom we had kept in touch from time to time by letters.

Under the new regime the country had been closed to visitors for several years. As soon as we heard that the regulations had been relaxed to allow tourists to stay for just seven days, including arrival and departure days, we decided to take advantage of the opportunity to return. We were anxious to see our friends again, and also to see for ourselves the changes barely hinted at in the news columns and referred to only obliquely in our friends letters. We also wanted to return to the meditation center in Rangoon where we had studied a type of Buddhist meditation, or mind training, called *satipatthana*. This method had been initiated by the Buddha and reintroduced into Burma by Buddhist priests, or Mahasi Sayadaws as they are called. On our earlier visit we had been privileged to take a short course of meditation under the direct supervision of the acting Mahasi Sayadaw, which had proved to be such a rewarding experience that we hoped to be allowed to repeat it, if only for a few days.

This second stay was a complete contrast to our previous one in every way. As soon as we arrived in Rangoon we were deeply shocked to see many signs of the way this lovely country had been allowed to deteriorate in every area. We were particularly aware of the change in the people, whom we had remembered as being some of the most delightful, friendly, hospitable and happy people we had met anywhere in the world. Now, as we looked around on the streets, we observed an air of gloom and hopelessness. We had alerted our friends ahead of our arrival that we would be visiting again, so we got in touch with each family as soon as we had settled into our hotel. They were all overjoyed to see us again, as we represented a breath of fresh air from the outside world from which they had been cut off for so many years. But we were also keenly aware of their barely concealed fear of being seen with foreigners, and learned that they now lived under constant surveillance by the military police. Once, they had been successful citizens of a thriving country, and had alternated regular periods of retreat in a meditation center with their work. They were now, literally, prisoners in their own country, afraid to speak to anyone for fear of being reported to the police for the slightest transgression of the rigid rules. On our last day they threw caution to the winds and we all gathered together for a farewell dinner. We enjoyed a gay evening reminiscent of those we had shared with them the first time. The next morning when we had to leave, they all insisted on seeing us off at the airport. Our last glimpse of them, as they clustered in a tight little knot waving to us and smiling with tears in their eyes, made us feel guilty. We were leaving them locked into a life without hope of relief while we were free to travel anywhere we wished in the world, secure in the knowledge that we would be returning to a country where we were not only free, but able to live a full life with comparatively few restrictions. As our plane took off, and they appeared like small dots on the ground, we wondered if or when we would see them again.

In this heavy mood we flew to Calcutta for a very brief overnight stop before continuing to Darjeeling. As I looked down from the plane to catch a last sight of the country I had previously enjoyed so much, I suddenly recalled my own frustration before leaving home when I had realized that I should not be able to see Baba during this particular trip. I compared it with the heavy daily frustrations which darkened the lives of the Burmese people who had little hope of any relief in the near future and I felt thoroughly ashamed of my own impatience. I learned much later that such insights are typical with many people after first hearing about Baba. In some strange way, defying explanation, he reaches out to teach those who make even a slight contact with him, wherever they may be.

As if to prove this point a strange thing happened while we were in the hotel in Calcutta that one night. Before dinner we decided to stretch our legs, which were stiff from the flight, by wandering around the hotel lobby and shipping area. We found an antique shop still open, so we went in to look around. I was really startled to see a large photograph of Sai Baba on the desk of the proprietor, who stood up to greet us as we entered. The thought went through my mind that I would not have recognized Baba if I had not so recently read the book about him. The owner had noticed my interest and asked with surprise if I knew who Baba was. I in turn asked if he was a follower of Baba. He replied that not only was he himself a devotee but so were several members of his family. He wanted to know how I had heard about Baba. I told him about Arnold Schulman's book, and he in turn suggested that I read another book, *Sai Baba, Man of Miracles* by Howard Murphet, an Australian, as it had been responsible for introducing him to Baba. He gave us the address of a bookshop situated not far from the hotel. He thought it would still be open and might possibly have a copy in stock.

Before taking our leave of him I asked if he carried any pieces of antique Moghul jewelery in his shop. He replied that he did not have any at the time but that one of his brothers, who operated a similar shop in New Delhi, had a fine collection. On hearing that we would be going to that city, he gave us his brother's business card. When we looked at it, we were astonished to see that his brother was a man whom we had met when we were in India in 1967 and whom we planned to see again this time. We had kept in contact with him by letter and had also seen him in the States from time to time since our first meeting. We were genuinely surprised to learn that he and his family were also devotees of Baba. In fact, we found that news very hard to believe as he had always been very sceptical of spiritual beliefs and gave the impression that he was agnostic and left religious pursuits to his wife. I clearly remember thinking that if Baba could make an impression on this man he must be extremely powerful and convincing.

We thanked the owner of the shop for his help, and hurried to the bookshop hoping it would still be open and have in stock a copy of the book he had recommended. We were to discover, more and more as we became further involved with Baba, that in some strange way things would work out so that we would find something we needed at exactly the right time. As a perfect illustration, we found that the shop was still open and an obliging salesman was able to find a copy of the book, tucked in behind some others on a shelf. It was very dusty, but fortunately intact. I could now look forward to reading more about Baba, even though I could not see him on this trip.

From then on, I began to notice that wherever we went pictures of him appeared in the most unexpected places as if he were greeting us along the way. It occurred to me that he was accompanying us in spirit by way of his pictures and the book about him.

For many years I had been seeking a method to help me to advance further along the spiritual path. My search had taken me to many places and exposed me to numerous teachers and methods. In all of them I had found something of interest but never enough to involve me completely, or convince me that I had found my right way. So I continued my search whenever an opportunity presented itself.

Before leaving on this present trip, besides planning to return to Burma to revisit the meditation center, we had also arranged to meet Gopi Krishna who lives in Srinigar, Kashmir. I had been in correspondence with him after reading his interesting book, *Kundalini*. In it he recounted his personal experiences, of inadvertently arousing his *kundalini* after many years of meditation. He described in vivid detail the extraordinary affect this occurrence had on every aspect of his life. When he finally learned the nature of it, he eventually managed to steer his way through it to a state of unusual clarity. He expounded upon his theory, born of his own experiences, that it culminates in a condition of expanded awareness. He felt certain that it was equally possible for many other spiritual aspirants to attain this state if they were provided with the necessary instructions on how to control the process, and thus avoid the tumult into which he himself had been thrown. He also felt very strongly that the discoveries he had made along the way were of interest to science and religion alike. He envisioned helping to unite these two disciplines in a joint attempt to discover a method to help mankind to offset the negative forces which are becoming increasingly active in the world. He had attracted the attention of several prominent scientists, and hoped to enlist their aid in initiating a research project. By using the available ancient writings on the subject, along with his own personal experiences and observations, he hoped to develop a safe course of instruction for those men and women who elected to participate in the proposed experiment, and who were judged by a select committee to be suitable candidates.

When we arrived in Srinigar we telephoned him. He invited us to spend an afternoon with him at his house and told us about his hopes and plans for the experiments he had outlined. They were very interesting, but almost as soon as we met, I became aware of a strong feeling mounting within me that although this was one more method which had much to recommend it for others, it was not for me. So, after joining him for tea, we thanked him and went on our way.

Our next stop was New Delhi. We telephoned our friend, the antique dealer, and told him about our unexpected meeting with his brother in Calcutta. He was surprised and delighted, and suggested we meet as soon as possible. After we had exchanged greetings and given him news of his brother, we told him of our conversation about Sai Baba. He then told us how he and his family had gone to see Baba and were now his devotees. He regaled us with stories about Baba and his miraculous powers, his over-powering love, and his simple yet profound teachings, all of which whetted my appetite even more for personal contact with him. I suffered a fresh pang of regret that it would not be possible at that time. Our friend was most sympathetic and gave me a picture he had taken of Baba during a recent visit to his many devotees in New Delhi. I was delighted to receive my first picture of him, which was more personal than those in the books.

During our lunch together I mentioned that I was suffering from an upset stomach probably caused by some food I had eaten, at a dinner on a houseboat the previous night. Our friend gave me a tiny envelope with Baba's picture printed on it. He added that it contained *vibhuti*, or holy ash, which could be used as a medicine. He instructed me to dip my finger into the lightly scented greyish powder and put a little of it in the center of my forehead, and a pinch of it on my tongue. He added that I could use it as a healing agent whenever the need arose. This was my first introduction to Baba's *vibhuti*. I accepted it gratefully, and used it as directed without any hesitation. I later realized that this was most unusual, as I am very cautious about taking anything which might possibly cause an allergic reaction.

He next suggested that on our return home we should get in touch with an American whom he had met while at Baba's *ashram*, who could tell us about his experiences. He gave us his name and address in San Francisco. As we parted he used a strange new phrase, "Sai Ram", which we were to hear many times, used both as greeting and farewell. It means simply, that Sai is God, since Ram is for Rama, an accepted divine *avatar* for the Hindus. It is usually accompanied by a gesture in which both hands are placed with palms together, as in prayer, and held in front of one. It conveys a greeting from the in-dwelling God in one person to the in-dwelling God in the other. This gesture, called *namaskar*, is more usual in India.

CHAPTER TWO

SOON AFTER WE returned to Los Angeles we flew to Oakland to visit our elder daughter, Sheila. While there we decided to try to get in touch with the man whose name and address we had been given by our friend in New Delhi. He had apparently moved several times and, when we finally located him, we were disappointed to be told that he was no longer a follower of Sai Baba. He had joined a group attached to another master. However, when he heard that we lived in Los Angeles he told us that there were several active Sai Baba centers in Southern California. He gave us the address and telephone number of the one in Hollywood, nearest to where we lived at that time.

After returning home, I telephoned the center and spoke to Janet Bock. She and her husband, Richard, were the center directors. She very kindly outlined the weekly schedule and suggested that we might like to attend an open meeting. These were held every Friday evening for the benefit of anyone who, like us, was interested in hearing more about Baba. We decided to attend the next Friday.

When we arrived at the center, we found that the meeting was being held on the ground floor of a large rambling house. As we approached the front door we could hear the sound of singing and smell the scent of burning incense. The door was quickly opened at our knock, and we found ourselves facing a group of people sitting cross-legged on the floor, singing in a strange language which we assumed was Indian. We hastily sat down on the floor with them but I was immediately asked to move. It was quietly explained that at such meetings it is customary for men and women to sit separately, the men on one side of the room and the women on the other, with a narrow space left between the two groups. In my ignorance I had sat down next to my husband on the men's side, a mistake I took care never to repeat.

Much later, in answer to our question about this seating arrangement, it was explained that it is a custom at religious gatherings in India, and one which Baba honors. It originates from the fact that any unnecessary distraction makes it difficult for most people to concentrate on spiritual practices, particularly during meditation. The close proximity of a person of the opposite sex can be one of the most powerful distractions, especially when people sit in rows on the floor, often so close together that their bodies touch. This close contact can set up a stimulating current which makes it much harder to quiet the active mind and to draw thoughts away from the outer world in order to concentrate within. We understood the reasoning, though at first we still found it strange, because of the Western custom in churches and temples for whole families to sit in the same pew. However, after a short time it lost its strangeness.

This first meeting was also our introduction to the singing of *bhajans* which are devotional songs similar to hymns. As we did not know the words or tunes we could not participate in the singing, so I took this opportunity to look around the room.

There were quite a number of pictures of Baba hanging on the walls. At the end of the room towards which we were all facing, an altar had been set up. On it were vases of flowers, lighted candles in containers, burning sticks of incense, and more pictures of Sai Baba. I experienced a twinge of anxiety as I recalled the altars I had so often seen during my childhood in England, displaying pictures of Jesus Christ, his mother Mary and the Cross instead of pictures of Sai Baba. I thought I had left all that behind when I moved to the U.S.A. Was I becoming involved in another religion after I had turned away from formal religion as soon as I left England because it had not provided the answers I sought? Obviously, I would not be able to answer that question until I had experienced more of Baba and his teachings. So, with that thought, I pushed aside my doubts.

The *bhajans*, however, were very different from the hymns I had sung as a child, so I gave my full attention to them. I noticed that several people, both men and women, were accompanying the singing with Indian drums, small bells, hand cymbals, and harmonium. The combination of these simple instruments created a very interesting and pleasing effect, very different from the somber organ music of my youth. I also became aware that a man and a woman would alternate in leading the *bhajans*. Each one introduced the *bhajan* by singing one line which was then repeated like a chorus by all those who knew the words. This pattern was repeated several times at an increasing tempo until the last line was again sung very slowly. The whole performance was very moving.

I looked at the people gathered there and observed that they represented many different types and were from varied backgrounds. They were of all ages, from babies lying asleep on the floor beside their mothers to old people sitting at the back of the room in chairs which had been thoughtfully provided for those who might find it difficult to sit cross-legged on the floor. Two features everyone seemed to have in common were a great enthusiasm in singing the *bhajans,* and a clearly perceptible love for Baba shining from their eyes.

I must admit that I began to feel very strange in participating, even to such a small extent, in a group so obviously worshipping the figure Baba as if he were God. In the inner work in which I had been engaged for many years, I had been constantly warned against worship of a human being, however advanced he may be. Yet here I was with a group of people vocally adoring Sai Baba who certainly possessed a human body, though a very distinctive looking one! But despite my doubts I felt irresistibly drawn to him and especially to one picture of him in the center of the altar which depicted his radiantly smiling face framed in its halo of black hair. As I looked at it I became aware that I was quite irrationally certain that he was smiling directly at me. I also felt that in some strange way he knew everything I was thinking, doubts and all, yet understood, and could smile indulgently, as if to say, "Yes, it is natural and right that you should question, and even doubt now, but you will soon comprehend."

My silent reverie was abruptly broken when the singing came to an end, and a man I later learned was Dick Bock announced that there would be a short meditation. I was now on more familiar ground as we had practiced several different forms of meditation during our many years of searching for more understanding of life. I was glad to have this opportunity to withdraw within after having been assailed by so many strange experiences. After what seemed like a few seconds, but was closer to ten minutes, the meditation was brought to an end by more singing, this time of a chant intoned by everyone. While it was going on I noticed a movement among the lines of people, and observed that a small jar containing the same lightly scented ash, or *vibhuti,* I had been given in New Delhi was being passed around. When it was handed to me, a woman sitting next to me motioned to me to put some in the middle of my forehead and a little on the tip of my tongue. I dipped my finger into the soft grey powder, and as I did so I was reminded of the first time I had done this. I realized with a jolt that I had recovered from the stomach upset from which I had been suffering at that time much more quickly than would ordinarily have been expected. Was my fast recovery due to the fact that I had taken the *vibhuti*? At that thought I felt a slight shiver slide down my spine. Maybe my imagination was playing tricks on me, or had the *vibhuti* really helped? I passed the jar to the woman next to me, and watched as it made its way down the lines and was finally taken back to the altar, where it was placed beside a similar jar which had been passed on the men's side.

The meeting ended with the showing of a film taken by Dick Bock in India. It depicted Baba moving among the crowds of people who had flocked to see him, both at his house near Bangalore and at his *ashram* in Puttaparthi, the village where he was born. I was fascinated by this first sight of him slowly walking in and out among the adoring visitors. Sometimes he was smiling or stopping to talk to a person in the crowd. He frequently held up his hand in a gesture of blessing, while all the eager faces were lifted up in the hope of attracting a glance or word from him. I soon became aware of an electric quality emanating from him even through the film. I was reminded of the similar sensation I had felt while reading the two books about him, as if he were reaching out to me from the printed pages. The more I watched his slight orange-clad form glide gracefully here and there among the crowds, as the film proceeded to show him in different places, my original desire to fly to see him was further increased. I knew with a deep inner certainty that I would not be satisfied until I could have my own firsthand experience of him.

As soon as the film ended everyone started to move around. The Bocks had noticed us come in to the meeting and, as we were strangers, they came over to welcome us. This was not only the beginning of a friendship, but a step towards Baba for us.

We attended meetings from time to time, and began to meet and talk to other devotees. Some of them had already been to see Baba, while others, like ourselves, were interested in learning more about him from those who had already met him. Many people had stories to tell about their experiences to which we eagerly listened.

From then on my mind was full of all I had seen and heard about this remarkable being. We plied the Bocks and other devotees with more questions. In this way we learned about his many facets and the countless different ways in which he affected those who came in contact with him, either in India or at home. It appeared that his influence was not limited by time or place. The more we heard, the more inexplicable he became to us.

As I look back to that first exposure to Baba, I am so thankful that my overwhelming desire to rush to see him when we were in north India was not fulfilled. By the time we did meet him, we were so much better prepared for his actual presence, having attended meetings, talked to other devotees, seen more films depicting his daily life, listened to tapes of him singing *bhajans* or giving a discourse, and read about his teachings from the many Indian books translated into English.

One result of this gradual preparation was that we learned the meaning of many new words and phrases and were also able to pronounce them before we went to India. At first, when we heard them being used so casually by those who were familiar with their meaning, I wondered if I would ever be able to pronounce them with such ease, or use them in the correct context. As they were once so foreign to me they may also be to others.

The word *devotee*, though not an Indian word, should be explained first. I have already used it to differentiate between those people who were already followers of Baba, and newcomers like us who had heard about him, but wished to know more details before forming an opinion, or making any kind of decision or commitment. The word "devotee" means a person who is wholly devoted to someone or something, and whose life is given over entirely to the chosen person, cause, ideal, or interest.

To be a true devotee of Baba means being so deeply interested and involved with him and his teachings that they take first place in that person's life. Obviously, there are many different degrees of devotion and therefore many types of so called devotees according to their understanding of his message. They range from those who are attracted to him in a very superficial way to the very few who have surrendered their lives to him and seek his direction. The latter, Baba says, "are so few in number that they can be counted on the fingers of one of my hands!"

He himself defines three kinds of devotees. First, there are those people who hear what he teaches, but put nothing into action, and so remain unchanged.

Then there are those who hear what Baba tells them to do, but take his words so literally that if he were to tell them to follow a certain path they would follow directions without considering how to circumvent any obstacles blocking their progress. They would attempt to force their way through, or try to push the obstacle aside, instead of using their common sense to find a way around it, or overcome it in some other way, by intelligently applying his teaching.

The third group are those who hear his teaching and apply it in the best possible way to each situation they encounter in their lives, by adapting it to fit the case. This group tries to live Baba's teachings instead of merely hearing and thinking about them. Baba urges all would-be devotees to choose to be this last kind.

One big mistake which many people make is to expect that as soon as a person says he is a devotee of Baba, or some other teacher or system, he immediately and miraculously becomes absolutely honest, wise, unselfish, reliable, loving and, in fact, perfect. Obviously this is not the case at all. The necessary growth which leads to change is a slow, step by step process if it is to be lasting. Therefore, it is most unjust to expect instant perfection either from others or ourselves. This warning, if taken to heart, can save future devotees from a great deal of disillusionment and bitterness. I have heard of many instances of disappointment and resentment resulting from trust mistakenly placed in a person because he professed to be a follower of Baba. It would appear that we must still use our native intelligence and powers of perception to judge for ourselves whether a person is likely to be trustworthy, instead of assuming that he has become pure as driven snow from the moment he met Baba.

Another word which we heard often during those first few weeks was *Avatar* when referring to Baba. It was explained to us that a divine *avatar* is an incarnation of God come to earth in physical form to inspire people anew at a time of great stress. This concept is mentioned in the *Bhagavad-Gita*, which in Sanskrit means "Song of the Lord", and is part of the *Mahabharata*, one of the great Hindu classics. The Gita, as it is often called, is a dialogue in lyric form between Krishna, the divine *avatar* at that time, and Arjuna, a warrior whom Krishna instructs.

Baba has paraphrased Krishna: "For the protection of the virtuous, for the destruction of evil-doers, and for establishing righteousness on a firm footing, I incarnate from age to age."

Darshan is another word frequently used in conversation among devotees. We often heard someone say that he had received Baba's *darshan*, or had attended *darshan* when in India. We were told that it stems from the Sanskrit word *darshana* which means "a seeing," and has come to mean the virtue, uplift or blessing which it is believed the beholder receives when in the presence of a great person. It is a Hindu concept and a little difficult for Westerners to understand, as we have nothing equivalent to it in our culture. The closest comparison is the blessing given by the Pope, most often from a balcony, to the crowd waiting below to receive it.

Most Indians will go to great lengths to achieve even a fleeting glimpse of their chosen teacher, *yogi*, or other charismatic figure, often walking great distances to receive this boon. It is in the hope of receiving Baba's *darshan* that huge crowds gather wherever he is expected to appear, often assembling many hours ahead of his scheduled arrival. We witnessed this phenomenon first in the films shown at the Sai Baba center, and later in India when we experienced it directly for ourselves, and felt the magnetism of his presence.

The word *vibhuti* was at first strange to us. It literally means marvel or wonder. When in the form of ash, it symbolizes the end product to which all material things can be reduced, primarily by fire, which at the same time purifies them. It is then a reminder that all those things we may crave to possess will eventually be rendered into ash or dust, and being therefore without lasting value, cannot provide permanent pleasure or usefulness. As ash is the basic substance, it can represent anything and everything. In this context it can be used to heal, protect, sanctify, or assume whatever symbolic role is needed at any time.

I have already mentioned the singing of *bhajans* at the meetings we attended. They are songs or hymns extolling a particular aspect of God. It is believed that by repeating one or more of the many names of God together with the virtues connected with that particular aspect of the God-force, the singer literally tunes into the power behind it and receives a blessing therefrom.

The word *ashram* also needs to be explained, particularly as it has no exact counterpart in the West, the nearest being a hermitage or monastery. Its literal meaning is a place where man has no *shrama* or struggle, conflict, or effort; a place where peace can be found, a haven. In India it usually includes the whole area surrounding a *guru* or teacher, where people can come to stay while receiving his teaching. *Ashrams* are usually situated in remote places away from the bustle and strife of a big city, so that the visitors have the least possible distraction while meditating or applying the teachings given by the *guru*. Most *ashrams* are extremely simple. They provide the minimum of shelter and food for the pilgrims, the emphasis being on the inner life instead of the outer, as in the case of worldly life.

A *guru* is a teacher. When the term is applied to a spiritual teacher, it means one who leads students from darkness to light, and acts as a guide to spiritual liberation by indicating the path which can lead to the destruction of illusion.

Sai Baba is a divine *Avatar* and a *guru* who lives in an *ashram* where his *devotees* receive his *darshan*. He produces *vibhuti* to heal their bodies, minds and spirits, and sometimes leads them in the singing of *bhajans*.

In addition to Indian words there are various customs, rules and guidelines outlining the appropriate behavior, attitude, and mode of dress required at the *ashram*, which we needed to know.

Towards the end of 1972 we started seriously to discuss the best time to make our first visit to Baba, and decided to go in January, when we invariably arrange to be away for our wedding anniversary, on the 30th.

Ever since I was free to travel with my husband I have made a point of including in each trip at least one place or person of an inspirational nature to ensure that it would be a meaningful experience and not solely a sightseeing tour. But this coming trip to Baba would be the first one we had ever planned for the sole purpose of meeting an inspirational figure. For that reason the preparations needed to be different from previous ones.

As soon as it became known among the local devotees that we were planning to go to India we were offered plenty of helpful advice from those who had gone already. Janet Bock gave us a copy of a pamphlet she had compiled containing helpful hints and instructions of a very practical nature.

We were warned that it is impossible to be sure ahead of time where Baba is likely to be. We would have to wait until we arrived in Bangalore to find out if he was at his residence in Whitefield, near Bangalore, or at his *ashram* in Puttaparthi in Andhra Pradesh, about four hours' drive from Bangalore.

We were also told about the specific codes of behavior and dress suggested for visitors to Baba's house and *ashram*. Many of the customs in India are very different from those in the West. It is therefore imperative that we be made aware of them before our arrival to be sure of avoiding any embarrassment to the Indians or to ourselves, by making mistakes, however unintentional they might be. As the places we would be visiting were in effect places of worship, visitors were expected to treat them as they would churches or shrines. We found that these simple guidelines were based on common sense and good manners, and included just a very few rules to adhere to local customs. We had already become used to the separate seating arrangement for men and women in the meetings we had been attending. As I do not smoke, drink alcohol, use drugs, or eat meat, these restrictions posed no problems. However, the mode of dress to which we were expected to adhere was very different from our customary style. Indian women wear *saris,* so most Western women prefer to do likewise. However, if for any reason wearing a *sari* is a problem, a permissible alternative is a long loosely fitting dress, *mu-mu* or *kaftan* worn with a shawl or stole covering the chest and arms to hide the outlines of the female form. As with the separate seating plan, the idea is to avoid any unnecessary distraction. I decided to buy a length of material for one *sari* before leaving, and wait to buy others in India, where there would be a much better selection of fabrics from which to choose. I was assured that I could have the little blouses, or *cholis,* made up in as short a time as one day at any of the many tailor shops with which India abounds. There is very little in the way of ready-to-wear clothing for women, except the cotton petticoats worn underneath *saris.* Most shops where *saris* are sold have a tailor on the premises for the sole purpose of making *cholis.* They will also hem the rough end of a *sari* and often add a fall along part of the hemline to ensure that it hangs in neat folds. This is particularly helpful with thin fabrics.

Ready-made men's clothes are available, but tailors also make shirts and simple pajama-like trousers in a very short time, assuring a better fit. Men usually wear white around Baba as a symbol of cleanliness, as he advises, "If you keep the body clean the mind will more easily follow its example." He also directs, "When you visit my *ashram* you have to accept the code of conduct prescribed for visitors."

There is now a booklet available titled, *Preparation for the Presence,* which sets forth Baba's directions, and is most helpful for those planning to go to Puttaparthi. There is also a booklet of health and medical suggestions compiled by Dr. Michael Goldstein. It lists various health measures recommended to be taken both before departure and while in India. It includes preventative measures and useful medicines to take along in case of sickness.

It is advisable to check with the local health office to ascertain the recommended shots. They always have a current list of areas throughout the world where there are known to be outbreaks of some of the more serious diseases, such as cholera. Hepatitis is very common in India so it is wise to take a gamma globulin shot just a day or so before departure, as it is effective for only a few weeks.

As we planned only to visit Baba, our luggage would be very light and simple. Later we would hear one of his favorite sayings, "Travel lightly, arrive quickly."

CHAPTER THREE

WE CHOSE TO enter India at Bombay chiefly because it held very significant memories for us from an earlier visit. It was there that we met Nyaya Sharma, a *guru* who had instructed us in a meditation technique, and had also taught us a special method of healing. I had kept in close contact with him by letters until his death. Just before he died he had written to ask me to befriend a young Indian student from Bombay who was at that time attending M.I.T. in Boston, but later moved to the University of California at Santa Cruz to continue his studies. We wanted to meet his parents who lived in Bombay to give them firsthand news of their son, and at the same time ask for more details of Sharma's death, which had come as a great shock to us.

As if to cement our decision, one day while we were discussing our forthcoming trip, Dick and Janet Bock casually mentioned that on their last visit to Baba they had been given a reading from the Book of Bhrigu, a copy of which was owned by a pandit living in Bombay.

We had heard from a friend about this remarkable book a short time before leaving on a prior trip to India. We had then learned that there were several copies of the original text in the care of pandits who were able to translate it from the original language in which it was written. At the time of our earlier trip we included in our itinerary two of the places where copies were located, one in Khatmandu in Nepal, and the other in Poona, not far from Bombay. However, that had apparently not been the right time for us to consult it. In Khatmandu we had been informed that the King's sister, in whose house it was kept, was away on an extended trip, and had locked it in a room and taken the key with her. In Poona we were greeted with the news that the pandit in charge of the book had contracted polio, and was therefore unable to see us.

We had been told that this extraordinary book is mentioned in the Bhagavad-Gita and had originally been written on palm leaves by a sage named Bhrigu who is reported to have received the contents during deep meditation. It describes the lives of certain people who would arrive at some future time to consult it.

When I first heard about this book I was fascinated, but at the same time, disbelieving. I wanted to see it with my own eyes, and hear with my own ears any message it might have for me, unlikely though that appeared to be. I decided that only then could I believe that a man who lived thousands of years ago could somehow project into the future and be able to describe people who are living now. The Chinese *Book of Changes*, or *I Ching*, is the only book I know which is anything like it, though the information is more general, and no specific names and dates for actual people are given.

After the disappointment at our failure to receive a reading on that trip, it now looked as if we were about to be given another chance to locate a copy in Bombay. We had not been aware that one was available when we were there before. How strange that no one had mentioned this one then. It seemed even more obvious to us that it had not been the right time to consult it earlier and we hoped that this time it would be.

It is a custom for devotees to send personal letters to Baba with anyone who is leaving to visit him as this ensures that they will be placed directly in his hands, rather than left to the mercy of the unreliable post. We were given a large packet of letters from the Hollywood center to take with us to deliver to Baba. I rarely get excited at the thought of leaving on a trip until I am actually on board the plane and it has risen into the air. Only then am I certain that we are really on our way as so many things can occur to delay departure. But this time it was very hard to remain calm, and even more difficult to realize that we would soon be in Baba's presence and hopefully receiving our first *darshan* of him.

As this was not our first time in India we did not experience to the same degree the original impact which this very different culture first made upon us, and which I can still vividly recall. All the senses are literally bombarded by the sights, sounds and smells of this vast country and its teeming population, both human and animal. India has a very distinctive smell which assails a visitor immediately upon arrival. Actually, it is more a pervasive atmosphere than a distinct aroma, being composed of many odors, no one of which predominates. There is the stench of unwashed bodies and urine, and the pungent aromas of many different spices, the perfumes worn by the women, and the smell of various foods being cooked. Over all these hangs the strong acrid smell given off by the thousands of small open fires used for cooking. As there is a shortage of wood in India, it has become customary to use cow dung for fuel. Thousands of cows roam the streets unattended. As well as collecting the dung to use as fertilizer for the crops, it is therefore also the custom, as in many other countries, to gather it for fuel. Women and children pat it by hand into patties which are dried in the hot sun until they are hard enough to be used as fuel. It gives off a slow even heat for long periods of time. However, the strong-smelling choking smoke hangs heavily in the air, especially in the evenings when families gather for a simple meal.

In Bombay, which is a coastal city, the year-round heat and humidity combine to create a situation similar to the much publicized smog which envelopes Los Angeles when there is a climatic inversion. But despite all this, Bombay is a very interesting city and one we enjoy.

Shortly after we arrived we made inquiries about the location of the Book of Bhrigu and were given the name and address of the pandit who had charge of this copy. Since he speaks only Hindi, the Bocks had kindly given us the name and address of the interpreter they had used. We telephoned and asked her to make an appointment for us to see the pandit, and to be our guide and interpreter.

As soon as the three of us arrived at his house the pandit took us out into a tiny back garden, and proceeded to measure our shadows with an astrological ruler. This procedure apparently gave him the information he needed to find the pages in the book in which we might be mentioned. Back inside his house, we were fascinated to see hundreds of rows of closely stacked palm leaves, each covered with an ancient script and strange signs. The pandit began to search through the rows, and finally brought out three of the leaves and started to ask us questions to help him to ascertain if we were mentioned in any of them. His questions related to specific events in our lives, such as the year we were married, the number and sex of any children, and dates of major incidents, such as accidents or serious illnesses. By a process of elimination, he chose two of the leaves, both of which, he informed us, referred to a couple who would arrive together at the present time to consult the book. They also matched the other data we had given him. He then started to read from the leaf supposedly relating to my husband.

He could have had no prior knowledge of either one of us, yet he told us many things which were correct, including my husband's age when we had come to Bombay together in 1967, and the fact that we had at that time met a meditation master with whom we had studied. He then informed us that we were now on our way to meet an even greater master from whose pictures ash sometimes flowed. Neither of us said a word to indicate whether he was correct, and after telling us some further personal details about my husband, he picked up the leaf which supposedly referred to me. He repeated the part about meeting the first meditation master and that we were on our way to meet a second much greater one. Then he added that this one would give me a ring, photographs of himself, holy ash, medicine, and his love and blessings. At that point, I must confess I lost all interest, as what he had just foretold seemed altogether too improbable. At that point we did not even know where Baba would be, or even if we would see him, let alone receive gifts from him. Besides it was not gifts I hoped Baba would give me, if I were fortunate enough to meet him, but help on my inner path towards enlightenment or oneness with God.

I thought back to our first meeting with Shri Nyaya Sharma, our former *guru*, who reportedly also materialized objects as gifts for certain people. I recalled with some embarrassment in retrospect that I had made quite a point of telling him that I hoped to receive from him spiritual teaching rather than psychic phenomena or magic, and a meditation practice in preference to tangible gifts. He had smiled kindly and nodded his head from side to side in the typical South Indian way, indicating acceptance and understanding. Thereafter, he concentrated on daily sessions in which he taught us a meditation method suitable for both of us.

Unaware of my negative reactions, the pandit proceeded with the reading, and I continued rather mechanically to take notes of what he said. He concluded with some flowery predictions for both of us, after which we made a hurried exit.

As we drove back to our hotel we discussed our recent experience. I told my husband that I was genuinely ashamed of consulting a fortune-teller, especially as I had always avoided them in the past, preferring to discover my fate as it unfolded day by day. When we reached our room, in disgust at my childishness, I threw the notes I had taken during the reading into the back pocket of my suitcase, hoping to put it out of my mind. I do not know what prompted me to keep them instead of destroying them.

During the remaining few days of our stay in Bombay we visited the parents of Sharma's young protegé, and learned from them the real cause of Sharma's death. He had been helping to free one of his followers from the clutches of a black magician. In retaliation this man turned his negative power onto Sharma and caused him to suffer a fatal heart attack. My first question was, "Why couldn't he protect himself?" They replied that he had tried to do so, as he had known his horoscope indicated that the specific time was approaching when he would be vulnerable to attack and might die. They hazarded a guess that the black magician was also aware of this critical time and made use of that knowledge to strike from a distance at Sharma's heart, which his chart also showed was his weakest organ.

This insight into the possible cause of his sudden death helped to clarify it for me. I had been extremely shocked and saddened when I first heard of his passing, yet I was also puzzled when I reread his last few letters to me. These, I began to realize, had indicated that he may have been aware of his approaching demise. The suggestion that it may have been caused by the use of black magic, coming as it did so soon after we had consulted the Book of Bhrigu, further convinced me that I wanted nothing to do with magic in any form, including the reports I had heard and read of Baba's ability to materialize objects. In this mood we prepared to take the next step, to Bangalore to find Baba.

CHAPTER FOUR

WE FOUND BANGALORE to be one of the cleanest and most attractive Indian cities we had visited. It most certainly lived up to its reputation of being "The Garden City of India," with its dozens of parks, and many varieties of flowering trees and shrubs lining the streets. We learned much later that it is a comparatively new city, and that parts of it were actually planned instead of being allowed to expand in all directions like so many other cities. It also has the advantage of a pleasant climate during most of the year, due to some extent to the elevation. Altogether, we decided that it is a most appropriate setting for Baba and his message to the world.

As soon as we reached our hotel we telephoned Dr. Bhagavantam, a renowned physicist and one of Baba's devotees and chief interpreter. We learned from him that Baba was at his house in Whitefield. He suggested that we might like to hire a taxi to drive us out for the afternoon *darshan* which should take place some time after four o'clock. He explained that it was Baba's custom to come out of the house each morning around nine o'clock, and again each afternoon, to give *darshan* to the crowds who wait outside the house each day for him to appear. We thanked him, and quickly figured out that we would just have time to unpack our luggage, freshen up, change into suitable clothes, and drive out for the afternoon *darshan*. I was delighted at the prospect of being in Baba's presence so soon. I shook out the length of material I had brought with me to use as a *sari* and felt thankful that I had had the foresight to be prepared in this way. I had as yet no *choli* to wear with it, so decided to wear an ordinary blouse until I could have some made in the city. Before I left home I had been shown how to drape the length of material around my waist and fold a length of it into pleats which hang down neatly and slightly to one side to allow room for walking. However, it was a new experience to try to repeat the steps alone, and turned out to be a most frustrating one, especially when I was in a hurry to arrive in time for *darshan*. I finally managed to wind it into place, but felt very nervous, and most fearful that I might lose it at the wrong moment. It felt so insecurely supported, merely tucked into the drawstring at the top of a petticoat. Much later I was introduced to a new use for large safety-pins, and since then, and with more practice, I have lost my earlier qualms, and have more confidence in handling a *sari*.

Finally, properly arrayed in my new mode of dress, and with my husband clad in a white cotton shirt and trousers, we set off in a taxi for our first trip to Whitefield, about which we had heard so much. The drive was fascinating, but also quite nerve-wracking, as our driver swerved from side to side of the bumpy roads to avoid hitting pedestrians, children at play, cows and dogs. They all meandered along in the middle of the road oblivious to the approaching car, despite the incessant honking of the horn, one of the most strident noises in India, we were to discover.

When we arrived at the gate leading to Baba's house we were miraculously intact, though somewhat shaken after our hair-raising ride. We alighted from our taxi and entered the main gate where we were immediately faced with the sight of hundreds of people already assembled and sitting on the ground in neat lines waiting for a sight of Baba. I noticed that the men and women were seated separately on the right and left of the tree-lined driveway which led to a pair of heavy iron gates. Through the gates could barely be seen the outlines of a large sprawling house. We started to walk forward to find a place, but were quickly stopped by a man and woman who hurried towards us to ask us to remove our shoes. We had been warned to remember to do this, but in the excitement of actually being there, had promptly forgotten. Flustered by our mistake we dropped our footwear in the separate piles for men and women on either side of the gate, and once again moved toward our respective seating areas.

For many years I had heard that it is the Master who chooses his disciple rather than the reverse, so before leaving home I had made up my mind to do nothing to attract Baba's attention. I resolved to remain in the background, and mentally ask to be given a sign to show me if he was to be my next teacher. As I walked forward barefooted on the rough uneven ground to the women's side, my feet faltered from the unaccustomed pain inflicted by the sharp little stones and gravel. I looked ahead and carefully picked out a place to sit in the shade of one of the beautiful old trees which used to line the driveway. I wanted to avoid sitting in the front rows where my light hair and pale face would be conspicuous among the dark-skinned and black-haired Indian women. In those days, I was one of only a very few Western visitors. I very carefully lowered myself to the ground, taking care not to step on the hem of my *sari*, which I feared might cause it to fall around my feet. I sighed with relief when I had managed this first step, but wondered how I was going to stand up again when the time came. Everyone waited patiently, silent and still, and I began to question how long I would be able to sit without fidgeting. The bare ground was already feeling harder the longer I sat there, and my bones threatened to poke through my flesh and skin as I am not too well padded. To distract myself from my uncomfortable body I looked around at my surroundings. Overhead in the trees monkeys were swinging from the branches, making funny little chattering sounds, and throwing down leaves and bits of bark onto the heads of the people gathered below, to the immense delight of some of the children. As I looked at the rows of women sitting so patiently in front of me, I noticed that some of them were meditating, others were reading books about Baba, while still others were writing or copying the sign of *AUM* many times over in small notebooks. But the vast majority were just sitting; their gaze turned towards the house from which Baba would emerge, as if loath to miss a single second of the time when he would be visible.

There were also several people in wheelchairs or lying on stretchers, and many obviously sick children held in their mothers' arms, brought there as a last resort, in the hope that Baba would heal them. I remembered a visit to the healing shrine at Lourdes, and once again felt that same overwhelming compassion which had welled up inside me at the sight of all those desperately hopeful people praying for healing for themselves or their loved ones. The whole scene set me to musing. As I looked around at all those waiting people, I wondered what pain, sorrow, loss, or deep yearning had been the impetus to bring them all to Baba.

These silent musings in turn prompted me to ponder afresh my own reasons for coming here. When I first read about Baba it was not the miracles he was said to perform, the healings he brought about, or his materializations of such objects as rings, pendants, and lockets which drew me to him. My recent experiences in Bombay had emphasized that. The hope he held out to all who would be willing to follow his teachings, of achieving liberation from attachment to the material world and eventual enlightenment, was the magnet which attracted me to him. I had been seeking a method to achieve such freedom most of my adult life. Now, as I sat there, waiting with the crowd for Baba to come out, I wondered if he would prove to be the right guide to lead me to that goal.

After what seemed like hours but was probably less than an hour, an almost audible hush came over the crowd which had grown even larger by then. By craning my neck I was just barely able to catch a fleeting flash of orange as Baba approached the ornate gates which gave his house a measure of privacy. Then he emerged into full view, my very first sight of him in person. I had many different reactions in far too quick succession for me to grasp them all at once. But of one thing I was certain, he was more vibrantly alive than anyone I had ever seen in my whole life. I was, however, surprised to notice that he was even shorter than I had expected, both from his photographs and the films we had seen. Now, as I watched him from a distance, I saw that his thick neck and shoulders and head, with its shock of black hair standing out all around it like a dark halo, all gave the impression that he was a large man. Yet I observed that his body was slight and extremely graceful. His customary simple robe, like a long straight orange sheath, reached to his feet, unadorned except for two tiny gold studs to fasten the opening extending down from the collarless neck.

He moved forward through the gates and onto the driveway, which had been decorated with intricate patterns composed of flower petals of many colors to form a floral carpet. He appeared to float rather than walk along it, and slowly drifted from one side of the driveway to the other between the rows of densely packed men and women. Sometimes he stopped to speak to someone, confer a blessing, draw the symbol of AUM on a child's slate as it was eagerly held up to him, or perform many other little loving gestures, just as we had observed him in action in the films. But this time he was doing all these things in person, right in front of our eyes, and in an atmosphere made electric by the ardent anticipation of the crowd. Perhaps what most impressed me was the way his eyes darted here and there over the heads of the people, as if watching and listening to tune in to their needs and conditions. Now and then he would pick out a person with a wave of his hand, and give him or her verbal directions to go to his house and await him there for a private interview. In such cases the sheer delight expressed on the faces of the chosen ones was a rare sight to behold.

I watched fascinated, but was still determined to make no effort to attract his attention. Instead, I prayed silently for him to give me a sign to indicate if he was the Master I should now follow. He continued to move gracefully back and forth between the two sides of the driveway. I held my breath as he lightly drifted over to the women's side at a point just short of where I was sitting, but at no time looking in my direction. Then he moved past me and several feet beyond. As I watched, I thought to myself, "So that is my answer. He is not my *guru*." Heavy-hearted, I realized that I must continue to seek further. No sooner had I accepted this decision than he wheeled around until he faced me directly, and said, "So you have come!" With this observation his face broke into the most radiant smile I have ever seen, like the sun suddenly coming out from behind a cloud and lighting up everything it touched. I was so dazzled by it, that I seemed to lose all sense of time or place, and my mind went blank, empty of its habitual busy thoughts. I have no idea how long it was before he turned and continued on his way between the lines, for time seemed to stand still.

So now I knew! Since he had made the contact as I had silently requested, he must be my next *guru*. I let the full significance of this realization sink into my mind, and felt a profound sense of relief that my fervent quest was ending right here. But I did not yet know that this was the beginning of an extremely painful period of soul-searching which lay immediately ahead of me.

As soon as Baba had made his rounds and gone back into his house the crowd began to disperse and we drove back to the hotel. This time I was oblivious to the wild drive, the constantly blaring horn, and the sudden jolts and swerves as we careened over the rough roads. I was still glowing inside and out from the radiance of Baba's smile which had pierced to the core of my being.

After that first momentous contact we drove back and forth twice a day between the hotel and Whitefield. I would find a place to sit in the shade of one of the trees, and quickly slip into the daily routine. I began to feel quite at home among the hundreds of Indians. I also noticed a very subtle change taking place in me, as if, by a kind of osmosis, I was absorbing some of their slower and more relaxed attitude, which is in such sharp contrast to our hurried and time conscious way of life in the West. Before our arrival I had often wondered how I would ever be able to tolerate the long hours of sitting and waiting, which I had heard made up a large part of the daily routine both at Whitefield and at the *ashram*. But now that I was here, I was pleasantly surprised to discover how quickly and easily I was adjusting to the change of rhythm. Instead of missing my customary busy daily schedule, I found that I was actually enjoying the unaccustomed luxury of just sitting, and allowing this change of pace to take over. I would never have believed it to be possible. I have always needed to learn to be more patient, so this would be excellent practice.

I never tired of watching the daily flow of visitors of every description who streamed into the grounds of Baba's house from every part of India, and from many other countries.

Another source of interest was the Boys' College situated on the grounds near the women's *darshan* area. From the very first day I had noticed the neat, white-clad boys noiselessly scurrying in and out of the various buildings, carrying stacks of books under their arms. When I asked some of the Indian women about the college they told me that, together with one for girls at Anantapur in Andhra Pradesh, it was one of the first of a series of colleges which Baba planned to start in every state in India. I was told that he intends to revive and teach the old values as expounded in the Vedas and other ancient writings. In this way, he hopes to reverse the current trend in the Indian educational system of imitating the competitive and materialistic methods of current Western education. His goal is a revolution in the entire educational system with more stress on human values and moral and spiritual concepts, in addition to the regular academic curriculum. He foresees that the students who are exposed to this way will in time permeate the various institutions of government, education, law, medicine and commerce. They will act as a kind of yeast to raise the overall level of consciousness of the country and its people. As I observed the boys moving about the grounds during those first few days, I was most impressed by their immaculate appearance and decorous demeanor, and particularly by their shining eyes and cheerful faces. From this, my first very limited view of them, they appeared to be a credit to Baba's system, a conclusion I have since found to be justified.

We did not visit the Girls' College until several years later, when we had an opportunity to compare them, and learn more about Baba's program for women. Also at a later date we were introduced to the vast network of programs designed to expose children of various ages to Baba's teachings.

During this first visit we were catching merely a tiny glimpse of the far reaching effect of Baba's influence. We would learn more each time we returned.

CHAPTER FIVE

A FEW DAYS after we arrived, Baba called us for our first interview by stopping in front of my husband as he sat in the *darshan* lines, and telling him to be at his house at nine o'clock the next morning.

From where I was sitting I could see Baba stop and talk briefly to him, and was most curious to hear what had transpired. After *darshan* had ended and the crowd was beginning to disperse, I hurried to find Sidney, eager to hear what he had to report. When he told me about the interview scheduled for the following morning, I was overjoyed.

We already knew that when Baba calls either a husband or wife for an interview, the other is automatically included, unless he specifies to the contrary. I was as excited as a child over a seemingly improbable dream about to come true.

Thoughts and questions began to race through my mind at the prospect of talking directly to Baba. I knew I must not waste such a precious opportunity—but what does one say when face to face with him? Several people had related how their minds had gone blank during an interview. I was familiar with that experience from the time when he first greeted me. I only hoped that it would not be repeated during the forthcoming interview, for I would certainly be reluctant to miss anything that happened, or that Baba might say to us. I finally decided simply to wait until we were called in, observe what happened, and decide what to say or do then. In other words, I instinctively seemed to know that we should follow Baba's cue rather than try to prepare ahead.

The day after our arrival I had purchased several *saris* including some of inexpensive drip-dry materials. So by the time we were called to the interview, I felt secure knowing that I was correctly dressed in the Indian style, and had also had sufficient time to get used to wearing it.

The next morning we arose early, bathed and dressed with care, and arrived outside Baba's house a little before nine o'clock. As we approached the iron gates through which we had seen him appear each day to give *darshan*, they were opened to allow us to pass. Baba must have left word that we were expected, or they would have been barred to us. We walked the short distance to the front door and were ushered into a long starkly simple verandah like room which stretched along the front of the house. My husband was motioned to the left of the door to join a group of Indian men already sitting cross-legged ranged along the wall, obviously waiting for Baba to appear. I was directed to the right of the door, where I took my place in a similar line of women sitting on the floor, leaning against the wall.

I noticed that my lady companions on that first day were all Indian. They smiled and nodded, but did not speak, so I occupied myself by looking around the room. Immediately opposite the front door was an archway leading to the back of the house, through which could be seen the entrances to several rooms, with women moving to and fro attending to household duties. On the wall facing us were many pictures of Baba, each one showing a different aspect of his ever changing personality. A little to the right of the archway stood a large, solidly built armchair and matching footstool, both covered in deep red plush. A folded white handkerchief hung over one arm of the chair, and on both arms, and in the center of the footstool, a tiny posy of flowers had been neatly placed. It was clearly reserved for Baba's exclusive use.

Simple rough textured carpets with brightly colored patterns covered the floor, and a clock hung over the archway audibly ticking away the minutes as we all sat waiting for Baba to appear.

Suddenly there was that familiar hush overlaid with excitement, and all heads quickly turned to the right. Baba appeared at a doorway, through which could be seen a flight of stairs leading up to what I later learned were his private rooms.

He swept into the room, and as he passed where I was standing with the other women, he smiled, and asked, "How are you?" and moved quickly towards the men's side of the room before I could gather my wits together in time to answer him. I have since been told that this is a very common occurrence. Baba invariably takes people completely by surprise however hard they may try always to be prepared. It appears to be one of his many different teaching methods. It reminded me of the way a Zen master will deliberately deliver a shock to a disciple, in an attempt to catch him off guard and create a "space between two thoughts" through which to penetrate the barrier set up by the disciple's busy conscious mind and reach the real person within. I have seen Baba throw an apple or some other object at someone to try to achieve the same result. One day he lightly tossed a package of betel nut at me, as if to say, "Wake up out of your dream and into reality."

As he moved over to join the men he greeted them with some remark in Telegu, his native language. It made them laugh, and relaxed their stiff postures. They had all been standing erect, their hands held up in front of their faces in the customary gesture to greet Baba as he entered.

From then on Baba moved in and out of the room attending to the scores of things demanding his attention. Sometimes he would stop to talk to the men, greet any newcomers who had slipped in from time to time, and listen attentively to whatever they needed to ask or tell him. Invariably there were heads of states, politicians, principals of colleges, heads of large companies and other prominent men, all of whom sought Baba's advice about some aspect of their work or lives. Sometimes he would sit in his red plush chair sorting through the huge pile of post which arrived daily. He touched some of the letters lightly with his hand as if blessing their senders, opened others and glanced through the contents, and left others untouched for the time being, to be attended to at a later time, I presumed. As I watched, I was filled with gratitude to be given this opportunity to observe him thus occupied with his daily round of activities. I marvelled at his seemingly inexhaustible energy and unruffled calm. He was obviously in complete charge of every minute of the day, and I wondered if he ever needed to rest.

I soon fell into the rhythm of standing whenever he appeared, and sitting on the floor while he was out of the room, taking my cue from the other women, who were more familiar with the daily routine. Sometimes, when he was popping in and out at frequent intervals, we were not always quick enough to stand up in time and he would laugh and wave his hand in a downward gesture for us to remain seated.

After a while I lost track of time until suddenly one of the college boys dashed into the room through the front door, grabbed the handkerchief from where it lay over the arm of the big red chair, and hurried outside with it. One of the women leaned over to explain that Baba must be ready to go outside to give *darshan* to the waiting crowd, and needed the handkerchief to wipe from his hands traces of *vibhuti* after he had materialized it for those who needed it. I was able to visualize the scene when I remembered watching the films shown at the Los Angeles center that depicted one of his close devotees walking behind him, holding a handkerchief ready to hand it to him after he had materialized *vibhuti* for someone.

We all settled back to await Baba's return. When he reappeared he looked around the room, and catching sight of Dr. Bhagavantam, called him to his side and beckoned to my husband to join them. I wondered if this was a signal that he was about to give us the promised interview. Without looking in my direction, he started to move toward the doorway leading to the interior of the house. Of course I started wondering if I was supposed to follow them, which was probably his intention for, smiling teasingly at my uncertainty, he motioned to me to come too.

He led the way into a small sparsely furnished room to the left of the doorway, and told us to sit down. We started to sit separately as usual, but he reached out his hands to draw us close together and, with an indulgent laugh, said, "Here, with me, you can sit together." The warmth of his tone and his broad welcoming smile put us at ease immediately. We sat side by side on the floor at his feet as he took his place in a large red chair, similar to the one in the outer room. With Dr. Bhagavantam also sitting on the floor, acting as interpreter, our first interview began.

We have since learned that invariably Baba's first question is, "What do you want?" usually addressed first to the husband when he is seeing a married couple. I have often heard him say that he gives people what they want in the hope that they will eventually want what he has come into this world to give: liberation from the thrall of *maya*, the illusion of the world of desires, or unreality.

When Baba asked this question of my husband, he quickly replied that he hoped Baba could cure me of the severe headaches I have had since childhood. Baba looked penetratingly at me for a moment and with a sympathetic nod said, "Yes! Yes!" He then launched into a detailed diagnosis of my physical problems, which Dr. Bhagavantam translated from Telegu into English. Baba spoke very fast and used complex medical terms which neither of us was able to comprehend, and which I would not have been able to spell even if I had tried to take notes. I also had the distinct impression that he was having a conversation with Dr. Bhagavantam, almost as if we were not even present. He finally turned to me and in English informed me, "You have five headaches, not one." This news came as a real surprise to me, and I must have shown my consternation, for Baba quickly leaned over towards me, and gently said, "Don't worry. I will help you." With that promise and a smile at seeing my obvious relief, he stretched out his right arm and, looking pointedly at my husband, a typically sceptical lawyer, he ostentatiously pulled the sleeve of his robe up above his elbow. Then with his palm turned to the floor, he drew several small circles in the air between us. Motioning to Dr. Bhagavantam to pass him a used envelope, he quickly drew his fingers together and dropped into it a small quantity of *vibhuti* which he had apparently just produced out of thin air right before our eyes. I had no time to react to this, our first experience of seeing him materialize something in our presence, before he handed me the envelope and started to tell me how to use the *vibhuti*.

With Dr. Bhagavantam translating, he instructed me to mix a very small pinch of it with water, milk or some other liquid to form a paste, and apply it to the bridge of my nose each morning upon awakening. At the same time I was to concentrate on the center of my forehead and visualize the same area on his head. He then lifted his right hand from his knee, where it had been lightly resting since the materialization of the *vibhuti*, and revealed a small circular badge made of a lightweight pale silvery metal bearing a picture of his head on its surface. I gasped with surprise at yet another materialization following so soon after the first one. He smiled delightedly at my fresh amazement, and gently said in English, "This will help you to concentrate," and pointing to the center of his forehead in the picture told Dr. Bhagavantam to tell me to use the *vibhuti* in this way for the next five days, while he was in Madras. He added that he would see me again after he returned to give me more instructions.

I shall never know how, at that point, I had the presence of mind to tell him that if he had asked me what I most wanted him to give me I would not have said a cure for my headaches, even though I would be overjoyed to be free of them. He laughed and asked what I wanted, so I told him that my most fervent desire was for him to help me to attain enlightenment and eventual union with God. He smiled, nodded his head and said again in English, "Yes, I know. But first the body must be made strong. After that I will teach you." With that promise he stood up to indicate the end of the interview, and held his hands over our heads as a blessing.

As we left the interview room to return to our places in the verandah, I was in a daze from all that had happened. Firmly clutched in my hand were the package of *vibhuti* and the badge bearing his picture. I had renewed hope of being free of the headaches, and was determined to use the *vibhuti* regularly each day and follow his instructions to the letter until his return, when he promised to see us again. I could hardly believe it. I was filled to the brim with all that had transpired. My mind was struggling to digest and put into perspective all I had experienced. I decided it was just as well that several days would elapse before we would see him again for I doubted that I would have been able to handle much more at that point.

CHAPTER SIX

DURING BABA'S ABSENCE we decided to see some of the other *ashrams* in the south about which we had heard. I am very glad we did. It enabled us to evaluate the effect of the teachings expounded by the particular *guru* around whom each had developed, and also helped us to compare their methods with Sai Baba's.

We first drove to Aurobindo's *ashram* in Pondicherry. At that time it was presided over by the Mother. She was by then very old and feeble, and was granting interviews only at very rare intervals until her death a year or so later. However, her powerful presence could be felt brooding over the *ashram*. From the window of an upper room she could look down onto Aurobindo's tomb, or *samadhi*, which was surrounded by masses of the countless varieties of her favorite flowers, many of which she had whimsically renamed. She was born in France, and had brought with her to India, not only a love of perfume, but the knowledge of how to make it. She had started a small factory and taught some of the resident disciples how to manufacture and sell it as an added support for the *ashram* community.

There were many other small but thriving enterprises being run by devotees, including a printing shop where Aurobindo's books were printed, a bookshop where they were sold, a laboratory where *ayurvedic* medicines were made, a clinic where they were dispensed, several cafeterias and bakers, hotels, and many other establishments. They were scattered throughout the city, often at some distance from the main *ashram*. We were taken on a tour of several of these institutions by some of the residents, both Indian and Western, and told more about the teaching, customs, and codes of behavior. We were informed that on entering the *ashram* each resident was expected to donate a sum of money to be used towards the overall upkeep of the community, out of which the donor's daily needs would also be met. We were introduced to several married couples who occupied the same sleeping quarters, yet had taken the required vow of celibacy while they were living at this *ashram*.

However, at Auroville, a nearby model town in the process of being constructed by an international team of workers, celibacy was a matter for individual choice. While we were being shown around the growing community we saw many happy children already attending the beautiful modern schools being built for their use.

The overall impression we gained at the Aurobindo Ashram was of a thriving community whose members were dedicated to a spiritual life, and who, at the same time remained active and helpful in a self-supporting group within the city. Their mode of living seemed to be halfway between living in the outer world and completely withdrawing from it. Actually, it was not too surprising that, with a practical French woman at its head, this *ashram* would be different in that respect.

On our way back to Bangalore we drove to Tiruvannamalai where Ramana Maharshi had founded an *ashram*. It nestles at the base of Arunachala, a sacred hill, reportedly the site of one of the earth's power centers. The *ashram*, though one of the most primitive, was notable for the very powerful atmosphere pervading it, which we felt as soon as we stepped inside the grounds. We wondered if it could be due to the proximity of the sacred hill and the natural power center. It is customary for visitors to circumambulate the hill, preferably barefoot. Fortunately, we had arranged to stay overnight, so we had sufficient time to take the walk. When we had walked about halfway around it, we came to another smaller *ashram* presided over by a resident *yogi* and his assistant, who was also a healer. They were both vibrant and dedicated to spiritual pursuits, yet we did not feel the same strange power that was so apparent in the Ramana Maharshi Ashram, even though we were just as close to the holy hill. After a brief but pleasant stay with the two *yogis*, we returned to our starting point, having made the ritualistic circle of the hill.

Back at Ramana Maharshi's *ashram*, one of his original disciples appeared and we started to talk. He told us that the Master had promised to watch over the *ashram* and his followers after he left the physical plane, and that it was evident to the residents that he was keeping his promise and was still very much present in spirit. He then took us into the meditation room in which the Maharshi used to teach his disciples. A large, almost life-sized photograph of him was propped up on a sofa on which we were told he used to recline. As I looked at it I had the distinct and slightly unnerving impression that his eyes were following me wherever I went in the room, as if he were really still there in person. From then on, as I walked around the *ashram*, I continued to have a strange feeling that I would only need to turn a corner, and there he would be coming towards me, so strong was his unseen presence.

We were also taken halfway up the side of the hill to visit the tiny cave in which he had spent many years in deep and almost continuous meditation before he started to teach, a practice which most holy men have followed during their early years as preparation for their mission. Our escort suggested that we might like to sit and meditate for a while in the peace and quiet which surrounds this place like a soft and soothing mist. Even though I had practiced meditation for many years, I have rarely slipped so smoothly and easily into this state, or remained at such a deep level for so long. It was a powerful experience and one I shall not easily forget.

We heard that the widow of Arthur Osborne, author of several books about holy men and spiritual subjects, was living a short distance outside the *ashram*. We were told that she enjoys meeting Westerners, so we decided to visit her. She was a most charming and gracious hostess who invited us to stay for afternoon tea. Though I was born in England, I do not enjoy drinking tea, so I was relieved when she made it with the leaves of the sweet basil growing abundantly in her garden. She told us it is very soothing for the nerves and we found it delicious. We were introduced to her two pet mongooses as they cavorted about the garden very playfully. But she told us they could turn into vicious attackers whenever a snake came into sight.

When she heard that we had so recently visited Sai Baba, she asked if we had read her late husband's book on the life of Shirdi Sai Baba. We were aware that he was allegedly a prior incarnation of Sathya Sai Baba, but knew little else about his life, so we bought a copy of the book. We thanked our hostess for her warm hospitality and returned to the *ashram*, where we joined others for the evening meal in a large hall. We all sat on the floor in front of palm leaf plates. Several young boys came around carrying large buckets of steaming food which they ladled out onto the leaves; first a helping of white rice, followed by a thin vegetable soup poured over it. We all ate with our fingers, using only the right hand, as is the Indian custom. We watched some of the other guests, and tried to copy the way they rolled the rice into a small ball, dipped it into the liquid, and popped it into their mouths with a quick flick of the hand. We managed a poor version of this dextrous trick. It was a very simple repast though quite filling. We learned that at most *ashrams* it is permissible for a person to stay for three days and nights and partake of the simple meals without charge, if one cannot afford to pay, before continuing on one's way. After the third day a small sum is expected. Many wanderers live by walking from one *ashram* to the next, staying three days at each, and moving on. That night we slept on the floor on thin mattresses in an opensided hut which was pleasantly cool after the oppressive heat of the day. The next morning, after a simple breakfast of *idlis*, the South Indian equivalent of pancakes, we continued on our way back to Bangalore.

I had been faithfully carrying out Baba's instructions, by applying the *vibhuti*, and using his picture each day, for the prescribed five days, so I was curious to hear what he wanted me to do next. However, on our return we learned that he had allowed himself to be swayed by the entreaties of his devotees in Madras, and had consented to extend his stay with them for a few more days.

So we decided to take another short trip down to Mangalore to the Ananda Ashram founded by the late Papa Ram Das, and since his death, presided over by his consort Mother Krishna Bai. I had always wanted to meet a spiritually developed woman. I have always firmly believed that women are as equally suited to spiritual pursuits as men, and maybe even more so! I therefore welcomed the chance to meet such a woman.

The Ananda Ashram was another of the more primitive ones as far as the creature comforts were concerned. However, it exuded an air of peace and tranquillity which I had expected to find pervading all *ashrams* until I experienced for myself how much they all differ from one another.

Mother Krishna Bai was a tiny, frail, elderly woman. She had a persistent hacking cough which necessitated her spitting frequently into a bowl placed at her side for that purpose. We later learned that she was suffering from advanced tuberculosis. There were quite a number of devotees around her, mostly older women, and a few young people who were touchingly attentive to her needs. We were granted an interview, during which she said very little, but just smiled and nodded her head most of the time. I had the distinct feeling that the energy in this *ashram* was diminishing in direct ratio to her failing health, but that this serene place offered the devotees a peaceful haven in which to live out the latter part of their lives. It was almost too peaceful to be healthy.

Some of the other visitors mentioned Shakti Devi, another spiritually evolved woman, whose *ashram* was situated on the other side of Mangalore. She was reputed to be very powerful and quite different from Mother Krishna Bai, so we decided to visit her on our way back to Bangalore. We stayed overnight at the Ananda Ashram, in a bare room similar to the one we had occupied at the Ramana Maharshi Ashram. By this time we were becoming a little more accustomed to sleeping on the floor and eating from palm leaves placed on the ground, though we began to notice a twinge or two in our lower backs caused by bending over to eat. We arose early, again ate a breakfast of *idlis*, and after receiving the Mother's blessing to protect us on our journey, left this peaceful place and drove to the nearby town of Mangalore.

There we made inquiries as to the location of Shakti Devi's *ashram* and were told that we were fortunate to have arrived on a Sunday, as it is a very special day when the Mother blesses all the young married couples who come eagerly to receive her *darshan*.

When we arrived at the beautiful new building which houses her and some of her devotees, we were taken into the main hall. It was already full of people, but a place was immediately made for us by everyone moving a little closer together in a good natured way, with smiles and little nods of appreciation that we had come to see and hear their beloved Mother.

After a while she entered from behind a curtain at the back of a platform in the center of which a chair had been placed so that everyone could easily see her. What a contrast between the sick little lady we had just left and this woman now facing us, smiling her acceptance of the enthusiastic greeting being given her. She was tall, buxom, and vibrant with energy. She had a deep reso-nant voice and flashing eyes which seemed to take in everyone in one sweep as she looked around at her assembled flock. She started to speak in her native tongue, but after a few minutes changed to halting English. She said, almost apologetically, "Mama has very little English and hopes you can understand." This was addressed directly to another Western couple and ourselves, the only non-Indians in the room. An elderly Indian lady sitting in front of me leaned back and whispered that the Mother had attended school only up to the third standard. She confided this piece of information with the same pride and love as a mother would relate her child's achievements.

Suddenly, the Mother leaned back in her chair, took a deep breath, and rolled her eyes up and back in their sockets until only the whites were visible. She then withdrew into a state of very deep meditation, apparently the signal for everyone present to meditate too. Once again, I found it surprisingly easy to go quickly to a deep level of consciousness, and concluded that the Mother must be lifting everyone in the room to a higher state, as she herself went to even higher levels of awareness.

After about an hour she began to stir out of the altered state of consciousness and moved into one different from either the latter or the fully conscious state in which she had first appeared. She now seemed to be unusually wide awake and alert. To our immense surprise, she began to speak rapidly in fluent English, obviously being inspired and directed by a force beyond her own conscious self.

Her talk was on the sanctity of marriage and the sacred mutual responsibility of both parents for the wise rearing of their children. It was delivered in a strong and forceful manner and greatly impressed the audience, judging by the way they drank in her message. When she had finished speaking, many young couples, some accompanied by their children, either on foot or held in their parents' arms, began to walk towards the platform, and up a short flight of steps, to receive her blessing for the coming week. She placed a hand on each of their heads and addressed a few words to each one, which often made them laugh. Each couple quickly moved back to their places to allow others to be blessed. When all those who wished had received her blessing, she turned towards us, and smiling, beckoned us to come up to her. We walked up onto the platform. As she placed a hand on each of our heads, I felt an electric current flowing from her hand down my spine. At the same time I was aware of an outpouring of love from her eyes as she smiled warmly at us.

After these very different experiences at the two *ashrams*, we drove back to Bangalore, eager to see Baba, hoping that he would, as he had promised, invite us for another interview. On our way we discussed the various *ashrams* where we had stayed during the past week. We had both noticed one tendency common to the devotees at all of them. They were fiercely loyal to their chosen *guru*, often to the extent of belittling all others in an attempt to enhance the one of their choice. I could very easily understand and respect their loyalty to their own *guru*, but their need to criticize the one chosen by other people greatly disturbed and saddened me, especially when Sai Baba was included in their attack. I made up my mind to try to ask him how to handle such criticism, if I ever had the opportunity. I did not receive an answer during that visit, but at a later time I heard Baba say in one of his discourses that on one side of him is a large number of people who love and praise him, while on the other side is a large group who wish to defame him. Asked how he handles the situation, he answered, "I bless both groups."

When we arrived back in Bangalore we found that he too had just returned from Madras and would resume daily *darshans* the next morning.

CHAPTER SEVEN

AFTER OUR VISITS to the other *ashrams* and Baba's return from
Madras, we soon fell back into the daily routine of driving out
each morning and afternoon for *darshan*, and taking our places in
the crowd of devotees who eagerly awaited the anticipated
blessing conferred by the mere sight of him.

Before coming to see Baba I had, in my ignorance, imagined
that he would be surrounded by an atmosphere of peace and calm,
and that everyone would radiate love and compassion. How wrong
I was! I was genuinely shocked to discover that the reverse was
the case. At times it appeared that chaos reigned instead of peace
and love. Everyone seemed to be frantically intent on catching a
glimpse of Baba and, above all, on attracting his attention and
silently begging for an interview or whatever else they desired. I
watched as people vied with one another to secure the best places
to sit, according to where it was rumored that he might walk each
day. To accomplish this they did not hesitate to push, elbow, or
jostle each other with anything but a loving or unselfish attitude.
The volunteers, men and women appointed to help and direct visitors and generally keep order, were with a few exceptions equally
unloving. At times they seemed to go out of their way to be
unpleasant and harshly authoritative.

At first I was appalled and began to wonder if Baba's love
had affected any of these so called devotees at all. Then I began to
hear stories which seemed to indicate that Baba himself often
seemed deliberately to stir up in people all kinds of negative emotions. At the same time he teaches that these very emotions are
contrary to the spiritual way of life he expounds and should therefore be eradicated. I was, to say the least, bewildered by all that I
was observing and wondered if I might be over-reacting or
whether my conclusions were correct. If so, what was the reason
behind it? Gradually, a fragment at a time, the picture was clarified
for me as I watched and talked to people and observed Baba in
action.

In my meditation and counseling work I have discovered that
most people are completely unaware of their own negative attitudes, emotions and actions. It is not until they begin to see themselves clearly and accept responsibility for their own lives, that

they are able to initiate the necessary changes in themselves. Could it be that Baba was stirring up all the suppressed negativity hidden within people to allow it to erupt into the open and become clearly visible for all to see? That certainly appeared to be a possibility.

Following that insight I began to notice that people were frequently placed in the *ashram* in close proximity with those who were most likely to arouse in them such emotions as anger, jealousy, envy, and a host of other negative reactions. Sometimes a mutual learning experience would result as they interacted with one another. But often very ugly situations would arise to their mutual discomfort. I heard such comments as, "I don't know what got into me, but so-and-so drove me to the point where I completely lost my temper, which never happens to me, as I always strive to keep it under strict control," or "I have never thought of myself as a jealous person, but I was consumed with jealousy today when Baba smiled at so-and-so and ignored me sitting right next to her."

The more I observed the scene around me the more insight I gained into the role Baba plays in people's lives, either directly, or through other people and situations. I made up my mind to remain as aware as possible of my own negative aspects lying hidden within, which would undoubtedly be brought out into the light while I was in close daily proximity to Baba and his extraordinary energy. I soon discovered that this process was not at all comfortable. In fact, at times it was positively painful.

Baba acted like a giant searchlight, shining on us all and exposing everything both inside and outside of us in minute detail for all to see. One day, while I was struggling with a new insight into myself, I suddenly realized that there was absolutely no place to run away to hide, even if I wanted to. I could wriggle and squirm, but I knew in my heart that I needed to be shown my faults and weaknesses before I could let go of them and replace them with more positive attributes. I tried to watch my reactions to people and situations and to consciously surrender the negative ones as soon as I became aware of them instead of being shocked or critical of other people. As soon as I started this process I realized I was being offered a golden opportunity to carry out this most difficult task right there in Baba's presence where it could be more easily and swiftly accomplished than if I attempted it alone and at home. From then on I tried to concentrate on my newly discovered task instead of being lured away from it by the distraction of all those around me.

After a few days Baba called us to another interview, this time approaching me as I sat in the *darshan* lines and telling me to be at his house the next morning at nine o'clock, and to "bring the band." My mind was instantly set awhirl with questions. How could I possibly hire a band in time? Where would I be able to find one? What kind of band did he want me to bring? He had lightly tossed out this invitation to me as he walked towards where I was sitting and had then continued quickly on his way. Suddenly, he turned around and, obviously thoroughly enjoying my confusion, added with a broad smile, "Hus*band* , of course," at which I joined in the merriment of the Indian women sitting near me. They had evidently heard him play this joke before and were highly amused at the little scene just re-enacted in front of them.

The next morning, once again, we arrived at his house a little before nine o'clock. The morning passed and then it was noon, and time for him to go up to his room where his lunch would be served by those college boys who had been granted the privilege for that day. As he moved to depart and all the other guests started to leave, we both wondered what we should do. As if reading our minds, Baba stopped, called over to my husband that we should come back in the afternoon, and swept out and up the stairs to his room. We asked some of the Indians when we should return and were informed that Baba usually came downstairs again around four o'clock.

We drove back to our hotel for lunch. Then we took a short walk as we were stiff from sitting on the hard floor all morning. We arrived back at the house shortly before four o'clock and sat down to wait for Baba. When he breezed in on his way past me to the men's side, he gave me a cheerful smile and said, "*Atcha.*" This was a new and strange word. Later, I asked one of the Indian women sitting near me what it meant. Apparently, it has several uses. It can express approval, consent or agreement, and is somewhat similar to our okay, or good. He proceeded to go about his business as usual, and we all relaxed into the daily rhythm of sitting while he was out of the room and quickly standing as soon as he re-entered.

After quite a while he appeared in the doorway leading to the interior of the house and beckoned first to my husband and then to me, to follow him into the same room where he had taken us for our first interview. Again he indicated that we should sit close together on the floor at his feet, while he sat in his chair. With Mr. Kasturi translating, he immediately began to tease my husband, who is an inveterate reader, by pretending to pick up an imaginary book, turn the pages at great speed, close it, put it down on the floor at his side, quickly pick up another, and hurriedly scan it as he flipped over the pages. He repeated this pantomime several times, saying, as he did so, "SO much book knowledge, but not enough devotion. Devotion is very important." His teasing way of play-acting to deliver his message was so delightful that my husband could not take offence or be hurt by the implied criticism. We both had a good laugh at Baba's perfect pantomime.

He next turned to me, but said to my husband, "Your wife has devotion." With this remark, he again startled us by making several small circles in the air with his hand and quickly catching a shiny object to prevent it from falling to the ground. He held his hand out towards me and I saw, lying in his palm, a silver colored ring set with a pale luminous stone. He tried it on several fingers of both my hands and finally decided on my left index finger. Satisfied with the fit, he left it there where it has remained, except for the times when I clean the indentation behind the stone. He then instructed me to rub the stone in the center of my forehead whenever I had a headache in that region, to heal the original cause.

My mind instantly flew back more than twenty years to a time when I had been involved in a process of recalling what appeared to be some of my past lives. In one of these regressions I had identified with a Tibetan monk. As the experience had unfolded I sensed that as part of his spiritual training he was voluntarily immured in a cave for a specific length of time. The purpose of this solitary confinement was to reduce to a minimum all outer distractions in order to concentrate on visualizing symbols of all his desires and thus relinquish attachment to them. This assignment was supervised by his instructor, a high *llama* who lived in the nearby lamasery and kept in telepathic touch with his disciple. In this way the disciple had gradually learned to observe mental images on an inner screen behind his forehead. One day, when the telepathic connection between him and his teacher was inadvertently broken, he was unable to continue to control the flow of images. When they threatened to overwhelm him, in a frantic attempt to stop the process he banged his head against the wall of the cave so violently that the injury to his brain eventually caused his death.

As I made the connection between this experience and what Baba was telling me to do with the ring I exclaimed sharply, "Oh Baba!" He smiled gently, and replied, "Yes! Yes! I know all about it. I will help you." Still stunned, I silently asked myself, "How could he know about it?" Baba smiled and nodded his head as if he had been listening to my thoughts. Apparently he did know and since then there have been many similar instances of his powers. With each new experience I am awed anew by his awareness of intimate details, not only of my present life, but also of past incarnations.

The ring is made from a special alloy called *panchaloha* which is used for ritual objects in India. It looks like silver but, unlike that metal, it does not tarnish. The stone is a moonstone, which I discovered much later was a most appropriate and significant choice. One day, when I was leafing through a book on the symbology of precious stones, I came across the meaning of the moonstone. I was fascinated to learn that it is an ancient symbol for the third eye, which is reputedly situated in the middle of the forehead, exactly where Baba had told me to rub the stone in my ring when I suffered from a headache in that area. The so-called third eye was the inner screen which the Tibetan monk tried to break in his frantic attempt to stop the flow of images from flooding his mind and driving him insane. Was the moonstone in the ring designed to heal the old injury? I certainly hoped so. Baba had told my husband that I had devotion. I hoped I had learned from that experience that it must be devotion to God and not to a human being, even a teacher, for only God is completely dependable and always available to help whenever we ask.

Sometime later I remembered another most significant fact. When I was a young student attending a college in England, where I was born, I was given a ring which was almost identical in shape to the one Baba gave me. It was made of silver with a simulated stone also made of silver. It had been given to me by the person who years later I had identified with the high *llama* under whose telepathic tutelage I had been working while immured in the cave. By giving me this new ring, was Baba showing me that the past life I had uncovered was indeed correct as I had recalled it?

Baba ended the interview by telling us to come to his house every day until it was time for us to return home when he would give us a farewell interview. I was still in a state of shock from all that had just happened and only later felt the impact of what he was now telling us to do.

CHAPTER EIGHT

FOR THE NEXT two weeks our daily routine underwent a change. Instead of sitting outside in the *darshan* lines, we went directly to Baba's house and sat with others whom he had invited either for an interview or on a daily basis. On some days we actually saw less of him than if we had still been outside, where he would often wander in and out of the men's and women's *darshan* lines for half an hour at a time. On Thursdays and Sundays, which were *bhajan* days, he would sometimes stay outside for as long as an hour.

Nevertheless I was delighted to be given an opportunity to sort out some of my impressions and reactions and, even more important, to continue to observe in myself whatever Baba's searchlight would bring to my attention. So I silently thanked him for providing me with the chance to concentrate with less outer distraction.

However, once inside the house, I was in for a surprise, for the closer we were to Baba's presence and tremendous energy, the stronger and faster the tension built up. It was like being in a pressure cooker!

When Baba was not physically in the room, we would talk to one another in low voices to ease the long periods of sitting cross-legged on the floor. I soon realized that in the house a smaller, but more intensified scene than the one outside was being enacted daily as the devotees reacted to one another and to Baba. It was much more restrained, but that only made the emotions more intense. Where was the peace and calm, the love and compassion which I had expected to find, and which we had experienced at the Ananda Ashram? As if in answer to my question came the thought that it does not help to spread a sugar coating on top of a mass of seething emotions. Surely, in the long run, it was more beneficial to be faced squarely with our unconscious faults and weaknesses while we were here in Baba's presence. Here, we could silently seek his aid and absorb his energy to help us to develop the wisdom and strength with which to overcome them. Such insights sprang up spontaneously in my mind in answer to some of my questions, but they did little to alleviate the discomfort and depression resulting from the daily X-ray view of myself that being so close to Baba brought about.

It was also during this period of sitting in the house for hours at a time that a swarm of doubts assailed me.

As I have already mentioned, for many years before I had heard about Baba I had been receiving guidance from within. The most important aspect of this teaching was instruction in breaking dependence on people, objects, places, in fact, anything which acts as a security symbol and prevents one from seeking security solely in the indwelling God or High Self. I had used this method for many years as a type of therapy to help people to achieve such independence. Many of them testified to the freedom they gained when they cut the ties to transitory security symbols which, by their very temporary nature, are bound to cause disappointment.

So I suffered a severe jolt when I became aware that here I was fast becoming attached to Baba, an Indian teacher. Though he was a self-proclaimed divine *Avatar*, he appeared in the form of a very real and vital human body. As I recalled all the warnings I had received for so many years, a veritable battle began to rage inside me between reliance on all the invaluable teaching I had been given in the reveries and the unmistakably strong attachment to Baba I was rapidly developing. What about the warning I had been given from the Tibetan life?

As if this were not enough, I felt absolutely certain that my inner turmoil was being observed by Baba. At the same time I was clearly aware that he could not solve this particular problem for me. Its very nature demanded that I find my own solution to it, apart from him, since he was the cause. As I sat there in his house squirming on the hard floor, I prayed for help in finding a solution to my unrest. It didn't help matters when I recalled how I myself had asked Baba to give me a sign to indicate if he was to be my teacher.

As he moved to and fro about his house, attending to the hundreds of demands on his time and attention, he often paused to say a word to someone. Sometimes he would sit down to talk to the group of men, mostly heads of Sai Baba centers, influential leaders in Indian affairs and teachers and students from his nearby Boys' College. These talks and conversations were usually in Telegu, but for more general topics in which we could all be included, he either spoke in English or asked one of his interpreters to translate them.

He has often said that he rarely chooses a specific subject for his talks, preferring to answer the unspoken questions and needs of the individuals in the group he is addressing. At that time I had not heard about this method of tailoring his speeches to fit his audience. I was, therefore, taken by surprise when he would weave into his talks a message or an answer to some of the questions with which I was wrestling, and then look across at me as if to say, "Does that help you understand?"

One point he frequently stressed began to have an effect on me, and eventually led to my release from the ambivalent predicament in which I was trapped. He stated unequivocally that we are not the body and therefore should not identify with it. He repeatedly emphasized that our real selves merely occupy the bodies into which we are born. These are like residences or sheaths making it possible for us to live in the material world. He further explained that we are attracted to a different body each time we enter the earth plane according to our *karmic* needs, and that each is transitory, whereas our real selves are deathless. He also mentioned another very interesting point. He said that all our problems are caused by our desires, which are directly connected to our personal or bodily needs, and do not originate from our true Self. He promised that if we will but try to understand and accept this truth, we will be better able to transcend our desires and become free from their dominance, a necessary preliminary to the eventual attainment of enlightenment.

One day he sat down on the floor on the men's side of the room, usually the signal that he was about to give an informal talk or initiate a question and answer session. On this particular day he began by saying in English, "Some of you quote me as saying that I am God, but fail to finish the quotation. I also say that every one of you is also God. The difference between you and me is that I know I am God, but you do not yet know that you are." To illustrate a point he often announces that he will tell a little story. This he proceeded to do in Telegu which was then translated. He started by likening people to electric light bulbs of varying wattage. Then, pointing to himself, he explained that he can be likened to a thousand watt bulb, which can carry a great deal of power, whereas we are like twenty, forty, sixty and one hundred watt bulbs, according to our individual development. He then pointed out that the important thing for us all to remember is that the electric current which illuminates all the light bulbs is the same, whatever their individual capacity may be. In other words, the light within everyone is God, but we all reveal that light in different intensities. He further expanded this theme by urging us to beware of worshipping his physical form or any other as the only form of God. Instead, he advised us all to acknowledge God as the Self in everyone, no matter how hidden or buried. Having made his point, he said again in English, accompanied by one of his dazzling smiles, "This is the message I have come to give to the world."

I was familiar with this concept both from past reading and the teaching I had been receiving by means of the waking dream technique. I had firmly believed that I understood its meaning. However, something about the way Baba expressed it suddenly brought it into focus for me so that it made perfect sense in an new way. Quietly and effortlessly I felt the pieces of a vast jigsaw puzzle slipping into place to reveal a little more of the whole picture. As a result I could see more clearly what Baba symbolized for me. He was the outer and visible manifestation, or embodiment, of my own God-Self or *Atman*. He was therefore a tangible reminder of Its inner eternal reality, as opposed to the physical body with all its appetites, weaknesses and eventual dissolution into ashes.

The *llama* in the Tibetan life had not known this truth, so, in his ignorance he had placed his faith in a human teacher who failed him when he most needed him. Because he knew of no higher authority to whom to appeal for help when the mortal one failed him, he was overwhelmed by the very desires he had been trying so hard to dispel and which he was unable to control solely with his own will.

A flood of relief poured through me and swept away all my remaining doubts. I realized on a still deeper level of my being that Baba was indeed a manifestation in human form of the God within all of us. As such he would never fail or disappoint us as human teachers, by their very nature, are liable to do.

As I relaxed with this solution to the riddle I had been struggling to resolve, I looked across at Baba with a new attitude. As I did so he turned his head and looked at me with his searching eyes. A knowing smile lit up his face, and he nodded his head as if to say, "Now you are beginning to understand." Shortly thereafter he left the room to attend to his many daily tasks, which allowed us to ruminate on all he had been teaching us.

From then on I was free to participate more fully in the daily routine. I was also more open to receive whatever Baba chose to give us, whether in his informal talks, or on the more subtle level of his love an energy which emanated from him so vibrantly and unceasingly.

As I look back at this first visit I doubt that I was fully aware of how blessed we were to be given the opportunity to be in his presence each day and to absorb all we could contain of his love and blessings. In recent years he has become increasingly occupied with his mission, primarily in India. As a result he has had less time to spare for intimate meetings and individual interviews.

As soon as I had, with Baba's help, become free of my doubts, and began to understand and accept his role in my life, I was enchanted at the opportunity to observe him. His countless changes of expression, running the whole gamut from extreme severity to melting sweetness, were wonderful to watch. I have seen him draw himself up to appear much taller than his actual height and look positively God-like: his Shiva aspect, as he himself calls it. At other times he was like an impish little boy, laughing and teasing, and setting us all at ease with his playful ways, very much as the young Krishna must have been.

I also marveled at his tireless and effortless activities. But perhaps what amazed me most was his apparent awareness of literally everything and everyone, which gave the impression that he was constantly tuned in to the whole world and everyone in it.

I also observed that when he spoke to someone he gave that person his whole undivided attention so that each one felt that he or she, at that moment, was the only person in the world for him. Then the spell would be broken and he would move on, soon to be equally concerned with someone else.

At times, with his head slightly inclined, he would appear to be listening to audible voices, and at other times he could be seen making signs in the air with his hand or forefinger, as if in contact with invisible beings.

Other Western visitors arrived from time to time. Jack and Victoria Hislop, who had been devotees of Baba for several years, came into the house one morning together with another American couple. As soon as Baba entered the room, Jack rather breathlessly started to speak to him, saying, "We want to thank you, Swami, for saving our lives last night. " Baba smiled and said, "Yes, that was a close one. You were all so shocked that not even one of you called for Swami. But Swami saved you anyway." Baba often refers to himself as Swami. He then turned to the men already sitting in the room, mostly Indians, and animatedly recounted the incident in Telegu.

Later that day we also heard the story from the two couples. It seemed that at one moment they all expected a head-on collision with a fast moving car which they could see approaching them. Just as they all braced for the crash, miraculously, the car was already behind them. They decided later that this was absolutely impossible as there had not been sufficient space for the cars to pass one another as a large bus was in the way.

They had all looked shamefaced when they realized that Baba was right, and that they had all been too shocked to do anything but wait for the crash, which they were all certain was about to occur.

In some strange way Baba's observation produced a disproportionately profound affect upon me, as if his words had been branded into my brain. I instantly made a silent vow to try to remember to call on him if I were ever in need of help. I would recall this scene and Baba's words so indelibly etched into my memory just a year later, after our next visit, when the plane on which we were flying from Bombay to London was hijacked.

Why did I react so strongly to Baba's words? Could it be that he was warning me to remember to call on him for help, to emphasize that, unlike the teacher in the Tibetan life, he would not fail me? I only know that it made such a deep impression that I have remembered to call on him for help on several occasions. Each time aid has been immediately forthcoming.

During the time when Baba was in Madras and we were visiting the other *ashrams*, I had a very severe headache and nausea, which, at the time, I attributed to the heat and humidity. But after we had been back in Bangalore for a few days, where the weather is more clement, another really violent attack occurred. We went as usual to Baba's house that morning despite the headache. I hoped he might give me some relief from the excruciating pain. As soon as he caught sight of me he quickly materialized some large white pills and told me to eat them. Then he called for Nanda, one of the women who lived in the house. When she came hurrying, he instructed her to take me to lie down in one of the rooms and stay with me. The headache became even more violent, so much so that

I was completely unaware that Baba came in from time to time and rubbed the front of my head with his hand. I heard about it later after I had recovered. Apparently I was so ill that Nanda was worried. She later told me that Baba had reassured her by saying, "Don't worry. She won't die. She has a long life." Following Baba's orders, I remained in her loving care the entire day without going back to the hotel for lunch. In the evening, when it was time for everyone to leave, we returned to the hotel.

The next morning we were back in the house, and as soon as Baba saw me sitting with the other women, he said, "So you are still fighting me!" I was horrified and blurted out, "Oh no, Baba, I am not fighting you, " to which he replied, "No, not you, the sickness. You were not even there yesterday."

Meanwhile I had figured out the cause of the headaches. I had always been extremely allergic to monosodium glutamate, a taste enhancer, marketed in the U.S.A. under the trade name of Accent, and lavishly used in Chinese restaurants. We had eaten Chinese food both in Mangalore and again in Bangalore the night before the attack. Undoubtedly that was the cause of both headaches.

The next morning Baba tossed me a small packet of betel nut as he passed by on his way across to the men's side of the room. As he did so, he said, "Indigestion, not Indra Devi." This remark puzzled me for many years until I began to understand that indigestion is resistance to accepting food. My body was certainly resisting M.S.G., but I now see that there were deeper levels of resistance to which he was referring. I am the only child of an exceedingly dominating mother who was so afraid I would be spoiled that she thwarted any desire I might express. My only recourse was to resist her in order to retain my own identity. But I withdrew within rather than risk asserting myself, and deliberately became as unobtrusive as possible to avoid attracting unnecessary attention from her eagle eye. Consequently I always avoided the limelight and was terrified of talking lest I let slip something which would bring down her anger upon my head.

Indra Devi had no such hesitation about talking or being visible. She is outgoing and enthusiastic and has been instrumental in introducing Baba to thousands of people by giving lectures whenever the opportunity arose. When I finally saw the significance of Baba's remark, I marvelled at his insight and was better able to understand his method of repeatedly urging me to come forward, speak and be willing to be visible, to teach me balance between resistance and assertion.

A few days before we were scheduled to return home, Baba asked us when our plane would be leaving. When we informed him that we were scheduled to leave on the morning flight to Bombay on a certain day, he told us to pack our luggage, load it into a taxi, and drive out to his house for a farewell interview. We have since learned that this is one of his favorite little games which Hindus call *leelas*. It has caused many of his devotees hours of anxiety until they learn the lesson he intends to teach them—patience and trust that he will allow sufficient time for them to catch their flight. However, this was our first experience of this test, and we were completely unprepared for the stress which ensued. On the morning of our departure we did as he requested and drove to his house in a taxi stacked with all our luggage.

I had been faced with the additional and typically feminine decision of what to wear! How could I wear a thin *sari* for the interview, yet be sufficiently warmly clad for the flight which entailed stops in cold climates? I finally decided to wear a *sari* over my other clothes and slip it off later, either in the taxi or in the plane. This proved to be an unwise decision for it was beginning to get very hot at that time of the year.

Baba greeted each of us when he entered the room that morning and smilingly asked again at what time our plane would be leaving. When my husband told him, he replied, "That is a late plane. I will see you." With that enigmatic remark, he left the room. For the next two hours, every time he reappeared we expected him to call us in for the promised interview, but he did not even glance at either of us. We were allowed to fret and worry, and become more and more frustrated and anxious as the minutes ticked away and we feared that we would miss the flight. To add to my discomfort, I was feeling the heat from the extra clothes I was wearing under my *sari*. Finally, when we had become resigned to the probability of missing our flight, Baba quickly entered the room and beckoned to each of us, with the most innocent expression on his face, as if he had no idea of the tension which had been building up in us. We felt sure that he not only knew how anxious we were, but had deliberately arranged this test of our patience and trust. I am afraid we did not do very well on this our first such test. As we followed him into the interview room, he smiled reassuringly to put us at ease after the strain.

That day my husband had been given a particularly appealing photograph of Baba taken by Sohan Lal, an old devotee from New Delhi, with whom he had been sitting and talking for the past few days. He was holding it in his hand and when Baba saw it he took it and wrote on it, "With love and blessings" and signed it "Sathya Sai Baba." He then continued with the interview.

Among other things, we asked him when we should return. Before answering, he pointed his forefinger straight at me, like a school teacher about to make a point. The he said, "First, understand that you do not need to come back to see this little body," pointing to himself. After a long pause he added, "Find me in your heart." He watched to see the effect of these words on me. I knew he was referring to my recent struggle with the idea of having a master in human form, which I had finally resolved with his silent help. Was he now corroborating the solution I had finally found, that he symbolizes the God within each of us? When he saw that I had understood his remark, he added, with his dazzling smile, "But you will come back to be regenerated." He then explained that being in his physical presence enables his devotees to be recharged with his energy. It was many years later before I realized that with this warning not to be attached to his physical form he had set the stage for the particular teaching he would be giving me.

We left with his blessings ringing in our ears and a large envelope full of small packets of *vibhuti*. We hurried out to the waiting taxi, hoping that the driver would be able to get us to the airport in time to catch our plane.

As I took off my *sari*, and exposed the Western clothes I was wearing beneath it, I felt this simple act to be symbolic of a change of attitude already taking place in preparation for our return to the West, and the mundane world of planes and time schedules.

Naturally, we arrived at the airport with just enough time to check in before our flight was called!

Our brief but eventful sojourn with Baba had come to an end, but I knew that I was not the same person who had arrived such a short time ago to see him in person for the first time. I had partaken of too much, both of him and of India, to remain unchanged. But most of all, I had come under his direct influence. I felt quite certain it would continue to affect me to the extent to which I allowed it to do so by remembering his direction to keep in contact with his counterpart within my own heart.

We had promised our friends in Bombay to stop off for a few days on our way home. When they heard we had visited *ashrams* besides seeing Baba, they suggested we might like to meet Ananda Mayee Ma, who happened to be staying with some of her followers in the city at that time.

I was delighted to meet another spiritually evolved woman. Our hostess took us to the house where Ananda Mayee Ma was staying. As we entered the gate, several very friendly Indians approached us. They told us that the Mother was seeing visitors and if we would like to receive her blessing, we could join a line of people who were filing into the house where she was sitting. As we inched our way along in the queue, my first sight of her through the open door was quite a shock. She appeared to be old and haggard, with unkempt hair, and her skeletally thin body wrapped in a greyish white cotton *sari*. However, when I moved closer to her and she looked up to greet us, her toothless, yet radiant smile lit up her entire face. I had a glimpse of how beautiful she must have been when younger. She seemed to encompass me with her eyes, and I felt she could see right through me to the core of my being, but without judgment, just as Baba had so recently done. She merely nodded her head in greeting, and handing me a flower she was holding, she smiled again, as I moved on to make room for others to receive her blessing.

I had now met three of India's spiritually advanced women, each very different from the others. I had felt the power emanating from each one, but to none of them was I drawn in the same way as I had been to Baba. With that realization, something settled down deep inside me, and I knew my search was at an end. I had found the one who could give me what I needed.

We left for home the next day. It was not until I was packing that I discovered the sheaf of notes I had taken during the reading from the Book of Bhrigu. I was about to toss them into a wastepaper basket but something made me hesitate, and I decided to read them before discarding them. I came to the part which supposedly referred to me, and read that I was on my way to visit a master, on whose pictures ash sometimes formed. As I read on, I was astounded when I came to the list of things which he reportedly would give me, for they were exactly what Baba had so recently given me: a ring, *vibhuti*, medicine, his picture, and his love and blessings. The ring he had materialized to heal one type of headache, some *vibhuti* to heal another kind, his picture on the tin plaque to help me to concentrate on the front of his forehead, and his love and blessings written on the photograph given to us by Sohan Lal.

This fresh evidence of there being so much in heaven and earth beyond human understanding made a tremendous impression on me.

I had scorned the message from the Book of Bhrigu, but now that Baba had verified at least part of it, I felt decidedly humble. But I still wondered how a man who had lived thousands of years ago had been able to see into the future and foretell that two people from the West would arrive in India and stop in Bombay on their way to Sai Baba to consult a copy of his book. And even stranger, how could he possibly have known exactly what Baba would give to one of them? I had more questions than answers at that point.

CHAPTER NINE

AFTER WE HAD recovered from the rigors of the trip and the jet lag, I tried to sort out the many and varied reactions and impressions of my first experience of Baba. I was quite certain his influence would have a strong impact on all areas of my life, as it is impossible to be in the presence of such a powerful personality without being deeply affected, either positively or negatively. My own reactions to him were definitely very positive. But to enable the experience to work in my daily life, instead of remaining merely a meaningful memory would, I was sure, entail great effort and dedication on my part.

His last words before we left him were constantly resounding in my head, "Find me in your heart!" That, I knew without a doubt, was what I must now endeavor to do if I hoped to avoid the trap of becoming attached to his physical form in India, instead of to his counterpart within me.

I knew from my reverie work that we have all been programed from early childhood to form attachments to people and things, and that such attachments must be broken before we are free to be fully connected to the God-within. But I was soon to discover to my dismay that this was no easy task for me or anyone else.

We gradually resumed our daily activities. We continued to attend the weekly meetings at the local Sai Baba center, with more understanding now that we had experienced being with Baba in person. We were asked by many of the devotees to relate our experiences but I hesitated to do so. Only when sufficient time had elapsed to digest all I had learned, did I feel I would be able to share my reactions accurately.

In addition, the teachings I have received over the years have repeatedly warned against talking too soon about any deep and meaningful experience. The reason for this precaution is that the energy carried within an experience needs to be contained and protected for it to be fully accepted, integrated, and to become an effective part of a person's life. Besides the danger of the energy being dissipated if an experience is related too soon, there is also the possibility that the person with whom it is shared may react in a negative way, with doubt, envy, jealousy or other similar emotions. Such reactions can cause doubt in the person who has had the experience, and may even negate it for him. Negative emotions have the power to wither and blight the new growth, which like a tender young plant needs nurture and protection until it is sufficiently sturdy to withstand the elements. When a meaningful experience has had time to settle and become an integral part of the person, such dangers are greatly lessened.

It is very difficult for some people to resist the temptation to talk about their experiences too soon. They may succumb to the persuasion of those who hope to catch a reflection of Baba's love; they may wish to express their own happiness at having been to see Baba; they may even desire to impress their listeners with the fact that Baba spoke to them, granted them an interview, or in some way made them feel important. If all such lures can be resisted and devotees are able to be disciplined and wait until they have digested their experiences, their account will be much more powerful and helpful. It will also be heightened rather than become de-energized by being shared.

Devotees often bemoan the fact that they have lost the initial feeling of fulfillment with which they returned home after seeing Baba. This is partially due to the impact of the culture shock resulting from their speedy return to the Western world. However, if they refrain from discussing their experiences too soon, this loss can be lessened to a great extent. The above warning applies to premature sharing with other devotees as well as with friends and acquaintances. With the latter I have found that it is even more imperative to watch for the appropriate time, and then to talk about Baba only if they show a genuine interest, or if I am strongly prompted from within to do so.

Many of our friends, on hearing that we had gone to India to meet a holy man, were curious or sceptical. Some were downright antagonistic, and decided that we were crazy—or worse, that we were headed straight for hell.

After returning the first time, I felt too newly exposed to Baba's influence and teaching to withstand the questions I was asked and the doubts expressed, often with raised eyebrows, so I decided it would be better to say too little rather than too much. Since that time, I have repeatedly heard Baba say that he does not need anyone to advertise him as he reaches people when they are ready to receive what he has to offer them. However, that does not mean that his devotees should hide the fact that they follow his teachings.

There is a very fine line between avoiding discussion prematurely or when the occasion is not conducive to sharing, and refusing to share when a person is sincerely asking to hear about Baba. Each person needs to find his or her own balance through trial and error.

The most difficult problem for me to handle was with many of the people with whom I had been working. Some of them were aghast at the way I appeared to be flouting all we had learned over the years about the problems attendant upon becoming attached to a teacher in human form. At that time, still so early in my relationship with Baba, I had very few answers to their objections. There seemed to be little I could say to satisfy them that I was not going against the teachings we had received. I tried to explain that Baba could not be placed in the same category as other teachers, and that for me he symbolized the God within each of us. But I had to wait until I had gained further insights before I would feel more secure in my belief.

Another area of great controversy was Baba's ability to materialize various objects at will and apparently from thin air. I was constantly being reminded by well meaning friends that in all ancient writings many warnings were given about the uses of *siddhis,* or inexplicable abilities. It is recognized that they can occur at certain points along the inner or spiritual path. However, if an aspirant becomes addicted to a feeling of satisfaction or pride in their use, his ego may be inflated. His spiritual progress towards enlightenment can be delayed if he stays too long at that level.

I tried, often in vain, to explain that since Baba is a divine *avatar,* he cannot be compared with ordinary seekers and that such rules do not apply to him. My own experience also led me to believe that there was usually an underlying reason for his materializations. For instance, the ring he produced for me was for the specific purpose of healing a particular type of headache. Likewise, the small metal plaque he had made was to help me to visualize that area on his head.

Several years later I read an account of an interview between Baba and the editor of an Indian magazine, in which he was asked to explain the reason for his materializations. Baba said, "What I did is neither magic nor is it a *siddhi* power either. For me it is a kind of visiting card to convince people of my love for them and secure their devotion in return. Since love is formless I use materialization as evidence of my love. It is merely a symbol."

The interviewer then said, "Still, I do not understand why you should materialize rings, bracelets, watches, and those kinds of trinkets." To this Baba replied, "Most people desire a talisman symbolic of my protection, so I provide them. When they are in trouble they feel the grip of the ring, bracelet, or watch to remember me and call me to their rescue so that I can help them. On the other hand if I give them something that they cannot wear they are likely to store it and forget about it. The main thing is that these trinkets or talismans, by whatever name you call them, give people a sense of security and protection they need in time of trouble or crisis and create a symbolic link covering the long distances between them and myself. When the devotees need me these objects flash the message as if by wireless and I instantly come to their rescue."

The ring he materialized for me would act as just such a link between him and me when we were hijacked the following year and I called desperately for him to help me.

Despite the fact that many people I knew did not believe in Baba, I soon began to discover positive evidence of his effect on my life, particularly in my counseling work. I had not mentioned this work to Baba and he had not referred to it. However, I felt certain that he was fully aware of it, judging by his obvious knowledge of so many other facets of my life.

One of the basic symbols of my work is a triangle. This is used to connect both the counselor and the person seeking help to their High Self or God-within. To achieve this connection both people visualize themselves sitting facing one another at points A and B, with a line of light connecting them at ground level, forming the base of a triangle. They then visualize a line of light flowing up each one's spine, out through the top of their heads and continuing on up to meet at C, the apex of the triangle. This point C (High C for High Consciousness), represents the God within, often referred to as the *Atma*, the Christ-self, the Buddha-self, and many other terms. It soon became High C, for High Consciousness. I found that most people, even self-styled atheists and agnostics, believed in a wiser aspect of themselves which made itself felt periodically in their lives, particularly in times of crisis. Consequently, they were able to accept the High C concept. Sometimes it would be symbolized by a figure such as Christ, Buddha, an angelic being, a wise one, or another more abstract symbol such as a bright light or star. It is important for both the counselor and the one seeking help to ask the High C to direct the session, so that neither person decides what should take place.

Now that Baba symbolized the High C for me, I started to visualize him at the top of the triangle each time I worked, and asked him to direct the session through me. I soon discovered that it was not important whether the people with whom I worked knew about Baba. They could still use their own symbol or figure to represent their High C. However, when I work with Sai Baba devotees we both visualize him at the apex, and ask him to direct the session through us.

As Baba has made it amply clear that he does not need us to advertise him or act as missionaries, I have never made any attempt to thrust my own belief onto those who come to work with me. However, there are photographs of him in various rooms in our house, so if anyone asks about him I feel free to answer their questions. But I have never urged anyone to accept him just because I do. I have worked with people of many different beliefs, some of whom have decided to find out more about Baba, while others have chosen to continue in their own belief system.

After I had been home for several months, I began to notice that the work was taking on a new depth. When I asked the Baba-within for guidance in helping those who sought my aid with their problems, thoughts and questions would quickly form in my mind to guide me more effectively than had previously been the case. It was as if the more specific form of Baba as the High Self produced more specific answers. As Baba in India was the power-house, I would also call on him for help from time to time and I slipped into the habit of rubbing the moonstone in the ring he had produced for me to make direct contact with him.

We had brought back with us several books about his teachings, and found others at the center. These greatly helped to fill out my understanding of his mission in the world.

I also tried to continue the self-scrutiny which had started while I was in Baba's presence in India. It began to have a perceptible influence on my life and work, similar to the subtle effect of yeast on a lump of dough. In this way a year soon passed. As January again approached we began to wonder if it would be too soon to go back to Baba to be regenerated. The more we thought about it the stronger became the desire to return, so we began to plan our second journey.

CHAPTER TEN

EVERYTHING WENT SMOOTHLY on the flight to India. When we arrived in Bangalore we heard that Baba was in Whitefield. As soon as we reached our hotel, we quickly changed into our *ashram* clothes, with much less trepidation on my part, even though it was a year since I had worn a *sari*.

Our taxi dropped us at the main gate and we hurried inside, deposited our shoes in the appropriate piles, and quickly found places in the neat lines of waiting men and women already assembled. This time again I chose to sit under the shade of a tree at the back of the women's lines, rather than in front where I would be conspicuous. We barely had time to settle ourselves when the now familiar figure appeared. As he emerged from the door of his house, his bright orange-red robe and black hair were clearly visible through the iron gates. The usual hush came over the crowds as people craned their necks to see him more clearly. Many people held their hands together, ready to greet him as he approached.

When he stepped through the gates and came into full view, I felt a quickening all through me. A ripple of happiness welled up from deep within and quickly expanded until I was enveloped in a warm glow of happiness at being in his presence again. It was like coming home and being reunited with my real Mother and Father, both contained in that one small body. That thought reminded me of a previous interview, when he had warned me not to come back to see "this little body," but to find him in my heart. Yet here I was, thrilling at the very first sight of his physical form approaching. Then I also recalled that he had added that we would come back to be regenerated. So that was what I was feeling! My battery was already being recharged at the very first sight of him. That must be what is meant by *darshan*. I had known the meaning of that term in theory, but now I was experiencing it in my entire being, and on many different levels of awareness. His power was so potent that the mere sight of him could set in motion an inner reaction when I least expected it. Perhaps the point I needed to see was that it was precisely when I was least expecting it that I was open to receive it. Whereas at other times, when my mind was clamoring with its questions, expectations and desires, the way was blocked to acceptance of his power and its action within me. At that point I was reminded of one of his pet sayings: "I will give you what you want in the hope that you will want what I have come to give you."

All these realizations came so fast that I was most surprised when I looked up to see that Baba had taken only a few steps beyond the gates while I was thus occupied. As I had observed so many times the year before, he meandered back and forth between the men's and women's sides, making a zigzag pattern as he advanced. In addition to being so happy to see him again I was just as fascinated as before by the grace with which he moved and the beneficent smile of welcome for everyone lighting up his face.

Suddenly I was aware that he had caught sight of me as he moved towards the place where I was sitting. As our eyes met, he flashed a big smile of welcome. Then, to my utter astonishment, he swept his hand across his forehead and asked me how the headaches were. I must have shown my utter amazement, which greatly amused him, and he smiled delightedly at having taken me so by surprise. I managed to mumble that I still suffered from headaches, though they were not quite as severe or as frequent. He nodded his head and promised to help me. With that reassurance he passed on down the lines. I was left speechless by the fact that he had not only remembered me after a whole year had passed, during which time he must have seen hundreds of thousands of people, but that he had also remembered that I suffered from headaches and was concerned enough to ask me how they were.

Incidents like this one convince those who have experienced them that he possesses extraordinary powers and a superhuman ability to tune into each individual. He knows exactly where they are in their inner development, how they are feeling, and what their problems are. Why he chose to give me this experience at that time I did not understand then. It is only since we have returned to see him several times that I have gained, just a little at a time, more insight into his actions. Perhaps the most important message to emerge is that there is a natural rhythm in each person's life and times when we are more receptive to teaching. Baba can detect and take advantage of such times, but however hard we try to do so with our own will, it is of no avail. The lesson is PATIENCE. How many times would I have to be reminded of that?

During the next few days we saw several people we had met the year before. I began to feel less of a stranger in the crowd as I found myself sitting near someone I knew. I also began to take careful notice of the people I happened to meet each day, for invariably the seemingly chance meetings would prove to be significant in some way. It was as if we were being used to teach one another by being like mirrors in which were revealed facets of ourselves needing to be scrutinized and dealt with.

I also got into the daily habit of taking with me one of the many books about Baba to read while I waited for him to come out for *darshan*. One such book was Howard Murphet's, *Sai Baba: Man of Miracles*, which I wanted to reread. I became deeply immersed in it and discovered that it had much more meaning for me now that I had met Baba and could relate to what was being written about him. From time to time I would stop reading in order to think about a particular point, hoping in that way to gain deeper insight. As I withdrew into my inner world to dwell on a particular incident, I was able to compare it with my own experience of Baba and his teachings.

One day I came again to the account of a Norwegian devotee who had inadvertently come under the influence of a black magician and had been rescued by Baba. While I was ruminating on the action of the forces of good and evil in the world and the use of magic to gain power over other people, I became aware of a tension around me. It was strong enough to penetrate my concentration. Looking up to seek the cause, I was horrified to see Baba standing directly in front of me, watching me with a quizzical look on his face. I was chagrined as I realized that I had been so immersed in the book that I had been totally unaware of his approach. Seeing my reaction, he smiled indulgently to put me at ease and jokingly asked if I preferred to read about him when he was here in person for me to see. He moved along on his way, followed by the laughter of all those who had heard his remark.

After *darshan* was over, and he had gone back to the house, my husband and several people I knew told me that they had all tried to attract my attention to warn me that Baba had come out to give *darshan*, but that I was too engrossed in the book to notice their efforts. I was mortified as I realized that one of my childhood habits had been revealed, of withdrawing my attention from the present time and place, and retreating into an inner world of my own, often with the help of books. As a child, I had unconsciously taken this means of escape to protect myself from being completely dominated by my mother. Though now over 103, she still tries in letters to dictate to me and my family. Books had been not only an escape but also companions. Now Baba was showing me that I must be willing to be fully aware of the outer world, consciously take my place in it, and be active in both the inner and outer, as the two together form a whole. This incident made such a deep impression on me that I vowed to put into practice the insight I had just been given. I was to discover, though, that it was not going to be easy to break an old habit. I have since learned that this can be accomplished only by taking one small step at a time with patience and perseverance and Baba's help.

A few days later we were again called to an interview at nine o'clock the next morning. We were now familiar with the rhythm of sitting on the floor for long periods, always alert to Baba's sudden entrance, a signal for everyone to stand up to greet him. We were also aware that though he had told us to be at his house at a specific time, it did not necessarily mean that he would see us then.

As I sat in the familiar room I began to think about the way he often appeared deliberately to keep people waiting. I had heard from some of the more experienced devotees that it was one of his favorite *leelas*. I remembered back to the year before when we had waited for a farewell interview, with a taxi containing our luggage waiting to take us to the airport, as Baba had directed. It had certainly seemed then that he had gone out of his way to keep us waiting to the very last minute before beckoning us in for the promised interview. I started reflecting on this particular *leela* silently asked him to show me what it was intended to teach.

I have always been a very impatient person. I hate to waste time, and become very nervous whenever I have to deal with time pressure. It now dawned on me that the reason must be because I myself try to decide or control the correct timing in my life, instead of allowing my inner time clock to set the pace. If that were indeed the case, then my will or ego must be blocking a more relaxed attitude toward time. How, I wondered, could I change this old pattern now that I had seen so clearly how it was affecting my life? If Baba is the outer symbol of my High Self or the God-within, was he bringing to my attention an area where my ego was still trying to be in control? If so, could I, with his help, let go of my own will and trust him to teach me how to surrender to his timing instead of insisting on my own? The more I considered this problem the more certain I became that I could not only trust Baba to show me how to deal with it, but that he would indicate other areas in my life where I was either still trying to retain control or allowing the will of another person to override my own true pattern.

This particular theme has recurred many times since that occasion, both in Baba's presence and at home. Whenever I saw the problem clearly, quickly let go of my will and followed my inner guidance, I discovered that I was immediately faced with a similar problem, but in a different area of my life. I can see that Baba used this way of slowly but surely chipping away at the control of my ego until I gradually became more and more free to surrender my life into the hands of the Baba within, or my own God-self. It has been, and still is, a long, slow, painful and continuing process. The effect of Baba and his teachings has been to make me aware of areas in my life where I need to establish "Thy will, not mine."

Nevertheless I soon discovered that just because I had caught a glimpse of the way Baba was teaching me, it did not mean I could immediately apply the insight and relax and wait patiently until he called us to an interview. Each time he entered the room I was alert for his signal to stand up and follow him into the interview room. Sometimes he would flash a knowing smile in my direction indicating that he was fully aware of my struggle to relax and wait patiently for his call. At other times he seemed to be oblivious to our presence, let alone the reason for calling us in. This cat and mouse game continued for the rest of that day. At noon he started to leave the room to go upstairs. Then, suddenly, as if just remembering we were still there, he wheeled around and told my husband that we should return in the afternoon. So we drove back to our hotel in Bangalore for lunch and returned around four o'clock.

The afternoon proceeded along the same lines and, toward evening, he called in the college boys to sing *bhajans* and motioned us to stay. I was delighted. I thoroughly enjoyed hearing the boys singing and more especially Baba leading several *bhajans* himself. I was temporarily distracted from the tireless activity of my mind as I happily lost myself in listening to his melodious voice and watching him mark time with his hand or clap his cymbals. Abruptly, he stood up at the end of a *bhajan*, indicating that the evening was about to end. What were we supposed to do? We could not come back the following day unless he invited us. Had he forgotten that he had told us to come? On and on raced my questioning mind. Again I resigned myself to the thought that my questions would not necessarily be answered and that we might have to leave without knowing what to do. As if reading our minds, just as he was about to leave the room, he turned and called to us to return the next morning. We both sighed with relief for we now knew at least what our next step should be.

We continued to sit in the house each day and I was finally able to relax and feel content to await his daily direction without always trying to figure out ahead of time what we would be doing. But this was only just the beginning of surrender. The questions still flooded my mind but I no longer demanded immediate answers.

One day Baba asked where I had bought the *sari* I was wearing. It was a hot day and I was wearing an inexpensive drip-dry *sari*. He drew my attention to the fact that it was almost identical to one worn by the young daughter of another American couple. I remember being rather puzzled by his remark, but at that time I had not had sufficient experience in interpreting his comments to probe for a deeper significance. It was not until a few days before the end of our stay that I was given further insight while talking to another American woman who always looked very well groomed. She told me when she first went to see Baba she assumed that she should dress very plainly as befitted a *sadhu*. So she wore no make-up or nail polish and only the cheapest of *saris*. She noticed Baba's searching gaze directed at her on several occasions. Then one day he smiled sweetly and said, loudly enough for all to hear, that in America Mrs.—always wore very attractive clothes and had her hair carefully groomed, but when she came to see Baba she did not care to make herself attractive. She told me that she immediately understood the point he was making. She added that she was most embarrassed at being shown that in her mistaken zeal to look the part of a *sadhu* she had given the wrong impression and had appeared to slight Baba. From then on, she took great pains to appear as attractive and well groomed as she did at home. I was most grateful for this helpful hint despite the fact that it was too late to apply it that time. I now realize that he had implied in a subtle way that I was dressed as a teenage girl instead of as a mature woman, the wife of a successful lawyer.

Now that we had returned, and would probably be coming back from time to time, I decided to buy some colorful silk *saris* more suitable to my age and station. I had a wonderful time choosing from hundreds of lovely fabrics, and having matching *cholis* made. Baba immediately noticed the change, smiled his approval and commented on my appearance the first time I appeared in one of my new acquisitions.

Then one morning, there he was, standing in the doorway beckoning to us to follow him into the little interview room. He made us comfortable on the floor at his feet, and without delay asked me how I was and whether I had any headaches. I told him I still suffered from them from time to time, but that they did seem to be getting a little less severe and frequent. With that he moved his right hand in a circle in the air and dropped some white-colored ash into my hand, telling me to eat it, which I promptly did. It was different from the *vibhuti* in the little packets, much whiter, tasteless, without scent, and granular in texture instead of smooth.

He then informed me that another cause of the headaches was some drugs I had taken which had precipitated the menopause prematurely. I was taken aback and blurted out, "Oh Baba, I never take drugs, as I am allergic to so many of them." He insisted that he was right, and abruptly changed the subject by asking my husband a question. This gave me a chance to collect my thoughts. I knew I had always been very careful to take as few medicines as possible, and had rarely taken even an aspirin for the headaches. When the interview ended Baba looked at me quizzically, as if to say, "What are you going to do about that?"

For several days after this incident I kept thinking about his remark and it continued to disturb me. Until then I had felt so sure that he really did know everything about me in this present life as well as in all my past incarnations. Yet he was now insisting on something I felt certain could not be true. Doubts now joined with the constant questions to torment me, until I became so utterly tired and sick of them that I just gave up the search for answers. I silently asked him to help me to understand what he meant by this latest riddle and whether he was referring to actual drugs or symbolic or psychological ones.

The next morning, just as I was awakening from sleep, I was jolted into full consciousness by the memory of a trip we had made to South America at least ten years earlier. At the suggestion of

Dr. Andrija Puharich we had visited Jose Arrigo, a famous Brazilian healer and psychic surgeon. Our friend, Andrija, had felt certain that Arrigo would succeed in curing my migraine headaches. Andrija himself had met Arrigo and had watched him perform many operations including one on himself, using only a small pocket penknife. Together with a team of medical doctors he had also examined and interviewed hundreds of the grateful people whom Arrigo had cured of all kinds of ills. So sure was he that I too would be helped that he offered to arrange to have a Brazilian friend of his meet us and escort us to the small village where Arrigo lived and worked and personally introduce us. As we were already planning a trip to South America, I decided that I had nothing to lose by adding yet another strange adventure to the long list I had already undertaken in my search for relief from the incapacitating headaches which had caused so much pain and confusion in my life.

When we reached Brazil we flew to the city where our guide lived and with his help rented a car to drive to see Arrigo. The drive itself was a real adventure, as our escort spoke Portuguese, and knew only a very few words of Spanish, and fewer still of English. Neither of us knew Portuguese, but my husband was able to speak a little Spanish. With this most inadequate means of communication we tried to explain to our companion our reasons for wanting to see Arrigo. Fortunately, we were all able to laugh about our strange situation, and resorted to sign language to make up for our lack of words.

When we arrived at the tiny village where Arrigo lived, and found his house, we learned that he had been sent to a prison in a neighboring town. We gathered that it was not the first time this had happened. His offence was performing operations without either a medical degree or a licence to practice medicine.

After coming so far to see him we were disappointed at such an unexpected turn of events, but our guide was determined to see what he could do to arrange a meeting. At his suggestion we drove to the town where Arrigo was jailed and found the prison. We waited in the car while he went inside. After almost an hour he reappeared and gleefully gestured that he had obtained permission for us to visit Arrigo that afternoon during the regular family visiting hours. He also mentioned that we must pose as members of Arrigo's family, which highly amused us since we would not be able to utter a word to him. Several hours later we were ushered into a bare room containing two bunk beds in addition to the rough wooden desks used by the prison guards. On one of the beds reclined Arrigo, clad solely in rumpled pajama trousers, a big welcoming smile on his unshaven face.

For the next two hours, my husband and I sat silently while Arrigo and our guide carried on an animated conversation in Portuguese. Finally Arrigo got up from the bunk, looked searchingly at me, and withdrew to a back room from which we soon heard the clicking of a typewriter. After a few minutes he came back holding two small pieces of paper on which were typed the names of nine drugs together with directions for taking them. He had apparently received these prescriptions from his spirit guide, Fritz, a deceased German doctor who often prescribed drugs when an operation was not indicated, or, as in this instance, not permitted.

On our way back in the car our escort managed to explain that some of the drugs were to be taken orally and others by injection. To our surprise he assured us that we could procure them at most of the main chemists without a doctor's prescription.

As soon as we reached Rio de Janeiro we hurried around to several chemists and were successful in purchasing a few of the drugs at each one until we had them all. Upon arriving in New York, we sailed through customs and went straight to our friend Andrija. He arranged for the translations into English of the ingredients and directions to be sure the drugs were safe for me to take. He himself gave me the first few injections and taught my husband how to administer the remaining ones. As I continued with the series I became sicker and sicker, but I persevered with them. After several weeks I rebelled and stopped the experiment, as I was feeling decidedly worse rather than better and preferred the headaches to my reaction to the drugs. Andrija had always felt that it was my failure to finish all the drugs that was the reason I wasn't cured. After the ill-effects had worn off I began to wonder if he was right.

As the memory of the whole unpleasant episode flashed back into my mind, I realized that these must be the drugs to which Baba had referred. How could I have forgotten? I had obviously suppressed the memory. As I thought back to that time, I suddenly remembered that my menstrual cycle had indeed stopped very abruptly about that time without any warning signs to indicate that the menopause was imminent. I had not connected its onset with the drugs Arrigo had prescribed until Baba drew my attention to it.

A wave of relief swept over me as I realized that Baba really did know all about me, even those things which I myself had either forgotten or had not fully understood. In this case he could hardly have been reading my mind, as some people prefer to believe.

It was hard to wait until we arrived at his house the next morning. I hoped to have an opportunity to tell him that I had remembered taking the drugs which he had insisted had brought on the menopause prematurely. As soon as he entered the room he looked at me with an inquiring smile as if to say, "What have you to tell me today?" I blurted out, "Baba! I remember taking the drugs you mentioned the other day." He smiled indulgently, and said, "Yes. Yes. I know. I will give you something to help you." He passed over to the men's side leaving me awe-struck at his power to know so much about one individual.

I had literally travelled all over the world seeking a cure for my headaches. I had consulted many orthodox sources as well as many highly unorthodox ones, all without success. Now here I was with Baba who knew all about my problem, had diagnosed the various causes, and promised to heal me. What more could I ask? I felt confident that my quest was coming to an end, though I did not know at that time how long it would be before I would be free of the headaches.

CHAPTER ELEVEN

IN INDIA SEVERAL religious festivals are celebrated at various times during the year, not only at Baba's *ashram*, but throughout the country. One of these is Mahashivaratri which falls somewhere between late February and early March, depending on when the moon is full, as the Hindu calendar is lunar. The festival is dedicated to Shiva, one of the aspects of God in the role of destroyer. The other two gods of the Hindu Trinity are Brahma the creator and Vishnu the preserver and protector. A lesser celebration to Shiva is observed each month at the time of the full moon and is called, simply, Shivaratri.

The first time we went to see Baba we had returned home just before this festival began. This year, we had arrived later, and the festival also fell at an earlier time, so we were going to be able to attend it. Because it attracts so many thousands of people it is usually held at Baba's *ashram* where there is plenty of space as well as ample accommodation for the huge crowds which stream in from all directions.

As the time for the festival approached rumors began to fly among the devotees gathered each day at Whitefield concerning the day and time when Baba would leave for Puttaparthi. Everyone wanted to know the exact hour so that no time would be lost in hiring a taxi and gathering food, bedding, and other essentials to take along for the length of the stay. A most coveted boon is to receive Baba's permission to drive in the cavalcade of cars which follows him to the *ashram*.

As we had not yet been to Puttaparthi we were curious to see it. One day Baba asked us how long we were planning to stay in India this time. When we told him, he smiled and said that in that case we would be able to go with him to the *ashram* for the festival and stay in one of the newly built three-room apartments being constructed for the convenience of visitors. A few days later he drew us aside and gave us permission to have our taxi waiting at the main gate ready to follow him on the day he would be leaving for Puttaparthi. He asked us not to mention to anyone else the actual day. At first we were puzzled by that request, then we realized the obvious reason for the precaution. He was anxious to avoid a large number of cars all swarming along the narrow roads at the same time. Such a procession would not only disrupt other traffic, but would cause distress to the villagers and their children and animals, who wander along the roads oblivious to the noisy approach of cars. Even when the horns are screaming a warning to them to move out of the way, they do so reluctantly.

As soon as Baba had told us when he would be leaving we hurriedly gathered together the necessary equipment and provisions to take with us. We had been warned by other Western devotees who had been there before that the very hot and spicy Indian food could very well prove to be a problem for me. At the hotel in Bangalore I could always order bland food, while my husband could have the hotter dishes which he enjoys. But we were informed that at the *ashram* only very hot food was available. In recent years milder food is served for the benefit of non-Indian visitors. Indians find it very difficult to understand how we can like food which to them is absolutely tasteless.

Among other items we bought a small kerosene stove on which to boil water and cook vegetables. This purchase, we were to discover, would lead to some very interesting experiences.

On the appointed morning, with the taxi loaded with our purchases and *ashram* clothing, we waited outside the main gate for Baba's car to appear to lead the cavalcade. We were surprised to find many other cars also waiting and began to realize that around Baba news seems to leak out in some strange way despite all the precautions. As soon as his car approached there was a mad dash as the taxi drivers jockeyed for a place in the line. As we all drove off they could be seen racing to overtake one another. Some of the occupants excitedly urged them to get ahead so that they could catch glimpses of Baba as he leaned out of the car from time to time to wave to the fast gathering crowds of people who came running as word of his approach flew ahead of him. News of the rare opportunity to receive his *darshan* always brought people hurrying from all directions. Baba, seeing their eagerness, ordered his driver to slow down so that he could confer his blessing on all who came.

In this way we drove out of the city and into the surrounding countryside, passing through many small villages along the way, each with its gathering of people eager for Baba's *darshan* as he passed through. When we came to a clear stretch of road between villages he stopped a couple of times to give us all a chance to get out of the cars to stretch and partake of a refreshing piece of fruit distributed by some of the college boys who drove with him.

Baba is invariably in a holiday mood on these drives, and this, our first experience, was no exception. Now and then he alighted from his car and walked back to look into some of the other cars, bestowing a smile, a word, or teasing the occupants about the large amount of luggage they were carrying. He has a pet saying: "Travel lightly, get there quickly. He intends his remark to refer to the load of attachments to material possessions which we all carry with us through life symbolized by the luggage being carried in the cars.

Baba's boyish, fun-loving side is uppermost on such occasions, and is a source of sheer delight to his devotees, just as an enchanting child delights relatives and friends with its *joie de vivre*.

In this light hearted mood, we finally arrived at the village of Puttaparthi where Baba was born and where his *ashram* has gradually grown up. Its name, Prasanthi Nilayam, means Abode of Supreme Peace. We were all hot after the long drive but not in the least tired, even though the roads were extremely rough and, as is the case with most Indian cars, the shock absorbers were almost non-existent. Baba's infectious holiday spirit had been like a tonic keeping fatigue at bay.

We all followed him in through the main gate and were met by a stark contrast to the dusty dirty villages through which we had driven. Before us could be seen a wide expanse of open ground with a group of three-story cement block buildings. At one end was a temple and at the other end some older buildings. We were directed to one of the latter and told to ask for a key to the accommodation reserved for us. We had been told that Baba, the perfect host, personally supervises many such details for the people he invites to his *ashram*. Sure enough, a key was handed to us when we gave our names to one of the men in charge of the admissions office, after he had consulted a list of expected guests. He pointed out the building in which we would find our apartment and directed us to go to the second floor where the number would be marked on one of the doors.

When we unlocked the door of the apartment which would be our home for the next few weeks, we received quite a shock. It was certainly very different from anything our Western standards had led us to expect of an apartment. Immediately in front of us was a starkly bare room about 12 feet by 14 feet. The floor and walls were of cement. To either side of the back wall were entries to two other tiny and equally bare cement rooms, one to be used as a kitchen, the other as a bathroom. Each one contained one cold water tap set halfway up a wall and a drain in the cement floor. The only feature by which we were able to differentiate between the two rooms was that the one to be used as a bathroom had a hole in the floor with two raised slabs at either side to accommodate the feet of the person using this primitive toilet.

Our first job was to clean and sweep our temporary dwelling before we moved in. It had obviously been shut up since the last occupants left, and had gathered dust and dirt, as well as a few spiders. As if our needs had been heard, a young Indian village girl stood at the door and with gestures, and a few English words, offered to clean it for us. She told us her price, a mere pittance compared to what we were used to paying for house cleaning. She had only a rudimentary broom made of a small bunch of twigs tied together with a ravelled piece of string, and a dirty rag, which she found hanging over one of the taps, left by the last occupants. Fortunately, we had brought some soap; and with these simple aids she was able to dispel the worst of the dust so that we could move in with our luggage and set up house.

We stacked our cooking utensils, stove, and provisions on the floor in one corner of the kitchen, and our towels and soap on the bathroom floor. We had brought with us two inflatable mattresses which we placed on the floor in the main room and spread sheets over them. Over each bed we laboriously suspended a mosquito net, attaching it by its four corners with pieces of string tied to nails hammered into the wood panels over the doors and windows. This was to be a daily task, as the nets had to be taken down each morning and put up again each night, to allow us to move about the room during the day. The next day we bought some rope and several simple wire hangers in the village. By stretching the rope across one end of the room from wall to wall, we fashioned a makeshift clothesline on which my *saris, cholis,* and petticoats, and my husband's white shirts and trousers could be hung. Everything else was left in our suitcases which were pushed against a wall to double as a table. During the day, the mattresses were placed against another wall to form a couch.

We quickly slipped into our new way of life, which could not have been more different from our usual daily routine at home. We take for granted the many conveniences and gadgets, which in India are still considered luxuries, if at all available. The daily routine at the *ashram* was also quite different from that in Whitefield. In Prasanthi Nilayam almost all of the guests lived on the grounds or close by in the villages.

I set up the kerosene stove in the kitchen area and started to prepare and cook some of the fresh vegetables we had brought with us. I had barely started to cook them when I began to feel very sick and my head started to ache. I stood up and walked outside into the fresh air and immediately felt better. But each time I returned to the cooking the symptoms reappeared. It finally dawned on me that I must be allergic to the kerosene fumes, just as I have always been sensitive to paint, varnish, cleaning fluid and other chemicals. What was I going to do if I could not cook or eat the hot food served in the *ashram*? I was at a loss to solve this problem.

As I was wondering what to do, a South African woman whom we had met at Whitefield came walking past our room. Seeing me standing outside, looking quite sick, she asked what was wrong. When she heard my dilemma she immediately offered a solution. She explained that she had brought with her from Bangalore a young village girl she had trained to cook and clean for her. She suggested that we take our food over to her room each day where the girl could cook for all of us. She was so insistent that we acquiesced, and from then on we ate with her and a young English girl she invited to join us.

Not only was our problem solved but we also enjoyed getting to know these two women. In the course of our conversations both of them revealed that they had in common a problem with paralyzing fears.

Until then I had purposely avoided any mention of my work. My decision was based on the belief that it would be in extremely bad taste to discuss it when we had all come here to receive Baba's help, healing and instruction. I had yet to learn that he uses all of us to help each other. Our meeting with the two women was to change my mind. Each day as we met for meals they both enlarged on the subject of their fears and described in detail how this negative emotion affected every aspect of their lives and continued to haunt them even in Baba's presence. They both bemoaned the fact that they had found nothing to help them with this distressing problem. As they talked about the many ways in which their fears manifested, I could keep quiet no longer, knowing that I had learned various methods which might help them. I suddenly found myself plunging headlong into a description of the type of counseling I had been taught in deep meditation. It was as if the words erupted out of my mouth and I was just as surprised as they were at my unexpected outburst. They were fascinated by what they heard, and eager to start to work with me now that they knew there were methods available to help them uncover the root cause of their fears.

However, I was now faced with a real dilemma. We were all guests at Baba's *ashram*, gathered there to seek his help and blessings. What right had I to offer my help, especially as I had not yet had an opportunity to check with him to find out if he approved of the method I used? I therefore told the women that I would try to obtain Baba's permission by asking him to indicate in some way what I should do.

Immediately, a swarm of doubts assailed me. Wasn't it Baba's place to help them? Wouldn't it be presumptuous on my part to undertake the responsibility of working with them? I was certain of only one thing: that I did not want to do anything in any way unacceptable to Baba. So I resolved to try to ask him personally the next time he came out to give *darshan*. However, it appeared to me that he deliberately avoided me, even to the extent of seeming to go out of his way to move away from where I was sitting. I remembered other people telling me of similar experiences when they were intent on asking him something which he was not ready to answer.

Meanwhile the two women were impatient to be released from their fears, which they noticed had begun to increase in severity. Finally, after failing for several days to catch Baba's attention, I sat early one morning in our room which faced the *mandir* (temple) above which Baba has his private rooms. As I sat there I tried to make mental contact with him, silently asking him to give me a sign to show me what to do.

After a few minutes of silence, while I settled into a quiet and receptive state, a vivid picture flashed into my mind. I seemed to be a spectator watching an extremely stormy sea from the safety of the shore. Huge waves towered and crashed onto the beach not far from where I stood. As I continued to watch this inner scene I became aware of a flimsy raft to which the two women were clinging desperately and calling out frantically for help. Inside my head I heard Baba's voice asking me, "If this were the actual situation would you hesitate to throw them a lifeline to help them to reach the shore?" I knew instantly that I would have absolutely no hesitation if that were the case. "Then why are you reluctant to help them to dispel their fears?" his voice questioned.

Here was my answer, clear and simple, received in the familiar way of the reverie. Satisfied that I had been shown what to do, I told the women about the experience and my decision to work with them. I also mentally asked Baba to give me a sign if for any reason he did not approve of anything I was doing. From then on I fitted a session with one or the other of them into the daily schedule whenever there was enough time between *darshan* and meals.

It appeared as if Baba continued studiously to avoid even so much as a glance in my direction, which again raised doubts in my mind about his reaction to what I was doing. I was certain he knew I was working with the women, as nothing escapes his attention, a fact which had been proved many times already. However, I still could not be completely sure whether he approved or not, so a nagging doubt persisted despite the fact that I had been given such a clear direction from the mental picture of the storm. But perhaps I had imagined it. Maybe my ego was getting in the way. On and on raced my doubting mind without respite.

Now I realize that Baba was forcing me to take responsibility by seeking direction from the God-force within me instead of relying on him personally to tell me what to do. What a necessary lesson after the Tibetan experience! But at that time I was more concerned with abiding by the *ashram* rules which I knew Baba expected his guests to observe.

As I continued to work with the two women, I noticed that the sessions flowed much more easily than was usually the case with new people. I decided it must be due to the extraordinary power which emanated from Baba at such close range.

Each day was very full, and slipped by swiftly. As the time of the Shivaratri festival drew near, the crowd rapidly increased as more and more people congregated at the *ashram*. Sometimes whole villages would arrive together, often having traveled hundreds of miles. Many of these people set up primitive camps on the ground or along the passages outside the rooms, as the existing accommodation was soon filled to overflowing. The whole area looked as if it were carpeted with people and it was necessary to walk very carefully to avoid stepping on a sleeping child or tripping over food supplies and bedding.

During Shivaratri at Baba's *ashram*, for many years it has been his custom to produce from inside his own body an oval-shaped object called a *lingam*. It represents symbolically the true form of the Supreme Reality which is all-pervasive, all-knowing, and all-powerful, and out of which, as from an egg, everything emerges, and into which everything returns. For the previous three years there had been no public demonstration of this extraordinary feat, though it was rumored that Baba had still produced a *lingam*, either in the privacy of his own apartments, or in a small intimate gathering of devotees whom he had personally chosen to be present.

We had seen a sequence in one of the films showing Baba producing a *lingam*, and would have liked very much to witness this rare phenomenon. But it appeared to be most unlikely that we would have that experience, as Baba had apparently decided to stop producing it before a large crowd.

Actually, the most important benefit to be derived from participating in this festival was the opportunity it offers to those attending it to relinquish the hold of the mind, and thus be more open to the God-within. To quote Baba, "Mahashivaratri is dedicated to the disintegration of the aberrations of the mind and so the mind itself, as each person dedicates himself to Shiva, as God." He explains that the moon symbolizes the mind. It has sixteen phases as does the mind. On Shivaratri fifteen of these have disappeared, and there is just a streak of the moon visible in the sky. The new moon that follows will not even have that streak visible. The mind too, must be mastered everyday. On the fifteenth day, fifteen phases of it will have disintegrated and only a streak remains to be removed by a final flourish of effort during the all-night *bhajan* singing. When the mind goes, no more deluding desires and attachments remain, and liberation follows. What an opportunity to break away from the fetters of the mind!

It is also one of Baba's customs to perform a ritual called *vibhuti abhisheka* on the morning of Shivaratri, to honor Shirdi Sai Baba, said by Baba to have been his previous incarnation. On that day, a silver statue of Shirdi Sai Baba was placed on the platform for this ritual. First, Baba materialized precious stones and grains of rice and threw these into a sacred fire burning in a container placed nearby for that purpose. Then he was handed a vessel containing water which he first blessed and then used to wash the statue. Next he took a large whisk, dipped it into the water and shook it out over the heads of the huge crowd sitting on the floor of the auditorium, sprinkling everyone with it. In order for each person to receive a few drops he walked up and down the aisles, bestowing a blessing on all those present. An attendant then walked over to the image of Shirdi Sai Baba and held inverted over it an empty urn. Baba approached, rolled up the sleeve from his right arm and thrust it into the upturned urn. He then started to move it in a churning motion. Immediately, showers of *vibhuti* began to pour out onto the figure in such quantities that it was soon almost completely covered, and the ash started to overflow on all sides. Suddenly Baba withdrew his hand and the flow stopped as abruptly as it had started. Next he proceeded to roll up the sleeve from his left arm and thrust that hand up into the urn and repeated the churning motion. The ash again began to flow, this time with astonishing force and the urn vibrated so violently that the man who was holding it aloft found it hard to keep steady. The flow continued until a huge pile of ash had collected all around and over the statue. As soon as Baba withdrew his hand again, the flow ceased and he walked off the platform leaving the crowd spellbound by the spectacle they had just witnessed. I was delighted to have had the opportunity of witnessing this extraordinary pre-Shivaratri ritual.

During the rest of the day there was a great deal of activity as more and more people arrived for the festival. By evening they were milling around everywhere. The volunteers were trying to keep some semblance of order among them. Some people tried to push their way into the auditorium. They hoped to secure a place on the floor from which to observe Baba officiate at the remainder of the rites and, even more important, to hear his discourse. He most considerately gave orders for the few Westerners who had traveled so far and at great expense to be allowed to sit in the first few rows. How very fortunate we felt, and so grateful to Baba for this thoughtfulness. We arrived early and sat quietly, my husband on the men's side as I took my place on the women's side of the great hall, waiting for Baba to appear. The usual audible hush settled over the packed auditorium as soon as he appeared from behind a screen at the back of the stage. He took his place in the big red velvet covered chair which he always used. A solemn ceremony was performed by several Vedic pandits and then it was time for Baba to speak. He delivered his discourse in Telegu, pausing at intervals for Dr. Bhagavantam to translate it into English.

As soon as it ended he broke into the opening line of a well known *bhajan*, leading the immense crowd. We all repeated it after him in thunderous tones which reverberated all around the hall. The tremendous energy thus released could be felt by everyone and seemed to lift us all up to a level beyond our everyday consciousness.

When the sound had reached a peak, Baba started to cough, and reached for a handkerchief placed ready for his use on the arm of his chair. We were all shocked to see him hold it up to his mouth and start to retch into it, his whole body contorted with the effort.

An electric current seemed to run like lightning around the huge hall as the silent question rose in everyone's mind simultaneously, "Was it possible that after a lapse of three years he was again about to produce a *lingam* in public for us all to see?"

As if following some silent cue, the tempo of the singing increased and everyone poured out in song their surprise and excitement at the great good fortune of being present at such a significant event. Each one seemed to be trying to help as Baba strained to set free the sacred symbol which had been forming within him. The tempo became faster and faster and a tremendous energy built up in the auditorium.

As I watched him intently, I found myself caught up in his effort to release the *lingam* and, for a split second, I became almost identified with him. I relived the birth of my two daughters, feeling again the tremendous pressure build up as I watched him retch again and again in an effort to give birth to the God-symbol. Finally he gave one last cough and quickly caught in the handkerchief a large shimmering opalesque egg shaped *lingam*. It appeared much too large to have passed out through his throat. He immediately held it up between his thumb and forefinger for us to see and then started to walk up and down the aisles to enable everyone to have the *darshan* of this wondrous creation. As we were given a close look at it, a light could be seen in its depths which seemed to move and change as he carried it around the packed hall. We were spellbound at having witnessed this extraordinary manifestation which produced a deep emotional impact on everyone present. After Baba had returned to the stage and disappeared through the curtains, everyone filed out of the hall, still in a daze, to prepare for the night-long *bhajan* singing.

The following evening Baba gave another discourse in which he announced that the *lingam* he had produced the day before was a very special one. It possessed the power to liberate from the bondage of life and death all those who were fortunate enough to be present at its emergence. However, he was quick to warn everyone that to earn that release we must, from this time on, live our lives in accordance with the grace we had won that day.

We were all profoundly moved by his words, each reacting in a different way. Some people were puffed up with pride at the thought of their good fortune, others felt burdened with the responsibility it imposed, and still others were overcome with gratitude. I doubt that any one of the thousands in attendance was left untouched by Baba's extraordinary message.

The next morning everyone assembled for *darshan*, sitting on the ground in long neat lines waiting for Baba to appear. When he came out he was followed by some of the college boys, each carrying a basket filled with little packets of *vibhuti*. We later learned that they were filled from the piles he had manifested at the *vibhuti abhishekam*. He walked slowly along the rows and personally handed each person some of the special ash as a gift to take home, now that the festival was ending.

During the last several days my mind had been so fully occupied with the events filling each day that I had not had time to give any further thought to Baba's possible attitude to the work I had been doing to help the two women with their fears. I had had no direct contact with him which might have enabled me to sense his reaction. But now, as I watched him walk slowly, with such patience and love, up and down the long lines of eagerly waiting people, I realized that he would soon reach the place where I was sitting. At that thought my mind started to raise the same old doubts. I was divided between eager anticipation of receiving the specially blessed *vibhuti* from his hand, and anxiety about his reaction when he saw me for the first time since I had started to work.

Finally, he was standing directly in front of me. As soon as I looked up at him, a wonderful smile spread across his face. As he handed me some packets of *vibhuti* he brought his right hand down firmly on top of my head and leaning over me, whispered so that only I could hear, "Good lady." Then beaming another smile at me he passed on down the line. No one else could have heard what he said, nor would anyone else have understood the significance of his words. A wave of immense relief swept through me as I realized that he had forced me to find out for myself what I should do, and now gave his approval of my decision after I had been willing to take the first step. This would continue to be his method of teaching me.

Baba rarely tells anyone what to do. Instead he prefers to leave each person to figure out for himself the best course to take. He comments, or gives them a sign only after they have made their decision, unless the results are so obvious that no sign from him is needed. I was most thankful to have his approval, not only of working at his *ashram*, but presumably also of the particular counseling technique I used as *seva*, or service, to God. What a contrast from my worried state only a few days ago!

Later that day Baba announced the close of the festival and gave permission for everyone to leave. We drove back to Bangalore and, after a few days of shopping for gifts to take back to our family and friends, we flew to Bombay, where we planned to see friends before returning.

CHAPTER TWELVE

WE HAD ALREADY made our reservations on a BOAC flight scheduled to leave on Saturday, March 2, to fly to London where I planned to see my mother. However, when we arrived in Bombay, we heard from some of the devotees there that Baba had sent word that he would be arriving that Friday evening for a few days. My immediate thought was how wonderful it would be to have one more *darshan* before we left India. I therefore suggested to my husband that we try to change our reservations to leave on Sunday instead of Saturday, which would allow us just enough time to drive out to Dharmakshetra, where he would be staying. To my delight, we were successful in changing our flight. I silently thanked Baba for helping to make it possible, a habit I noticed I had recently fallen into.

On Saturday we drove out to Dharmakshetra. It is situated on the outskirts of the city, and is one of the most beautiful and unusual of the buildings dedicated to Baba. When we arrived we were surprised to see a huge crowd already assembled and beginning to overflow the extensive grounds adjacent to the main building. Some people were sitting outside the walls, wherever they could find a space. We doubted that there would be room for us inside, but our fears were soon allayed when we were escorted by volunteers to places on the men's and women's sides of the huge open area. People moved closer together to allow us to squeeze in between them.

This was our first visit to Dharmakshetra. Many people had tried to describe it to us, and we had seen views of it in some of the films. Now I was being given the unexpected opportunity to have my own actual view of this remarkable building. It is hard to describe, and no description can do it justice. It is a large white circular cement building surrounded by a walled pathway at the base. Within this rises a lotus shaped structure with windows at intervals all around it, each one in the middle of a petal of the lotus. Immediately in front of the whole complex stands a very tall *stupa*, like a half open lotus at the end of a long stem. The whole effect is most unusual.

One of the Indian women seated near me leaned over and pointed out the exact location of the room in which Baba stays when he is in Bombay. Whoever she was, I wish I could thank her, as it enabled me to visualize it later the next day on the plane.

After some time the usual sudden hush heralded Baba's approach, as those who could see him emerge from the building sent back word to the crowd that he was on his way. Very soon thereafter he could be seen circulating among the eager throng. Some of them had been sitting and waiting for this moment for hours. At one point he came close and sent me a warm smile of recognition. What a perfect ending to our visit! Another Indian woman sitting in front of me leaned back and whispered, "You are blessed." I heartily agreed. Her remark removed any doubt I might have had that his smile was intended for me. I mention this small incident only because I was to flash back to it the following day when I was desperately trying to make contact with him and wondering if he could hear my call for help. When he had finished his rounds and gone back inside the building we went back to our hotel, the vivid memory of his small orange clad form clearly silhouetted against the white building imprinted on our memories.

The next day we boarded the plane for London. It landed in Bahrain and again at Beirut to allow some passengers to disembark and others to join the flight. We took advantage of these stops to stretch our legs. As we were re-boarding at Beirut, I remarked to my husband that the security check through which I had just come was a veritable farce. The woman inspector had merely riffled her fingers around in the top of my handbag and stamped my boarding card. I added that if this was an example of the precautionary measures being taken in Beirut, of all places, where there had been so much trouble lately, it would be very easy for a plane to be hijacked. Prophetic words . . . .

Soon after the stewardesses had finished serving a meal and had removed the trays, we happened to look up and were surprised to see a group of passengers from the first class cabin moving back into the tourist section where we were sitting. We both thought it rather strange and discussed possible reasons for it. My husband suggested that perhaps we were heading into rough weather, in which case it could be a precautionary measure to shift the weight. At that point the captain appeared at the rear of the group, looking grave. As he passed our seats we asked him what was happening. He replied in a grim voice that we would soon find out and with that enigmatic remark he moved past us to find a seat. As soon as all the first class passengers were reseated, a harsh voice speaking in very broken English came over the loadspeaker announcing that we were being hijacked.

This terse announcement produced audible gasps of horror from the passengers, followed by shocked silence as everyone began to realize the many frightening implications.

Into my mind flashed the memory from our first meeting with Baba in 1973, when he had reprimanded the two couples for forgetting to call on him for help when their taxi was about to collide with a big truck. I recalled my silent vow to remember to call on him if I were ever in trouble, and immediately began silently to call, "Baba! Baba! Baba!" with all the intensity and urgency I could muster.

Shortly after the hijacker's stark announcement, two toughlooking Arabs emerged from the cockpit carrying machine guns and pistols. They were obviously ready to shoot anyone who might attempt to resist them. I distinctly recall thinking that if they had been cast as villains in a film they would scarcely be believable. They were so grotesque that they were like caricatures. They commandeered the services of an Arabic speaking passenger who reluctantly raised his hand when they asked if there was anyone who could interpret for them. He was ordered to collect all the passports and place them in a pile on a seat in front of the hijackers. One of them started to check through them, and appeared to be separating them into the various nationalities. Most of the passengers were Indian, Arab or British, with a mere handful of Americans. The chilling thought went through both our minds that those of us who were traveling with American passports would probably be taken as hostages, because of the strained relations between the U.S.A. and the P.L.O. at that time. I also had my own private worry. My husband is Jewish, and in my anxiety I could not remember whether the fact was given in his passport. If so, he could be in even more danger.

Their next move was to have all our flight bags collected. Some were emptied, refilled with dynamite, and placed at various strategic points throughout the plane, such as outside toilets, and at intervals along the aisles. They next announced that no one would be allowed to go the toilet unless escorted by one of the stewardesses, and even then only one person at a time. Naturally, everyone needed to use the toilet at once. It is a well known fact that tension and fear affect the kidneys and bladder. This was particularly true under the eagle eyes of the hijackers, who pointed their guns at the bags of dynamite at the entrance to each toilet, ready to shoot into them if anyone tried to cause trouble.

By this time the mass fear was so strong that it felt like a tangible presence and was accompanied by a strong acrid odor. I had heard that animals are able to smell fear in a person, and now that so many people were held in the grip of it at the same time, I too could smell it. I realized that logically I should have been filled with fear myself and greatly agitated at the possibility of leaving our two daughters so suddenly and unexpectedly. However, I discovered with astonishment that I had absolutely no fear and moreover was positive that we would all be spared. This attitude made no sense whatever to me, so I searched within for the fear which I thought I should be feeling, as I did not want to delude myself. Miraculously, there was not even a trace, and with this discovery came the thought that Baba must have heard me call for help and had removed any fear I might have had. Comforted by that thought I surreptitiously opened my handbag and quietly withdrew from it a picture of Baba and some of the *abhisheka vibhuti* he had so recently given me at Shivaratri. I placed these in my lap, together with the ring he had materialized the previous year, hoping they were out of sight of the hijackers. I started to concentrate on them as links to help me make telepathic contact with him. I remember thinking how very fortunate it was that only a few hours earlier the room where he was staying had been pointed out to me. That now enabled me to visualize him there, at the very moment when I so desperately needed to make contact with him.

No one in the plane dared to utter a sound and the unnatural silence weighed very heavily. We later discovered that there were several small children on board, including a two-week-old baby, yet none of them even whimpered, probably paralyzed by their parents' fear.

Some time later, one of the hijackers began wiring the plane, presumably preparing to blow it up. He very ostentatiously wired all the escape hatches, a lighted cigarette hanging out of one corner of his mouth and a gun held in one hand. He was obliged to use his teeth to hold the wires as he manipulated them with his free hand. As soon as the wiring was completed to his satisfaction, he ordered the stewardesses to bring all the bottles of alcohol and scent from the duty-free supply. He proceeded to break open the bottles and spill the contents all along the aisles, with the obvious purpose of feeding the flames when the plane was set on fire.

During all this activity I had been concentrating on Baba, and at this point I seemed to hear his voice in my head telling me to send love to the hijackers. I was shocked at such a suggestion, especially when I looked at their faces and saw their eyes filled with fanatical, almost ecstatic hate. My first reaction was, "Oh Baba, how can I?" but I quickly added, "Please love them through me, since you alone can see the God within them which you assure us is in everyone." I then leaned back in my seat and began to feel Baba's love flow through me and across to those two hate filled men. As I watched the effect, the one who was emptying the bottles of alcohol and scent became so nervous that he cut his wrist on the broken glass. He was obliged to stop and bind the cut with an improvised bandage to stop the flow of blood. He took a handkerchief from one of his pockets, but would not put down his gun, so again used his teeth to help tie the makeshift bandage around his hand. From then on both men became increasingly nervous. They lost the air of bravado which had been so obnoxiously evident when they first took over the plane.

We could tell that we had been flying in a westerly direction for several hours, but could only guess at what our captors had in mind to do with us. Much later we learned that their first plan was to land in Athens where they intended to demand the release of some of their Palestinian associates imprisoned there, in exchange for hostages from the plane. However, they were refused permission to land so we next flew to Amsterdam, where their request was also refused. They then decided to fly over the North Sea and blow up the plane in midair. But the copilot, who was flying it under their surveillance, informed them that there was insufficient fuel in the tanks to take them that far. They again appealed to Amsterdam, reporting the low supply of fuel, which resulted in permission to land the plane at a remote part of the airport.

As we knew none of this at the time we were most surprised when one of the hijackers announced that we were about to land and that we should "take our feet in our hands, hold them up above our heads, and move out into the aisles." It took us all a minute or two to realize that they meant our shoes and not our feet. They then informed us that we had two minutes to get off the plane before they set fire to it. They opened one door through which they let down a plastic chute for the passengers to slide down to the concrete surface of the airfield many feet below.

At that point, with escape in sight, everyone tried to rush for door, jostling each other in a wild effort to get free of the plane before it caught fire. An hysterical man behind me tried to push past me, and in his anxiety to escape knocked me sideways down the chute in such a way that I had no control over my landing and hit the hard tarmac on my coccyx. The force with which I hit the ground was so severe that I could not stand up and was shoved to one side by passengers coming down the chute after me. My husband soon followed, and he and another man managed to carry me to one side, out of the path of the others and free of the plane, which was already beginning to burn.

Buses from the airport soon rushed out to pick us all up, but because of my injury we were far in the rear of the group. We were finally able to board the last bus but, to our horror, our driver, catching sight of two more people standing a little beyond the fast-burning plane, turned his bus around to pick them up. They were our hijackers! We could not speak Dutch, but my husband pounded on the glass screen separating us from the driver, and screamed, "Hijackers," one word the driver understood. He promptly turned the bus around and drove as fast as he could to the terminal. Our last view of the hijackers was seeing them standing limply a little distance from the plane. They appeared drained of energy, the very picture of defeat, with the plane smoldering behind them.

As we were prevented from taking anything with us when we got off the plane, handbags, coats and jackets, hand luggage, and even some people's shoes had been left behind. We had left hot and steamy Bombay only a few hours earlier and were now in Europe on a cold March evening. It had been raining and many people without coats or jackets were thoroughly chilled by the time we arrived at the terminal building. It was long after the last plane for the day was expected, so the airport was almost empty. However, word of our arrival was immediately circulated, and the whole place soon came to life as workers hurriedly arrived from all directions, exclaiming excitedly about the near disaster, and all asking questions at once.

We were given warm socklets, blankets to wrap around us, and steaming hot cups of coffee to warm us inside and out. Reporters from the local newspapers came rushing in to cover the event, and we were all asked to tell our version of the frightening experience. My back was still extremely painful so I wondered when we would reach London, where, by an odd coincidence I had already made an appointment to see a doctor who specializes in the Alexander Technique, a method of aligning the body. I had seen him the year before and wanted to take advantage of our time in London to have a few more treatments. I could certainly use them now! Just as I was thinking about this I happened to hear an announcement in English over the loudspeaker system that a scheduled flight was leaving shortly for London, and that all passengers should proceed to the gate. I quickly told my husband, and he asked one of the men in charge to enquire if there were two seats available on that plane. He explained that I had hurt my back and would prefer to see a doctor I knew in London rather than a strange one in Amsterdam. The man spoke to an airline official who agreed to try to arrange for us to leave on the flight to London. In a few minutes he came hurrying back to tell us that two seats were available and we should follow him as fast as possible as it was due to leave shortly. With him and my husband to help I hurried as quickly as I could and we arrived at the gate just in time. Our problem was quickly explained to the various officials waiting for us and we were rushed on the plane in time for it to leave on schedule.

We had no luggage, no handbags, no passports, and no identification. We were given handwritten passes to allow us to land in London where we would have to apply for temporary passports to allow us to fly home.

We sank gratefully into our seats. As the plane took to the air we both looked down, and there on the ground we could see the smoldering plane we had so recently left in such a hurry. I quickly sent my heartfelt thanks to Baba and was again aware of a sense of peace enveloping me as I acknowledged his help.

An acid foam was being sprayed into the burning plane from tiny cars designed to put out fires. A few days later, when we went to pick up our luggage at London Airport, on opening the cases we discovered that everything was ruined, either burned or soaked with acid and horribly discolored. We had to abandon everything, including the cases.

We were issued temporary passports. I kept my appointments with the doctor in London which enabled me to fly back to Los Angeles after a few days. It was, however, a long time before my back was free from pain.

Several weeks after we returned home we read in a newspaper that one of the food-handlers in Beirut had been offered a bribe of four hundred dollars to take guns, ammunition and dynamite onto the plane in food containers. He hid it all under the seats reserved for the hijackers.

During the months ahead we were able to follow their movements in the newspapers. When they were first detained in a prison in Amsterdam, the questions arose of where they should be tried and by whom. They were eventually tried in Amsterdam and imprisoned there. However, several months later we heard that another plane had been hijacked and the release of these two prisoners was demanded in exchange for hostages.

At the time of our escape I had felt profound relief at our narrow escape and an overwhelming sense of gratitude to Baba for answering my frantic call for help. I never for a moment doubted that he had done so. However, it was not until a whole year later that we were able to thank him personally for his help.

He has often said that he will never interfere with anyone's earned *karma,* but will soften it as much as possible and help them to bear it. He explains that we all have free will and with that not even he will interfere. So it is our personal responsibility to make the conscious descision to call on him to help.

For me, one of the biggest insights resulting from the hijacking experience was that Baba requires us to be willing to do our part. We must allow him to use us in various situations and in whatever ways he sees fit. I was sure that it was only the power of his love that was a strong enough force to divert the hijackers from their original plan to destroy the plane and all the passengers. It would be eight years before he actually confirmed that this was the case. It is so easy to forget that we also have a part to play by surrendering our own will and agreeing to let his will take over in our lives, and consequently in the world in which we live and with the people with whom we come in contact.

An interesting sequel to the hijacking occurred in October of that same year. It so happened that Dr. Gokak, a close devotee of Sai Baba, currently Vice-Chancellor of the university at Puttaparthi, was in California on a brief visit. He had been the guest of several devotees and was staying with us for a few days. He was a delightful guest and we thoroughly enjoyed his company. He and my husband shared a common interest in English literature, and we learned that he had attended Oxford University. He is also a poet, and paid us a charming compliment by composing a poem about the panoramic view of the mountains and distant ocean which he enjoyed from the window of the room he occupied in the twelfth floor apartment where we were living at the time.

A day or two before he was due to move on to stay with another family, we received a cable from a travel agent in London with whom we had been in contact regarding a possible tour to Red China. The cable informed us that we had both been cleared by they travel authorities in Peking, and space had unexpectedly become available on a tour due to leave that coming Thursday. However we would have to arrive in London by Monday to allow time for our visas to be granted by the Chinese embassy. In those days visas to travel to China were not available in the U.S.A. as the American government had not yet recognized Red China. The travel agent urged us to call him as soon as possible if we wished to join the group as he could not keep the spaces open for long.

Our immediate reaction was disappointment. It seemed to be out of the question for us to accept with so little time to prepare for such a trip, and with a house guest. We were also attending the various meetings at which Dr. Gokak spoke and were preparing to give a dinner in his honor on the evening before we would have to leave.

When Dr. Gokak heard about the trip he was adamant that we should take advantage of such an exciting offer. He pointed out that it was an opportunity that should not be missed, for in those days there was no guarantee that the U.S.A. would recognize Red China and thus make it possible for Americans to be granted visas to enter that country on a normal basis. He offered to move sooner if his visit was the cause of our reluctance to leave on the trip. We finally succumbed to his persuasion and telephoned the travel agent, telling him to save two places, and to request the Chinese embassy to prepare our visa applications.

Those final few days were really hectic, yet everything flowed smoothly. We were able to attend the meetings and still manage to prepare and pack for the trip. Many devotees joined in to help us make the dinner for Dr. Gokak a success. On the Sunday morning, as he was being picked up by his next hosts, we were ready to leave for the airport.

Imagine our reaction upon arriving in London, when we discovered that we would be flying to Hong Kong on a BOAC plane scheduled to put down in Beirut and Bahrain for refueling and change of passengers. It was the same airline and the same two cities where our ill-starred flight earlier that year had stopped. We were not a little dismayed at this news, but realized that there was absolutely nothing we could do about it at that late date. So I silently called on Baba to protect us. Everything went smoothly in London and we were issued our visas in time to join the group as planned.

When the plane landed at Beirut we were informed that for security reasons all continuing passengers must remain on board during the stopover. This restriction caused a great deal of grumbling among the passengers, as many of them had been looking forward to a chance to stretch their legs. My husband, who was standing near the open doorway, remarked that he for one was quite content to stay on board as we had been hijacked after stopping in this city earlier that year. He added that he was glad to see that the security measures appeared to have been tightened since then. An Indian stewardess standing near him wheeled around when she heard his remarks and asked if he was referring to the plane which had landed in Amsterdam in March. When he affirmed that it was indeed that one, she exclaimed, "I was one of the stewardesses on that flight." We all marvelled at the coincidence and wryly commented on the fact that apparently we were all willing to take another chance. She took the attitude that such an experience was very unlikely to happen to anyone more than once in a lifetime, so the odds were against it happening on this flight, with all three of us on it. Everyone within earshot fervently expressed the hope that she would prove correct.

Soon after we returned from China we began to plan another trip to see Baba the following January, which was fast becoming a yearly habit with us. I was most anxious to see him again and hoped for an opportunity to thank him for bringing us safely through our ordeal. We had not heard whether he had given any indication that he knew of our eventful flight home after we saw him last. I only had my own firm conviction that he had not only responded to my call for help, but had erased any fear I might have had and had prevented what could well have resulted in a disaster for the whole planeload of passengers. I realized that only he could verify this feeling of mine, and then only if he chose to do so. But I also knew there was no certainty that he would even refer to it when we saw him again. Our experience had shown us that no one can ever predict what Baba will do at any given time or about anything whatsoever. Besides thanking him, I also hoped for some word from him for another reason. The news of our experience had a very strong impact on other devotees who knew us. The most common reaction was one of shock that Baba had allowed it to happen and had not warned us, as he sometimes does when he sees what lies ahead for some of his devotees. His warm smile when he caught sight of me in the *darshan* lines at Dharmakshetra in Bombay made me certain that he could have warned us then had he deemed it necessary. For reasons known only to him he chose not to do so, possibly because he foresaw that it would be an important experience for us in some way. I was well aware that some people's faith in him was badly shaken, which I could easily understand. My own conclusion was that we cannot afford to labor under the delusion that as soon as we accept Baba we will henceforth automatically lead charmed lives and live happily ever after, free from all problems. I can only speak for myself and my own experience and, for me, this has been far from the case, as he has illustrated by his method of teaching me through such experiences.

CHAPTER THIRTEEN

WE LEFT FOR India again around the middle of January 1975. When we arrived in Bangalore we heard that Baba was in Whitefield so we changed our clothes and drove out for our first *darshan*. When Baba came out and caught sight of us in the *darshan* lines, he told my husband that we should be at his house early the next morning.

It was like coming home to be sitting in the house again. When he came down from his private rooms, he told us he was going to lunch at Dr. Bhagavantam's house and asked us to accompany him. When we arrived and entered the front door several men were already sitting on the floor waiting for Baba. I was the only woman invited, and no sooner had I begun to wonder where I should sit than Baba saw my dilemma and came over and graciously showed me where to sit by waving his hand in a large circle and saying with a twinkle, "This is the ladies' section."

After giving a short discourse, he beckoned to us and led the way to a small room. As soon as we were sitting on the floor at his feet, I started to thank him for saving us in the hijacked plane. But I got no further than the first two words, when he broke in, saying, "Yes, yes I know. I heard your voice calling, Baba! Baba! Baba!" He mimicked my voice perfectly with the English accent and inflection that, I am told, is more pronounced when I am excited and apparently slip back into my original way of speaking. He then launched into the interview with the usual comments, questions and stories, but with no further mention of the hijacking. He had made his point by underlining the fact that I had remembered to call on him for help. Evidently, that was all we needed to hear until our farewell interview, when he referred to it again, though obliquely.

When Baba brought the interview to a close we rejoined the other guests. There were two Western men in the group, neither of whom we had met. Baba was taking great pains to answer their questions and to explain his answers in detail. We later learned that they were two parapsychologists, Dr. Karlis Osis, director of the American Society for Psychical Research in New York, and Dr. Erlendur Haraldsson of the Department of Psychology at the University of Iceland at Reykjavik. They had traveled to India together on two previous field trips to study cases of *psi* phenomena. They had first come to see Baba in 1973. They were now continuing their observations of his powers and hoped to persuade him to give them permission to set up some controlled experiments with him.

When lunch was announced, Baba led us all into another room. Again I hung back uncertain where to sit. Baba wheeled around and waving me forward with his hand and said with an encouraging smile, "Hurry up. Don't hang back." As soon as I went through the door he hurried in after me to show me where to sit. He then took his place on a raised platform reserved for him where Mrs. Bhagavantam personally served his lunch. We all sat on the floor and were served by members of the household who carried around food containers from which they ladled out various foods. Again I was so grateful that Baba had shown me where to sit for, being the only woman present, I would have felt most insecure without his help.

When we had all been served Baba gave the signal to start eating. From time to time he looked over to me and with an understanding smile, motioned that I should avoid eating a certain food when I was just about to put it in my mouth, indicating in mime that it was too hot and saying, "Too much chilli for you!" Ordinarily I would have been embarrassed to be singled out for attention, but Baba managed to catch my eye and get his message across so quietly and imperceptibly that I doubt if it was observed by any others, all of whom were busy eating the hot Indian food.

Throughout the day Baba demonstrated the loving care of a devoted mother for her child. It was like a soothing balm, for my own mother had lacked this quality. How did Baba know exactly what I had craved as a child and never received, gentleness, loving concern and acceptance of my weaknesses instead of criticism? How could he also have known that even at the age of sixty I still needed to be encouraged to be less shy and retiring, and more willing to take my rightful place, having been intimidated into believing that to do so was selfish, and therefore a grievous sin? With Baba's gentle yet firm encouragement I took my first steps in venturing out from the safety of my protective shell. With his continued urging I have taken many more steps since then. This was the area where he knew I most needed his help. He treats people who have the opposite problem, of being too aggressive, in a very different way. His method of teaching each person according to the individual need is often overlooked and sometimes causes problems, when something he says to one person is taken and applied by another to whom it may not be applicable. Many seeming contradictions arise in this way and cause confusion when people quote him out of context.

After this memorable first day back in Baba's presence, we were again back in the daily rhythm. One day, shortly after our arrival, Baba came from the back of the house and sat down on the men's side of the room, usually the prelude to one of his informal talks or question and answer sessions. He mentioned that he had just performed a wedding ceremony for a young Indian couple. My husband remarked that they were just starting out on their life together whereas we would be celebrating our 33rd wedding anniversary in a few days. Baba asked on which day, and when my husband told him January 30, he said he would see us on that day.

Later, when Sidney told me of the conversation, I was overjoyed, I could not imagine anything more auspicious than to have Baba's blessing on our anniversary. A day or two later Baba told us that he would be leaving for Puttapparthi the next morning and that we should follow his car in our taxi. He repeated that he would see us on the 30th, which was then two days hence.

Early the next morning we joined several other taxis waiting outside the main gates for Baba's car to appear. Again we participated in his holiday mood. He stopped his car several times along the way, either to give *darshan* to the waving people who seemed to appear out of thin air as his car approached, or to alight and walk back along the line of cars to the delight of the occupants. He also sent the college boys who were with him to hand out fruit to refresh us all for the remainder of the journey. He was in his most jovial and carefree mood, laughing and joking with all of us.

Early on the morning of January 30 a messenger knocked on our door to tell us that Baba wished to see us that day and that we should be outside the interview room after *darshan*. The two parapsychologists, whom we had recently met at lunch at Dr. Bhagavantam's house, and several others had also been called.

After *darshan* Baba waved us into the room and signaled to us all to sit on the floor as he sat facing us, smiling broadly to welcome us. As we were settling ourselves into comfortable positions, his right hand began to make small circles in the air and he materialized some *vibhuti* which he distributed by sprinkling it into our hands. We all hesitated, not quite knowing what to do with it. He said, "Eat it," and we did. He was in a light hearted mood which was most infectious and helped us all to relax. He quickly engaged the two parapsychologists in an animated discussion, as if continuing an earlier conversation. It soon became apparent that they were most anxious to obtain a promise from him to participate in some controlled experiments to determine if his powers were genuine and not magicians' tricks.

Quite suddenly he interrupted the discussion and turned to my husband and me with a smile. He then announced to the group that we were observing our 33rd wedding anniversary that day and that he would perform a spiritual marriage for us according to Vedic rites. We could not have been more surprised. We had never heard of this custom, so had no idea what to expect. Baba was watching our reactions and enjoying our surprise. With a smile at us he waved his hand in the air in the familiar circular motion and materialized a gold ring with his head embossed on it. He held it out for us all to see and then beckoned to me to take it from him and place it on the ring finger of my husband's left hand. He next explained that Hindu women do not wear wedding rings. Instead, they wear a necklace called a *mangala sutra*, which means auspicious thread. Moving so that everyone in the small room could see him clearly, and watching for the reactions of the two parapsychologists, he pulled up the sleeves of his robe and held out both hands to show that they were empty. Then, with all our eyes intently fixed on him, he closed one hand and with the other slowly pulled out from it a long sparkling necklace which he deftly caught as it started to fall. Everyone in the room was completely astonished. He handed it to my husband to place around my neck. I was enchanted. It was so delicate and beautiful. It is 32 inches long and contains eight sets of nine precious stones, each set separated by a gold bead, making 81 altogether. They are attached to each other by a tiny gold link and, hanging from the bottom, is a picture of Baba set in a circular gold frame, surrounded by the outline of his logo representing five world religions. I was so overcome with emotion that tears streamed from my eyes. To cover my confusion he leaned towards me and gently told me to wear it inside my *sari*, out of sight, to avoid causing jealousy and envy. Everyone crowded around to examine it, so I asked Baba if it was permissible to show it here. He replied, "Yes, these are your brothers and sisters." He then went on to explain that it would give me the protection of the nine planets which had been propitiated and were represented by the nine precious stones.

Quite a bit later we learned that the second wedding, known as *shashtiabdi*, is a custom in South India. After a man has attained the age of sixty, he and his wife are given a spiritual ceremony at which they agree to help each other on the spiritual path towards the goal of realizing God. Baba explains that the first phase of life is known as *bhoga*, or fulfilment of desires, and the next phase as *yoga*, or union with God. I had just turned sixty on my last birthday, and my husband was then sixty-seven.

When everyone had had the opportunity to admire the *mangala sutra*, Baba looked towards the two parapsychologists and teasingly asked them, "Can you explain how this happened?" They shook their heads. He then went on to tell them that he was giving them repeated chances to observe him closely and to listen to him because he knew that they had good hearts and were interested in helping humanity by their investigations. There followed a lively question and answer period with the two men firing questions at Baba which he patiently and good-naturedly answered.

He explained that he materializes objects by his *sankalpa*, the will power that creates. He added that if we develop our mental powers and purify our hearts we can also do it, provided we love the entire creation as he does.

They asked, "What is the scientific explanation? Will science ever understand your materialization?" Baba replied, "Material science can never understand it. The scope of science is limited because it does not go beyond the manifest world. Science deals with experiments, whereas spirituality deals with experience and inner vision. I can see matter where the best microscope can find none. Even the best doctor needs the help of an x-ray film and the results of clinical tests of blood, urine and stool to diagnose a complicated disease. But I need none. I can give you the correct diagnosis straight away."

The two men again tried to persuade Baba to participate in some controlled experiments. He appeared to become impatient and turning to one of them said, "Look at your ring." As he did so a look of consternation appeared on his face. The inset picture had disappeared from it. They looked for it on the floor, but no trace of it could be found, yet the frame and the notches that should have held the picture were undamaged.

While the search was going on for the missing picture, Baba gave personal interviews in the adjoining room. When he had seen all of us he indicated that the interview was at an end and jokingly remarked to the two parapsychologists who were reluctantly giving up their search for the picture, "This was my experiment."

We all filed out of the room into the open, moving in a close group and still discussing the riddle of the missing picture which we concluded Baba must have removed in some way. We wondered what would happen next. Would he give the man a new ring? He had been known to do so at times when one was lost or broken. Or would he leave the setting empty as a reminder of his experiment?

I was still stunned from the impact of our unexpected remarriage and its many implications, and would have liked to hurry away to find a quiet place to meditate on the whole experience. But the length of the interview and our varied expressions as we all emerged from the room were noted by many of the people waiting outside. Some rushed over to ask what had happened. Immediately I found myself in a quandary. Baba had just told me to keep the *mangala sutra* out of sight, yet had indicated that it was all right to show it to the others in the interview room as they were my brothers and sisters. What was I to do now? This was the beginning of a lesson in discrimination. Somehow, I must learn to decide when I could show it and to whom. I quickly explained that I needed time to digest what had taken place. Everyone understood, as it is common knowledge that an interview is usually a very powerful experience. As soon as I could do so unobtrusively I slipped away and found a quiet spot. I desperately needed to sort out my emotions and concentrate on the significance of the way in which Baba had chosen to observe our anniversary. I knew from past experience that everything he ever does or says is significant on many levels. I wanted to try to recall as much as possible while it was still fresh so that I could gradually assimilate it in the months ahead. My first strong impression was of a heavy responsibility, though at the time I did not yet fully comprehend what it entailed.

Two days later we were called to another interview together with the two parapsychologists and several others. As soon as we were all assembled and seated on the floor, Baba looked over at the man who had lost the picture from his ring and, with a quizzical smile, asked if he wanted it back.

He replied that he did and at Baba's request gave him the ring. Baba took it in his hand and asked, "Do you want the same picture or a different one?" "The same," was the reply. Baba then closed his hand around the ring, blew on it three times, and stretching out his hand, opened it to reveal a ring. The man remarked that the picture was like the original but the setting was different.

The two men were so taken by surprise at the way in which Baba finished his experiment that their voices rose to a high pitch of excitement. Baba put his fingers to his lips to indicate the need to lower their voices, and gently ushered us all out of the room.

One of the women with whom I had worked to remove her fear during our last visit was there again with her husband. I started to work with both of them and was kept very busy as other people asked to work with me.

Towards the end of our stay it was rumored that Baba was planning to spend a few days at his women's college at Anantapur, also in Andhra Pradesh. On hearing this my husband decided to ask Baba's permission to leave as he might not return by the time we were scheduled to return home. As is often the case when someone wants to do something of which Baba may not approve, he seemed to make it impossible for Sidney to catch his attention. The more he tried, the more elusive Baba became. Finally, as he was walking to his waiting car to set forth on his journey, Sidney hurried after him to ask if we could leave. Baba drew himself up to his full height, and seemed to tower over my husband, who is actually taller. In an imperious voice he said, "No, you both stay here!" As he delivered this ultimatum, he brought his hand down firmly to emphasize his point, and away he drove.

The *ashram* seemed lifeless after his departure. The atmosphere underwent a sharp change as everyone relaxed from the customary intense alertness deemed necessary to catch his every move to avoid missing the comparatively few opportunities for receiving his *darshan*. No one had the slightest idea how long he would be gone. He rarely announces his plans, and even when he does, he is likely to change them without warning. We tried to relax, patiently await his return, and use the time and opportunity to catch up with all the neglected mundane chores.

Towards evening of the first day of Baba's absence, a young man with whom I had been working came breathlessly running to our room with the urgent request that I come quickly to where a young woman was creating a stir in the women's section in front of the *mandir*. He told me that the volunteers were unable to restrain her. He went on to explain that she had just arrived at the *ashram* under the care of an older man who had accompanied her on the journey from England. She was raving and quite violent, and needed constant supervision to prevent her from harming herself or others. Her escort or bodyguard had told the young man that he had known her for a long time. She had been a brilliant student and the youngest woman ever to be appointed as headmistress of a school in England before she became so disturbed. The drastic change had come about when she inadvertently became too involved with a group who practiced black magic, though professing to be Christian. She had realized her mistake when she was taken through the Black Mass. Her present condition was directly related to this frightening experience. While he was quickly relating these facts to us he was urging me to go with him to help. He had left her in the middle of the women's *darshan* section where neither he nor her male escort could remain as it was against *ashram* rules.

To say that I was horrified would be an understatement. I had not the faintest idea how to deal with such a situation. Besides, I had no authority to do so in the *ashram* and I could not ask Baba's permission since he had already left for Anantapur. It was obviously the responsibility of the women volunteers, as they were selected to deal with women's problems. They had been given responsibility to enforce the few rules to ensure order and propriety among the women. When I voiced some of these objections the young man pointed out that this was no ordinary problem, and that I was the only woman to his knowledge who might possibly be able to help her. I agreed to go with him to see what was happening and my husband insisted on accompanying us. As we approached the women's *darshan* area in front of the *mandir*, a wild scene greeted us. Several volunteers were trying to restrain the young woman. She was most inappropriately dressed and was ranting and raving right outside the *mandir*, where silence is strictly enforced. Baba's private rooms are part of the *mandir* building, as is the interview room, so it is even more imperative for silence to be maintained.

I saw that she was resisting the volunteers' efforts to control her so violently that they were obliged to keep at a distance to avoid her flailing arms and legs. It was indeed an impasse.

Before I had time to make a decision I found myself racing across the intervening space towards the scene as if propelled by a force other than my conscious will. In the same automatic fashion I took the disturbed young woman in my arms, very gently pulled her down with me onto the ground, and cradled her on my lap as if she were a hurt child.

As I started to speak soothingly to her, she looked up at me, obviously startled, and asked, "Are you English?" When I replied that I was born and educated in England, she sighed and relaxed against me.

At that point my husband came rushing up but was shooed away by the volunteers as he was on the women's side of the area. I could see that he feared that I might be harmed, so I quickly reassured the young woman that I would try to help her, and persuaded her to let me take her to another part of the *ashram*. She meekly acquiesced and, with the help of another woman, we half carried her to a place where we could all discuss what should be done next. The man who had brought her came hurrying up just then with a key to the room which had been assigned to them. I noticed that his face and arms were covered with scratches and cuts. We later learned that they had been inflicted by his charge during their flight to India.

It was not until we got her to the room that I had a chance to look closely at her. I was appalled at the sight. She looked like a skeleton, was filthy, her hair matted, her clothes awry and torn, and her face as white as a sheet. But it was the look in her eyes which spoke volumes of all she had suffered. My heart ached for her, but I still had not the vaguest idea of how to help her. All I knew at that moment was that she desperately needed love and compassion.

For the next few days the small group of Westerners tried to help in the more practical ways. Some of the women donated *saris* and showed her how to wear them, while others brought food and bedding. I helped her to bathe and comb out the tangles in her hair. When she slowly and fearfully began to talk about her experiences I was horrified to discover the extent of the hypnotic power wielded by the people behind the so-called Christian group with which she had unwittingly become affiliated. I was appalled at her complete subjugation and terror. I used every method I had learned to draw her out and show her how to dispel some of the ghastly symbols and apparitions which she reported "seeing" inside her head. I felt inexperienced in treating such a serious case and had absolutely no doubt whatever that it would have to be Baba working through me if she were to be freed from whatever sinister force was still controlling her from a distance.

Several people started to notice various very strange things happening to them. They reported that whenever they came in contact with her, or even passed by her room when she was inside, they became ill, depressed, confused or just weak. One woman who merely loaned her a handkerchief, felt very sick after it came back from the laundry, when she picked it up to put it in her luggage. Only after she had burned it was she free of further trouble. As more and more women told me these stories it suddenly dawned on me that I, who was with her a great deal of the time, had not experienced any problems like the ones they were having. This really surprised me as I have always been extremely sensitive, particularly to negative emotions or vibrations. Why was I unaffected while other people were having problems?

Then one morning, when she was more than usually disturbed and frightened, I instinctively reached for the picture of Baba hanging from my *mangala sutra*, in an effort to contact him mentally to ask him what I should do. Of course! Hadn't he told me that it would give me the protection of the nine planets? I had not fully understood that statement at the time. That must be the reason why I was the only one who was immune to the negative forces controlling her. I felt comforted by the thought but also very much alone, and more certain than ever that I must constantly ask for Baba's help.

Everyone was happy when Baba returned. We took it for granted that he would now take charge of this bizarre situation. We hoped he would heal her and free her from her oppressors. Instead, he gave instructions to the volunteers to seat the two of us for the morning and afternoon *darshan* against the wall of the interview room immediately below his private rooms. The effect of this position on the girl was extraordinary. Apparently, Baba's power, as it filtered through the wall of the building, began to stir up and bring to her conscious awareness hundreds of different symbols representing the experiences she had suffered at the hands of the black magicians. As the images surfaced and she was able to visualize each one separately, I found I was able to help her interpret them and release them by handing them over to Baba. The fear and horror which racked her during this process were so forceful that she trembled uncontrollably. Fortunately she was aware of what we were doing, realized how necessary it was, and co-operated most willingly to the extent possible at any given time. In this way she freed herself of enough of the buried memories to be able to take care of herself in a more normal way by the time we left for home.

I now realize that if Baba had made direct contact with her when she first arrived, the effect of his energy could easily have been more than she could tolerate. I heard later that he advised her to move out of the *ashram* during the approaching Shivaratri celebration, when the atmosphere is charged with the Shiva energy. He must have decided it would have been too strong for her to stand in her weak condition.

Shortly after we had arrived, Baba discussed with Jack Hislop and my husband the need for a committee to organize and supervise the growing number of Sai Baba centers which were springing up in the U.S.A. As more people went to India to see Baba, many, on their return, joined together in small groups to sing *bhajans* and share their experience with other devotees, and some formed centers. Now that the numbers of such groups were increasing they needed guidelines to help them to organize centers like the ones in India, but in a form that would be practical and appropriate in our country. Baba asked Jack and Sidney to work out together a brief outline of what they thought was needed, and present it to him for approval. They had several meetings to discuss it.

Towards the end of our stay Baba announced that the Second World Conference would be held at the *ashram* during the third week of November, immediately preceding his 50th birthday celebration on November 23.

When it was time for us to return home he gave us a farewell interview during which he invited us to attend the Conference. He also inquired about my headaches. On being informed that they still occurred, he materialized a small cylindrical plastic vial containing pills and instructed me to take one each day after I reached home. When I looked more closely at the container, I was intrigued to see that the only marking on it was a small triangle containing the letter K on the circular lid. When we got back to Bangalore we inquired at several chemists if this was the trademark of any known manufacturer. No one recognized it, so we concluded that it was another of Baba's riddles for me to solve. My immediate thought was that it was composed of two of the symbols I use most frequently in my work, the circle and the triangle, and that the letter K is the first letter of our surname. Was Baba again letting me know, in a most ingenious way, that he was aware of the methods I use?

I came away filled with his blessings. However I had a tremendous amount to assimilate from both his teaching and my own experiences before I could use them in my daily life. I have since become aware that some of the things he says, either in his discourses or to me personally, often take months, and in some instances even years, to understand. His messages need to be interpreted on many levels for the complete lesson to become clear.

CHAPTER FOURTEEN

WE ARRIVED HOME at the end of February and would be returning in November to attend the Second World Conference and Baba's 50th birthday. We had certainly not expected to be going back so soon, but there is something about the way Baba makes his wishes known which overrules personal plans, so we did not question it.

The next few months were very full of mundane activities. On our return from India we decided to move from an apartment into a house. We moved in August, which gave us just enough time to settle in before leaving for India again in the middle of November.

On our arrival in Puttaparthi we discovered that we would be sharing a room with two other married couples which really surprised us. It seemed so strange that men and women sit separately for *darshan* and all other gatherings, yet are housed together for sleeping, which surely placed them in the closest and most intimate proximity. When we reached our room we were happily surprised to discover that one of the other couples were our friends the Bocks who had arrived several days ahead of us and were already ensconced. A day or so later another couple arrived making quite a crowd in the small space. At night we had to place our bedding on the floor very carefully, as there was barely sufficient room to accommodate six mattresses. Even with the greatest care, if any of us happened to turn over in the night we could easily land on top of one or other of the sleepers on either side. It was certainly a taste of communal living. Not only did we all sleep in the same room but cooked, bathed, washed our clothes, and dressed and undressed in the same cramped space. We became experts at taking turns using the cooking and bathing areas, and quickly learned ways to be as modest as possible with our ablutions and dressing. Many comical situations arose as well as stressful ones, but we all managed to adjust to the cramped space. We have often commented since then that if our friendship with the Bocks survived such a test, it must be pretty strongly grounded in our mutual love for Baba.

The conference spanned a ten-day period, each day filled with diverse activities and functions. This was the first time we were given the opportunity to observe in action the members of the various branches of the huge organization which had developed around Baba. All over India, as people began to be exposed to Baba's teachings, a network of centers sprang up to enable devotees to gather together to sing *bhajans*, study Baba's teaching, and engage in *seva*, or service, to the community.

In 1967 the first All India Conference had been held for the purpose of working out a format to establish uniformity in all the centers. Baba suggested the following few simple guidelines to facilitate the process:

1. Men and women were to meet and work in separate groups.
2. The *samithis*, as these groups are called, were instructed not to collect any money for any purpose.
3. There were to be no membership dues.

Baba feels very strongly that it is inadvisable to mix financial dealings with spiritual activities and does not want his name connected in any way with monetary transactions.

A service wing of the organization called the Seva Dal was also formed, as Baba teaches that it is not enough to concentrate solely on our own spiritual path. It is equally important to be of service to others in the community, particularly those who are less fortunate.

As the organization grew, with more and more people being drawn to Baba, other branches were formed. The first of these was the Mahila Vibhag, or the women's wing. Under its supervision a Bal Vikas program was started to educate the children of devotees according to Baba's teachings. Out of this program grew the more advanced plan up to college level.

Gradually, as all these aspects of the organization developed, they began to work smoothly together towards Baba's goal of making people conscious of the indwelling God within everyone. Members of these groups were urged by Baba to put his teachings into practice in their lives. In this way they would act like yeast in a lump of dough in the community in which they lived, which in turn would affect the whole country. He says, "My life is my message," and he expects his devotees to follow his example.

The first World Conference in 1968 was attended by a very small number of devotees from other countries. In 1975, the number had increased to the point where it was deemed necessary to work out guidelines for the groups which were springing up in other countries as Baba had already indicated to my husband and Jack Hislop earlier that year. Members of the Seva Dal groups from all over India arrived at the conference early to help with the vast preparations. They worked day and night to sweep, clean, and decorate the buildings and grounds. They prepared sheds to be used as sleeping areas for delegates, aided the band of organizers in providing and maintaining sanitation and medical aid, and helped in the kitchens and dining halls. The spirit of devotion with which they carried out all these arduous tasks was an inspiration to behold, and showed the beneficial effect on them of Baba and his teachings.

In addition to the delegates many thousands of devotees and pilgrims streamed daily into the *ashram*, coming from all parts of the country. They arrived on scooters, bicycles, buses and cars, horse-drawn vehicles, and even bullock carts. The road leading to the gates of the *ashram* was so thickly congested that it became difficult to move in the streets. The whole *ashram* was alive with thousands of people, far too many to be accommodated in the apartment buildings and sheds which were reserved primarily for the delegates. To ease the situation, Baba sent word granting permission for temporary shelters to be erected, using whatever materials could be found or had been brought by the pilgrims to protect them from the heat during the day and the sharp cold at night. Strange looking structures began to spring up like mushrooms all over the ground, composed of various scraps and covered over with tarpaulins, rags and bits of clothing. Beneath these makeshift shelters, whole groups camped with their bedding, cooking equipment, food and all their belongings. Those who had no means of providing cover lived on the bare ground out in the open, exposed to the elements as well as to every passerby, whether human or animal. They performed all their daily activities in full view of everyone. They could be seen oiling their bodies in lieu of bathing, combing their hair, dressing, cooking and eating, sleeping, and caring for their many children of all ages. The ground was so densely covered that it became necessary to walk very carefully to avoid stepping on a sleeping child, a pile of clothes or a sack of food. Many also camped along the passages running outside the rooms on each floor of the buildings. We soon had to learn to get accustomed to the sounds of snoring, coughing, crying babies and other noises of the night as they were wafted up through our open glassless windows.

Each day groups from all over India as well as from other countries met together to discuss the many questions which had arisen in their centers. They also tried to discover ways to improve and expand their activities, particularly those relating to *seva*. For those of us who had come as delegates from overseas centers there were meetings to discuss ways in which the guidelines used in Indian centers could best be applied to our different cultures.

To and for and in and out of all these activities, Baba would weave his way, unexpectedly appearing in a doorway, listening for a few minutes, sometimes making a comment and moving on elsewhere, overseeing all that was going on.

A Sathya Sai Committee for America was formed with Baba's approval, with a central committee of three men, Jack Hislop as President, my husband as Secretary-Treasurer, and Richard Bayer as Vice-President. In addition, eighteen directors were picked to represent the committee in various parts of the country.

Besides the many meetings throughout the day, there were evening functions including concerts, plays, and regional folk dances presented by the Bal Vikas children and youth groups. But without a doubt the most eagerly anticipated events were the edifying and inspirational discourses given by Baba. He often ended by singing several *bhajans* which were continued by the whole gathering. The auditorium was filled to overflowing with delegates on these occasions. Many thousands of pilgrims assembled outside and were able to participate with the help of loudspeakers set up all over the area.

As the time drew closer to the highlight of the festival, Baba's 50th birthday, still more crowds streamed into the *ashram* to join the already densely packed masses. The excitement mounted. As this was a jubilee birthday, it was even more meaningful to the visitors.

When the day finally arrived the throngs of people, dressed in their finest clothes, sat patiently waiting in neat lines outside in the extensive grounds. We all wondered when Baba would appear and where he would stand to give *darshan* to such an immense crowd. We waited and waited, sitting cross legged on the hard ground. Finally the unusual sound of a helicopter was heard. All heads were turned up to watch as it circled overhead. Almost simultaneously everyone drew in a sharp breath in disbelief. Baba was clearly visible leaning out of the helicopter waving a white handkerchief to the crowd below, his orange robe recognized by all, and his black hair clearly silhouetted against the brilliant blue sky. This then was his way of solving the problem of giving *darshan* to the vast multitude assembled for this auspicious occasion. He knew that if he had tried to walk amongst them, or even to ride on the back of his pet elephant, Sai Gita, he would have been lost to sight in their midst, and only a few would have been able to have his *darshan*. By flying overhead, he was clearly seen by everyone. As the helicopter circled around, flew low and hovered over the heads of all the waiting people, many wept with joy as he waved his handkerchief, his face wreathed in a big smile of boyish delight at the effect of his surprise.

After satisfying everyone's desire for his *darshan* he directed the pilot to land in front of the *mandir* where he alighted and proceeded with the other plans for the day. His gift to every single one of the visitors was *prasad*, consisting of two kinds of rice confection, distributed by members of the Seva Dal, the college students and the volunteers. Considering the huge number of people to whom it had to be given in so short a space of time, it was an incredible feat, and one which could only have been successful when initiated by Baba and carried out by his devoted followers.

That evening the Poornachandra Auditorium was filled to the limit. We were all sitting on the floor hemmed in by bodies on all sides, making it impossible to move. Obviously no one considered the discomfort of being so cramped for several hours too big a price to pay for the privilege of hearing Baba's birthday message.

He began with a spontaneous song and then launched into a discourse which was translated into English. He first expressed his happiness that so many thousands of seekers had assembled for this occasion. He went on to say that some deep need or longing had brought them there in the hope of being given help and inspiration to lead their lives with more meaning. In so doing, they would help to bring about the revival of righteousness in the world, the mission for which he had come himself at this critical time.

He said, "Each of you must have felt a gap within; a thirst, a pang, an unfulfilled urge, a divine discontent, or a call from within, to persuade you to travel long distances, brave many obstacles, put up with strange discomforts in order to come here to secure strength and guidance."

On the evening of his birthday it has become a custom for Baba to sit on the platform in the auditorium in a large swing called a *jhoola* in Hindi, which some of the college boys gently push to keep it moving. For this occasion he wears a pure white robe instead of his usual orange one. In this way he seeks to personify and thus awaken the pure God-force within everyone, seated in each heart, awaiting recognition. He followed this ritual with another inspirational message urging everyone to seek contact with this inner force. The next day he gave formal permission for the crowds to disperse and return to their homes, resulting in a mass exodus.

The pageantry of these ten days with all the color, music, dance, excitement and strong emotions was designed to penetrate to the deepest unconscious level of each individual. Many were deeply moved, and none could have escaped being changed in some way for the better.

CHAPTER FIFTEEN

AS WE HAD made two trips to see Baba in 1975 we did not return in 1976. My husband was occupied with the various activities connected with the newly formed committee. I, too, needed time to digest and ruminate on all that we had experienced this year and to resume my work which was rapidly increasing.

I often recalled Baba's injunction during our first time with him in 1973, that I need not go to India to see his little body, but must find his counterpart in my own heart. He urges us to see him swinging in the *jhoola* in our own hearts. I knew that now, more than ever, I must try to put his advice into daily practice. It was even more significant now that I had actually watched him swinging in the *jhoola*. This imprinted the message deeply into every part of my mind, not only the conscious part, but more important, the unconscious part for which such a symbolic picture is particularly potent.

We were also busy making arrangements for our younger daughter Lorna's wedding early in January of that year. After our first meeting with Baba in 1973 both daughters became interested in him. They asked us to deliver letters to him each time we returned to see him. Sheila, the older of the two sisters, has always been career oriented, whereas, from the time she was quite young, Lorna dreamed primarily of being a wife and mother. Consequently, her first letter to Baba in January 1975 contained a request for help in finding the right husband.

Much to our surprise, on our return home, she excitedly told us that while we were in India she had met Ed Taylor whom she hoped to marry, as she was certain that meeting him was an answer to her letter to Baba.

Towards the end of that year the engagement was announced and the date of the wedding set for the middle of January. We decided to give them as a wedding present the down payment on a home and suggested they look at houses while we were in India attending the World Conference. We took with us a letter from Lorna asking Baba to help them find the right house. Again, on our return, they were eagerly waiting to tell us they had found a house they both liked, and wanted us to go immediately to see it.

In the middle of January they were married at a small family service. Thus the first step of Lorna's dream came true when she became a radiant bride. I thanked Baba from the bottom of my heart for her happiness and hoped all her dreams would come to pass. Later that year, I had a very unusual experience which again demonstrated Baba's ever present love and protection from a distance. It also further confirmed his explanation that the rings and other talismans he materializes and gives to various people do indeed act as links through which to ask his help in time of need.

On the morning of July 14 I awakened with the memory of the tail end of a particularly vivid dream. In it I was standing in a long line of people about to be tested individually by several judges, though I had no idea of the nature of the test. When it was my turn, the judges said with surprise that this one, meaning me, was able to breathe with the whole breath. Apparently this was the test. I remember being puzzled, as I do not practice *pranayama* or any other breathing exercises, and had not been aware of breathing in a different way.

Shortly after waking, my husband and I started our usual morning routine including a form of *Tai Chi* followed by meditation. A few minutes after starting the exercises I was strongly aware of Baba standing only a few inches in front of me. I was most impressed with the fact that although I did not actually see him I knew the space he occupied, and his size and height compared to my own. Next, I became aware that he was literally pouring into my solar plexus what felt like energy. I was amazed at how very easy it was to relax and breathe it in and hoped I would be able to continue to be as open to receive from him in this way as I now was. However, I did not connect this new kind of breathing with the dream I had just had until later. I had awakened with a headache, so, hoping Baba would help me with it, I silently thanked him.

The extraordinarily strong awareness of his presence continued throughout the exercises and into the meditation. I began to feel that he was deep inside me and that his energy was circulating all through my body, producing a tingling sensation rather like pins and needles. It was such a subjective experience that I did not mention it to my husband at the time. After breakfast I took a shower in his bathroom instead of the one I use, as it was being redecorated. As soon as I stepped out of the shower, he stepped in.

The next second I heard a crash. He had slipped on the wet and soapy tiles and fallen on his back across the steps leading down into the shower. He seemed hardly to breathe and only groaned as he lay inert.

As Baba's presence was still strongly with me I immediately called on him to help. Somehow I was given the necessary strength to move Sidney out of the shower and onto a mat and turn him over onto his stomach, a feat I realized I could not have managed with my own strength. I was horrified to see that his rib cage on the right side was caved in and two angry red marks were appearing across it. There were also black and blue bruises beginning to appear on his upper back. I quickly reached for a packet of Baba's *vibhuti* and my *mangala sutra*, lying on a counter in the bathroom. I placed them on his back and with another request to Baba for help, started to rub some *vibhuti* on his back, gently massaging it into the bruised areas. I was moved to tears as I watched the ribs begin to move under my fingers and saw the upper back resume a more normal shape. At that point he gulped in a big breath of air, and was able to speak and breathe regularly again. I continued to rub the *vibhuti* into the injured areas and as I did so I was amazed to see the bruises begin to fade as if they were being erased. However, I could feel broken bones move under my hands and heard the ends grate against one another.

As soon as I felt it was safe to leave him I telephoned our doctor. He told me to telephone the paramedics to take him to the emergency hospital. When they arrived and examined him they assured me that he had no broken bones. They also told me that he did not need an ambulance, but that it might be a good idea for me to take him to the hospital to be checked just to be on the safe side. I could hardly believe it, as I knew I had heard and felt those broken ribs.

The whole time we were driving to the hospital, as Sidney lay flat on the back seat of my car, I was imploring Baba to help, for I was afraid the jolting of the car might move the bones apart. When we reached the hospital he was X-rayed. The films showed he had three broken ribs. Amazingly enough, they had not punctured his lungs and were in perfect alignment so an operation was not needed. Surprisingly, there was not the least sign of the original bruises.

I feel certain Baba had known the accident was likely to happen, but as he will not interfere with our earned *karma* he would not avert it. He prepared me ahead of time (without my knowing the reason) so that I was alerted to call on him for help. I was already filled with his energy and could pour it into Sidney, to prevent the injuries from being more serious.

An important message emerged from this experience. Many devotees believe that as soon as they accept Baba they will, from that moment on, live happily ever after. When this proves not to be the case they are deeply disappointed and disillusioned. They often begin to doubt Baba, especially when it looks as if they are under attack with barely sufficient time to recover from one problem before new ones loom up to take its place.

Baba has frequently explained that he may decide to accelerate our negative *karmas* when we come to him to enable us to become free from them. He helps us to accept them and learn from them if we call on him and are certain that we cannot do so alone. With his help anything can be solved. In the above experience, he not only filled me with his energy but guided me to be right there, only inches away when Sidney fell. If I had been anywhere else in the house he might not have survived, as his condition made it impossible for him to call out for help. In addition, I would not have heard him fall with the bathroom door closed.

For me it is so much more realistic to know that Baba is always available to help us with our problems than to expect him to wave a magic wand to avert them. If he did so, it would take away our opportunity to learn the very lessons the problems present. I am touched as I recall the loving care he showed by arriving ahead of the accident to alert and prepare me to help as he had in the earlier experience with the hijackers and would do so again at other times.

Shortly after this incident our daughter Lorna called to tell us she was pregnant. She was overjoyed at the prospect of becoming a mother and thus realizing another of her ambitions. The baby was due in the middle of March, so she wanted to know when we were planning to go to India, and begged us to be sure to be home in time to welcome our first grandchild. We reassured her that we would probably be going at our usual time in January, but would arrange to go a little earlier this year, in order to be back in plenty of time for that joyful event.

CHAPTER SIXTEEN

WE FLEW TO India again on the 4th of January. A doctor whom we knew decided to accompany us for a very brief time. Baba is always very happy when doctors go to see him and usually gives them a lot of attention, probably because their whole lives are spent in service to mankind, a cause very close to his heart. His treatment of this doctor was no exception.

Baba was at Whitefield when we arrived. He invited all three of us into his house as soon as he caught sight of us. He included us in two group interviews during which he materialized a ring and a cross for the doctor and gave him a large packet of *vibhuti* to use for his patients. He returned home overwhelmed by the kind attention and love Baba gave him during his very short stay.

At one of these interviews Baba walked over to me and touched a tiny gold ring I was wearing. It is shaped like a figure eight, one of the most potent symbols in my work and was given to my by our daughter, Sheila. With an approving smile he said, "Figure eight is also letter S for Sai," which seemed to be another example of his indirect way of expressing not only that he was fully aware of the techniques I use, but that they came from him and bear his initial.

The figure eight symbol is used as a visualization exercise to separate each of two people into their own circle or territory to help them to withdraw their projections from one another. It is also used as a preparation before detaching from anyone or anything which represents a security symbol in preference to the Baba within. When we are attached to other people or to objects we are not free to put our entire trust in Baba, for no one can serve two masters. Baba himself has expressed this concept very clearly. He says, "Freedom is independence from externals. One who is in need of the help of another person, thing or condition is a slave thereof. Perfect freedom is not given to any man on earth because the very meaning of mortal life is relationship with and dependence on another. The lesser the number of wants, the greater is the freedom; hence perfect freedom is absolute desirelessness."

The more I learned about Baba's teachings the more I recognized that they are consistent with those I had been taught for so many years, long before I knew of Baba's human form in India. I greatly appreciated Baba's gift of indicating his recognition of the figure eight, thus sanctioning the method.

One day, shortly after the episode with the figure eight ring, he pointed to the watch I was wearing which has no numerals on the face. "No clock time, only inner time," he remarked approvingly. This was the introduction to a gradual process by which he has taught me inner timing in contrast to the more common slavery of watching the clock. I was to recall it many times as I watched him wait for the correct time, almost as if he were listening for it, before speaking or acting or granting someone's request. We in the West are so time conscious that we find it difficult to relax and listen patiently for the inner timing to be revealed to us.

Unsuspected by me he was also preparing me for a future task. This time I usually sat all alone on the women's side of the verandah each morning and afternoon, unless other women had been invited that day. I enjoyed the opportunity this solitude allowed for meditation and reading. But, at first, I felt very uncomfortable to be so conspicuous, having always been of an extremely retiring nature. Baba, however, had other ideas, and this was his first lesson in bringing me out of my shell.

My discomfort at my solitary state was further heightened by the fact that when the college boys came down from Baba's room they had to pass in front of me to go outside. As they did so they lowered their eyes and made a wide circle around me by walking close to the opposite wall. I knew that Baba teaches the boys to look upon every young woman as their sister and every older woman as their mother. I was also aware that he advises them to avoid unnecessary contact with members of the opposite sex lest it distract them from their study and worship.

After the first few days I became aware of poems quite spontaneously forming in my mind, seemingly without my volition. I began to write them down as if I were taking dictation. Since childhood I have been in the habit of composing jingles to commemorate birthdays and other occasions, but it always took time and effort on my part to fit the appropriate sentiments into the meter and rhyme. Now I was most surprised when complete poems came so quickly into my head, that I was absolutely certain I could not possibly have composed them myself. It was fascinating to watch the process taking place.

One day a charming little incident occurred which illustrates Baba's whimsical sense of humor. A large group of men who were waiting to talk to him were becoming very restless, because he had been out of the room for much longer than usual. Suddenly he appeared in the doorway and, strolling towards them, began scolding them for their impatience. They were completely subdued and all looked sheepish. Then he began to discuss with them the various matters for which they had come to seek his advice. When he had finished he started to walk towards where I was standing alone on the women's side. As he approached, such a mischievous expression appeared on his face that I wondered what he was about to say. When he was almost in front of me he raised his right arm over his head and started to bring it down as if he were going to spank me. But halfway down he changed the direction of his arm, and with an impish smile brought it swiftly down and sharply slapped his own thigh. He thoroughly enjoyed my startled reaction at the prospect of being spanked by him. All the men he had so recently reprimanded for their impatience broke into laughter at this little episode. My immediate thought was that knowing that I too was very impatient, he reminded me of this fact but took the slap himself. I joined in the amusement, as he turned to continue up to his apartment.

A day or so later he came up to me one morning and informed me that he would see us at an interview the following day. Then he asked if we would like to stay later for *bhajan* singing by the college boys that evening. It was always a joy to hear his students whom he has taught to sing like angels. This time he himself sang several *bhajans* and kept time with his hand cymbals. I was absolutely enchanted. I love to watch his small brown hands which almost seem to dance as they clap the tiny cymbals together. At the end of the session, he walked over to me and said, "Tell your husband I will see you tomorrow, and arrange to stay for lunch upstairs."

I was still so filled with the sight and sound of him singing and playing his cymbals that my joy overflowed and I spontaneously grabbed both his hands in mine and thanked him for the wonderful evening. Such a gesture was most uncharacteristic of me and must have erupted as a result of his daily encouragement to come out of my protective shell and be less shy and withdrawn. Instead of reprimanding me, as he does when devotees try to touch him or grasp his feet as he passes by, he merely smiled like an indulgent parent and passed on his way.

Towards the end of the following morning we were called in to an interview. We again discussed my continuing ill health. He assured me that the headaches were not the result of anything I was thinking or doing wrong, but were due to a weakness. He further stated that they were mechanical-physical and not psychological. This assurance was a great relief to me. As if reading my thoughts he added, "Don't let anyone tell you that." He promised to make me some more medicine. Then he really bewildered me by saying, "It will soon be your 25th jubilee anniversary." I replied that it would be our 35th not 25th. He only smiled and said, "No, 25th. Jubilee Year," and added that he would perform a special Vedic wedding ceremony with a *mangala sutra* and a ring. That completely confused me. He had already give us this ceremony on our 33rd anniversary. But there was not time then to pursue this puzzle further for he quickly asked for the package of letters from devotees.

Both our daughters had also sent their usual letters. This time Lorna asked him for a healthy baby and to help her to be a good mother. He held her letter unopened in his hand for a minute. Then with a pleased smile he said, "She is carrying a baby. I will help her."

I asked his permission to donate a scholarship for a boy to attend his college, explaining that we had two daughters but no sons. He quickly replied, "But you have many many sons. They are all your sons and daughters," presumably referring to the people with whom I work, since he then assured me that he was always with me when I worked. What a wonderful relief it was to hear that.

After everyone had left for lunch, we were told to wait. After a while one of the college boys came to escort us upstairs to Baba's private dining room. The table was already laid for lunch and Baba was waiting to seat us as soon as we entered. He waved my husband to a seat and directed me to sit at the end of the long table at his right. As I sat down the memory of a dream I had several weeks before we left home flashed into my mind. In it Baba and I had been sitting at a similar long table in exactly the same positions, but instead of eating he was teaching me. As I compared the scene in the dream with the present one, Baba turned to face me. He smiled and nodded his head knowingly, as if he too were comparing the two scenes.

Several college boys waited on us and sprang quickly to serve us each time Baba signaled to them that we needed something. I was most grateful that the food was neither too hot nor too spicy for me to relax and enjoy it. One of the dishes contained okra, a vegetable I had known as a child in England as lady's fingers. I was delighted to hear Baba referring to them by that name. When he saw that I liked them he urged me to have more servings. When I finally refused, he nodded approvingly and said, "It is better not to eat too much when you are over sixty."

He limited our conversation during lunch by telling us that talking too much while eating hinders the digestion. I was relieved, as I am sure we would have found light luncheon conversation with Baba a little ridiculous. Altogether it was an enjoyable experience. Baba was a perfect host, and attended to our needs like a father with his children.

The next day I was most amused to notice that the college boys who had attended us at lunch no longer walked around me in a wide circle. They now passed close by though still with eyes averted. I suspected that having heard I was over sixty put me beyond even the age of a mother and into the venerable grandmother class, and therefore no distraction. A day or so later we followed Baba to Puttaparthi, where we would remain until it was time for us to leave again.

Since the last interview my mind kept dwelling on Baba's announcement that he would give us a spiritual wedding on our forthcoming anniversary. So many questions seemed to demand answers. Had he forgotten that he had already given us one? Should I remind him even though it might imply that I thought he had made a mistake? Should I show him the *mangala sutra*? If he made me another one, what should I do with the one I already had? I was trapped as if in a net of questions. Finally, I released the whole problem and prayed to be shown on the day of the anniversary what to do.

While staying at Puttaparthi, I again had time to work with people, and fitted in sessions between the regular daily activities. Several members of our Los Angeles center were there at the time. We had a particularly meaningful experience with one of them,

Ed Dugan. It is usually very hot during the day at Puttaparthi but it cools off towards evening, and is sometimes quite chilly at night. My husband and I had fallen into the habit of walking around the *ashram* as soon as it was cool for exercise after the long hours of sitting.

Late one afternoon Ed joined us and we decided to walk up onto the top of the hill above the *ashram*. It was a wonderfully peaceful vantage point from which to look down and observe from a distance all the activity below. It was especially meaningful that day. *Bhajans* we were being sung in the Mandir and the sound of the many voices raised in worship was softly wafted upwards and seemed to envelop us. The hill also afforded an unobstructed view of the surrounding countryside. At dusk the colors of the sunset in the clear air are incredibly beautiful. We had just breathed in such a scene and, as the colors began to fade, we prepared to descend before darkness obscured our way along the narrow footpath. My husband was walking a few feet ahead when I became aware of a delicate scent pervading the air. I was surprised as we were walking along a particularly barren part of the path. I looked all around to see where it could be coming from, but there were no flowers or bushes which could possibly emit such a fragrance. Ed, who was walking close behind me, asked if I could smell a wonderfully sweet perfume which he too had just begun to notice. We both searched for its source but we found nothing. I called to my husband who had gone on ahead, and he retraced his steps. When he reached us we asked if he could smell anything unusual but despite the fact that he has an extremely keen sense of smell he detected nothing. Puzzled, we continued on our way wondering if we had imagined it.

Several days later we heard that other people had from time to time reported similar experiences. It was explained as Baba's presence making itself known by means of a perfume at a time when a person is especially relaxed or attuned to him. Ed and I were both deeply touched by the shared experience of Baba's presence in this subtle form when we least expected it, and were at a distance from his physical presence. It seemed to emphasize the fact that the all-pervasive spirit he expresses is everywhere, and can be sensed in a perceptible form whenever we are in harmony with it.

On the morning of January 30, our 35th wedding anniversary, Baba sent a messenger to our room to summon us to an interview. I began to wonder, all over again, what he intended to do this time.

At the specified time we made our way towards the interview room. As we approached we saw several other people already waiting outside. Shortly after our arrival Baba came out and beckoned us all to go in together for a group interview. He started with a short talk and asked each of us how we were. Then he quickly rose from his chair and walked over to me. Looking around at the others, he announced that this was the day of my jubilee anniversary of twenty-five years and that he was going to conduct a special wedding ceremony to mark the occasion. Again he had said twenty-five years instead of thirty-five, and by calling it a jubilee further emphasized that he really meant twenty-five. What ever did he mean? I got no further with my silent questions for he abruptly started to circle his right hand in the air in front of me. I thought, "Here it is, all over again. What shall I do?" As I watched intently, and I must admit nervously, he manifested a shiny gold ring set with a clear pale blue stone like an aquamarine. Taking for granted that it was for my husband I looked across the room to where he was sitting with the other men, expecting Baba to direct me to put it on his finger, as at our previous *shashtiabdi*. But Baba motioned to restrain me. Then he took my right hand, slipped the ring onto the ring finger where he left it, even though it was much too big. He usually makes quite a point of the perfect fit of the rings he makes for people. He then brought his right hand down firmly on top of my head, and said, "Blue light, green light. Be happy."

At the time my sole reaction was intense relief. I realized that I need not have worried, for Baba had not repeated the ceremony with the ring for my husband and a *mangala sutra* for me. This time it was different, but the full significance of the difference was not apparent to me until much later when I was deep in a working session with my daughter, Sheila. Suddenly the full meaning became clear to me. Baba had not remarried my husband Sidney and me, but had married me to my inner husband, or animus as Carl Jung called it. In the first ceremony he had given me a *mangala sutra*. Now, in this one, my inner husband was given a ring. I also realized that the "blue light green light" referred not only to the color of the stone but to the colors of two parts of a *mandala* used in my work. It is a symbol that helps to balance the four functions we all carry within us. In the *mandala* intuition is yellow, intellect blue, sensation green and emotion rose. I realized that, of course, the ring was too big for me. I still had a very long way to go before blue and green, symbolic of the more assertive and active attributes of my animus, were sufficiently developed to bring about a better balance. For some time, Baba had been very obviously encouraging me to drop my habit of hanging back, and replace it with self-confidence so I could take my rightful place in the world. Yes, I still needed to develop further the blue light-green light. I hoped that the union of my male and female parts in an inner marriage would enable me to achieve balance. Then my mind flashed back in sudden comprehension to the time, twenty-five years earlier, when I had just started on the inner search for meaning to life resulting in the work I have been doing ever since. In order to pursue the inner search, a woman has to use the inner assertive male part of the mind which Baba often likens to the inner husband. I had also learned that as soon as each part had been recognized and developed an inner marriage of the two can take place. The "child" of this union would be the new, more balanced and integrated person. Had Baba married those two parts? It certainly seemed likely, though none of these insights occurred to me at the time of the interview. I had since heard Baba say that our real birthday occurs when we first turn to God. By this reckoning it *was* my jubilee or twenty-fifth year.

After the brief ceremony Baba called individuals from the group into an inner room for private interviews while the others sat awaiting their turn. At one point when he came in to call another couple, he caught sight of my husband sitting on the floor leaning against a wall. With a mischievous twinkle he asked him, "Do you feel tied?" My husband thought he said, "Do you feel tired?" and replied, "No, Baba, I am not tired, just resting." Baba retorted, "Not tired—tied." To my complete surprise, I blurted out, "Tied to Baba." At the time I did not realize the full significance of that remark either. But much later it too became clear.

Each partner should be tied to the Baba within instead of to one another. Then I recalled an incident from a previous year which I had also not fully understood at the time. One day Baba had hurried into the room where we were all sitting. As he passed in front of me on his way up to his room, he turned and said almost scornfully, "Marriage ceremony! They want companionship, but God is the only companion." With that he had disappeared upstairs, to return in a few minutes with a neatly folded *sari* under one arm.

He had apparently performed a wedding ceremony for a couple whose motives for marrying he did not approve. Now I was aware that he had indicated that if the husband or wife became more important to each other than God it could obstruct their growth and prevent them from relying on God for their sole security. The *shashtiabdi*, or remarriage ceremony, was a rededication in which each partner promised to help the other on their spiritual path towards union with God.

When it was time for our private interview, my newly acquired ring almost slipped off my finger, so I said to Baba, a bit hesitantly, "It is too big." He looked quizzically at me and said, "Yes, I know. You will grow to fit it, " which, of course, I did not understand then.

As the time for our departure drew near we tried to ask Baba for permission to leave, but were never successful in catching his attention until the day before we were to depart, when he approached my husband and innocently asked, "When are you leaving?" as if he had no idea. When Sidney told him that we were due to leave the following day, he granted us a farewell interview for the next morning. That meant that we would have to be packed and ready to leave as soon as it ended.

When we arrived for the interview we found quite a number of Western men sitting waiting. Among them were doctors and psychologists. We were glad to see several devotees from California, including Ed Dugan, as we all filed into the room. As I was the only woman present I sat over to one side apart from the group of men.

Soon after we were all settled Baba entered with a jaunty step, singing a little tune, "Who is Sai Baba? He is love, love, love," which he repeated several times until, apparently, aware that some-one was missing, asked, "Where is the Italian couple?" He sent one of the men to look for them, but he soon returned saying that he could not find them and was told they had left. A few minutes later the couple entered breathlessly and Baba announced to the group, "Swami knew where they were."

It turned out to be a very long interview and was one of the most interesting and informative ones I can recall. Baba referred to the doctors as body doctors and mind doctors. For the benefit of the latter he launched into a discussion of the mind and asked, "What actually is the mind?" Everyone joined in with suggestions and an animated discussion ensued. Baba then switched to devotion and love, stressing the need to give up what he referred to as contraction love, or lust, which is the main part of human love and often mistaken for true love. He urged us all to move from love based on lust and attachment to divine love based on detachment which is expanding instead of contracting.

He then leaned towards the Italian man, and pointing to a *japamala* around his neck, asked, "Do you use it or is it just for decoration?" The man laughed and assured him that he used it. Baba took it and demonstrated to us how it should be used. A *japamala* is similar to a rosary or the prayer beads used in various religions to help count the number of times a certain *mantra* or prayer is repeated. *Japamalas* are composed of 108 beads with an extra one tied separately to a small tassel to mark the beginning of the strand. Baba showed how it could help us concentrate to detach from the world and be attached only to God. He explained that the thumb represents the indwelling God, the index finger the life of the individual including the ego, will and personality, and the other three fingers the *gunas*, or the three attributes of the material world. Moving the index finger away from the other three fingers and connecting it just below the tip of the inner side of the thumb indicates the wish to move away from the usual attachment to the world and make a firm connection with God. The *japamala* should be draped over the middle finger, thus separating the other three fingers from the index finger indicating that when the self and God are joined they can cooperate harmoniously together in the world. As each bead is advanced by the thumb and forefinger, he recommended that we repeat "*Aum, Aum, Aum,*" "*Sai Ram, Sai Ram, Sai Ram,*" or any other of the names of God. The practice of this separation of the self from worldly attributes and attachment to God will gradually allow such attachments to fall away. Whereas when we are attached to worldly qualities, God automatically becomes separated from our lives. We cannot be attached to both the world and God simultaneously. He urged us all to keep moving one step at a time away from the world and towards God.

He elaborated on this theme for several minutes and then asked, "Who really are you?" He quickly supplied his own answer, "You are three persons: there is the one you think you are, the one others think you are, and the one you really are. Work towards making all three the same. Then there will be peace and bliss."

During a lull a particularly aggressive young man seized the opportunity to ask Baba some very searching questions. He started by saying that he had a problem concerning Baba, to which Baba replied, "Many problems!" Unperturbed the young man continued, "My problem is that sometimes you have said you will talk to someone or see him tomorrow, and then when tomorrow comes you do not keep your promise. What does this mean?" Despite the questioner's abrasive tone Baba smiled sweetly at him and said, "Swami knows each one's program and how long you will be here. When he speaks to you that is the tomorrow he means. If he says he will see you after some days you will know it will be in a while, but if he says tomorrow then you will be happy and expect it, and each day will be tomorrow and tomorrow." The young man was not satisfied with this explanation and persisted with his cross-examination. He asked how the Incarnation of Truth, which he had heard Baba professed to be, could justify propagating an illusion by promising something that did not come true and misleading people with such promises. Baba, still unruffled and loving, patiently explained, "When you come here for the first time, perhaps as part of a group, you must be given some foundation for your faith. My duty is to call you in and speak to you so that you will not go away disappointed." He further elaborated on this theme by explaining, "Some come with so many problems that each day Swami speaks to them a little because he knows they have come such a long way and their anxiety must be consoled. When you are very hungry a little food should be given at first. If you are given too much all at once, to stop all your hunger, it will ruin your health. When you are thirsty you will want to gulp down all the liquid given you but you must be persuaded to take only one sip at a time. Sometimes it is best to give you only one sip at a time. When you are here it is your duty to wait. The real student will wait until he gets his interview and will have confidence that he will get it. Sometimes it is necessary to test students to build faith and confidence. Does he have the real desire? If he doesn't get the interview right away will he go away?

"When you knock a nail into a wall, " he said walking over to a nearby wall to demonstrate his point by pretending to hammer a nail into it, "you test it with your finger to see if it holds firm." He again pretended to test the imaginary nail in the wall, laughing at his own mimicry. Turning serious again he said, "My duty is to test you. When you are teaching a class, every once in a while it is necessary to give a test to see if the students are progressing and are ready to go higher. You must all be earnest enough to ask for tests and anxious to move up. Without tests you stay in the same place year after year. Real desire is to yearn for what you have come here for and to wait, although that may actually happen here, there, or anywhere; now, tomorrow, the day after, or another day. Have faith in the word given that you will get to see Swami, I will never disappoint anyone who has complete confidence."

The young man was still not satisfied, and as he persisted with his question his voice rose to become more and more shrill and strident. "Is it okay, " he asked, "to say you will give an interview tomorrow and not do it?" Patiently, Baba replied that the question was not clear. It was reworded with, "If you are a teacher isn't it important to speak the truth?" Baba replied, "If you are the teacher and you say you are going to give an interview, then it is the student's duty to wait." But this answer did not satisfy the young man either. He persisted, asking, "Is it okay to mislead if Baba knows he will not see the person?" Baba replied, "The yearning, the desire must be there. You must wait. It's called *tapas*. You have to have faith that you will get it. If not tomorrow, then someday you will get it." "Then it is permissible to mislead in certain circumstances?" the young man demanded. Baba answered, "God tests you so that you will go higher and higher." "Then isn't it the devotee's duty to test the Master to be sure if he is right?" challenged the young man.

At that point even Baba's patience seemed to be wearing thin and the rest of the group were becoming very restless and uncomfortable. Some of them made as if to top the young man's arrogant baiting, but Baba answered by saying, "The teacher knows how to test the student. If a man doesn't know the alphabet how can he know the words? The eyes see everything but they cannot see themselves. You need a mirror. You come to see me to get that. I am your mirror in which to see your own eyes. Many *gurus* tell you that you are weak, but I don't say that. I say that you have power. You are God! Follow the Master within you. Fight to the end."

Finally, the young man seemed to settle down. Baba continued to ask some of the others what they wished and the discussion became more general and less tense. He delighted everyone by materializing a ring for the Italian man and comforted his wife who was obviously very upset, apparently over a very sick child.

Then he turned to us and asked if we were leaving that day. We told him we were ready to leave but were waiting for his permission. He replied that we should go that afternoon, and waved us into the private interview room where he spoke to us on a more personal level.

Soon after we came out, he signaled that the interview was at an end. It had lasted an hour and a half, but the time had gone by so fast that it seemed more like a few minutes, such was the concentration he evoked and the energy he emanated. We were all filled with his love as we filed out of the room. He held his right hand up over each of us as we passed in the traditional gesture of blessing, and said over and over, "Bless. Bless. Very happy, very happy."

During the interview our friend Ed had been able to tell Baba how much his life had changed since he started going to the local center. This was his first time with Baba. He left the interview room so filled with Baba's love and energy that he was sure he could not absorb any more, and decided to leave with us instead of staying for Shivaratri as he had originally planned. The three of us started to hurry back to our rooms to finish packing. We were stopped along the way several times by people asking what had taken place during the interview to cause so much laughter, which could be heard in the *bhajan* hall above the sound of the singing. We stopped to give quick reports and hurried to our rooms. When we arrived we immediately noticed that a large life-sized photograph of Baba's head and shoulders had been hung in each room in readiness for Shivaratri. The likeness was so compelling and lifelike that I wondered if it was for sale and quickly went over to the bookshop to inquire. I was told that the photographs had been distributed at Baba's request and, as far as was known, there were none left. Regretfully, I accepted this information and continued to make ready to leave.

As we were walking towards our loaded taxi we heard our name being called. Turning around we saw one of the college boys racing towards us carrying what looked like two scrolls. When he reached us he breathlessly told us that Baba had sent them with his blessing for a safe journey. I unfolded one of them and, to my delight, it was a copy of the photograph which had been placed in our rooms. One was for us and the other for Ed. We were so touched to have our wish fulfilled in this way, just minutes before we were to leave. What a lovely end to our visit! We left regenerated once again, and ready to return to our daily lives and work in the Western world having been exposed again to a way to gain freedom from the thrall of the world, from *maya*.

We arrived home in plenty of time to welcome our lovely little granddaughter, Crystal Ann. Lorna and her husband were overjoyed, and we were not only happy to become grandparents but especially grateful to see our daughter's happiness and fulfillment.

CHAPTER SEVENTEEN

I HUNG THE photograph of Baba on a wall of my work room where it dominates all the daily activities, as if he were physically present. His presence became so very real that I slipped into the habit of greeting him each morning before a counseling session to ask him to direct both me and the person I was about to work with. In addition, often during a session I turned to his picture to ask silently for insight into a particularly knotty problem.

I became aware that more and more devotees had begun to call me when they heard how I work. So I was kept very busy performing what I began to understand was my *seva*. Baba assures us that service is an extremely important part of our daily spiritual practice. He states that it is as important as meditation, if not more important, but only if it is performed as worship and without attachment to the results or fruits. Only then does it incur no new *karmic* consequences.

With Baba's apparent awareness and approval of my work, I arrived at the point where I was willing at least to try to undertake the task of writing a book about it. One of the chief reasons for my delay had been lack of time, because of the number of people with whom I was working. I had begun to hand over all the problems to Baba asking him to help me to find their solutions, so I included this one.

Towards the end of the year we began to plan another trip to Baba at our usual time in January. As we started to work out our schedule, it suddenly occurred to me that I would have a perfect opportunity to begin writing the book while I was with Baba. Plenty of time would be available while waiting for his *darshan* each day. Starting it while I was physically in his presence would not only give me the benefit of his inspiration but also the increase of energy I had noticed whenever I was near him. I relaxed with this solution to the problem of finding time to start the book.

I decided to pack a supply of small note pads and pens which I could keep handy in my handbag for those odd times when I would be free to write. I still had very mixed feelings about the venture, as I had no idea how or where to start. How was I to present in written form such a seemingly unstructured and individual method? The only way I could do so was to seek direction from my High Self, and trust that a book would emerge transmitted by this higher source of wisdom which had for so many years proved to be valid. As Baba was for me the outer manifestation of the God-force within everything and everyone, surely starting the book while I was in his immediate presence would make it easier for me to be open to receive the contents. With this encouraging thought we set out once more on our yearly pilgrimage to Baba.

On the long flight to India I started to outline the steps by which I was first led to the quest for meaning to life resulting in my present work. As it was all factual it was simple to record.

Baba was in Whitefield when we arrived. As soon as he saw us he told us to go directly to his house and return everyday. He often tells people, "This is not my house. It is yours," meaning that everything he has is for those who may need it.

From then on, each morning and afternoon, I took my place on the women's side of the long room, frequently in solitary state as on the previous occasion. When I concentrated on writing the book I found, to my surprise, that words and sentences began to flow into my mind exactly as the teachings had been doing for so long. Sometimes the flow came so quickly that it was difficult to write fast enough to record it in my note pads. Whenever Baba came into the room I tucked my notes back into my bag and resumed writing while he was away.

About the third day, rumors began to circulate that Baba was about to leave for Madras on his yearly visit to celebrate Pongol, a festival when cattle are blessed. We arrived at his house early that day since no one knew when he would be leaving. While waiting for him to appear, I immersed myself in writing. After a while I became aware of an unusual stillness and, looking up, found myself staring up into Baba's face. He must have come down from his private rooms without my hearing him and was now standing looking down at me with a quizzical expression on his face. Thoroughly embarrassed, I realized that once again, as with the Murphet book, I had been so engrossed in what I was doing that I had been oblivious to his arrival. I started to rise to my feet, apologizing as I did so, but he restrained me with his hand. Then looking down at the small pile of notes on the floor at my side, he quickly moved closer to them and sharply and loudly clapped his hands over them three times. He then looked up and, with his wonderful smile suffusing his face, he said, "I am very, very happy." With that he swept out through the front door and into the waiting car and off to the airport.

It had all happened so quickly and unexpectedly that I was left in a daze. My husband came over to ask what Baba had said. As I told him I realized with an uprush of gratitude that Baba had not only given his approval of the book but had released his energy into it right at its inception by clapping his hands over the first few notes. I was now certain that with his blessing I would be able to complete the task. I also knew that I must trust the step-by-step process and avoid worrying about the outcome.

Baba was away for only a short time, but long enough for us to attend to the various errands so often neglected while we were driving back and forth to Whitefield twice a day. As soon as Baba returned we resumed our daily routine. Again I found myself all alone on the women's side most of the time, except for occasional visitors. This isolation was now a tremendous benefit. It enabled me to concentrate on writing for long periods at a time, and my pile of notes grew noticeably each day. As I continued to listen within and write what came into my mind, I was surprised to discover that a clear, step-by-step sequence was being revealed. As I had always asked to be shown by my High Self what to do each time I worked, I had not realized that there was a definite pattern. I was fascinated to discover that a complete method was emerging as I wrote.

Baba would come and go in his usual way. He sometimes stopped to smile or comment on my progress as he passed in front of me and referred to me as a hard worker. With so much encouragement I relaxed, and the pile of notes grew apace.

Oddly enough, all three of the officers of the American Central Committee, Jack Hislop, Richard Bayer, and my husband, had arrived within a short time of one another. None of them had known in advance that the others would also be there at the same time. Such seeming coincidences are very common around Baba. He appears to draw people to him at the right time not only for their own needs, but also for the unfolding and furtherance of his plans. Several of the directors of the American organization had also arrived, enabling many of the current questions about the progress of the centers to be discussed and checked directly with Baba.

At one meeting four women were included: Mrs. Hislop, Mrs. Murphet, whose husband had written two books about Baba, Mrs. Rajagopal from Ojai, California, and myself. As we all settled down on the floor, Baba looked around the room with a welcoming smile. A curious expression flitted across his face as his glance fell on the four ladies. Quickly he raised his right hand and with his inimitable gesture circled it in the air and quickly closed it. When he re-opened it, four identical lockets were revealed in his palm, in four corners of a square. After showing them to everyone, he turned with a broad smile and gave one to each of the four of us women, saying in English, "My latest portrait for my four daughters. All the same, so no jealousy," which caused much laughter. The lockets consisted of delicate oval gold filigree frames containing a thin piece of mother o' pearl, on the face of which was a picture of Baba's head and shoulders set against a pale blue background. The picture portrayed his Shiva aspect, his eyes boring intensely into those of the beholder. We all laughingly commented later that he had obviously given us a gift to keep us happy and prevent us from becoming bored with the long and tedious business meeting which ensued.

There was an interesting sequel to the gift of the lockets. The filigree frames were too delicate to hold the picture securely in place. Mrs. Hislop's and Mrs. Rajagopal's fell out after just a few days. Mrs. Rajagopal took hers to a jeweler in Bangalore to have a thin layer of gold added to the back to hold the picture permanently in place. She showed it to Mrs. Hislop who decided that she would like to have hers fixed in the same way. When she went to pick it up she noticed that the picture was different from the original one, and pointed it out to the jeweler. He insisted that it was the same one which she had brought him and refused to be persuaded otherwise. She was very upset and told her husband who showed it to Baba at the first opportunity. Baba took it, looked at it carefully, and agreed that it was not the one he had materialized. He then asked Mrs. Hislop if she wanted the original one back. When she eagerly said, "Yes," he held it in his closed fist, blew on it three times, opened his hand and handed it back to her. She saw immediately that the original picture was back in the frame. Later, when she was showing it to Mrs. Rajagopal, they both noticed that not only was the gold backing applied by the jeweler now missing, but the whole frame was heavier. It felt as if the gold from the jeweler's backing had been added to the frame. Here was yet another of Baba's little mysteries!

Around the middle of our stay Baba left for Puttaparthi and told us to follow him. I wondered how I would be able to continue writing while we were there. I soon discovered that I was able to balance the small pads of paper on my knee as I sat in the crowd each morning and afternoon waiting for Baba to come out to give *darshan*.

Shortly after our arrival at the *ashram*, a rumor began to circulate that Baba was planning to go to the Women's College at Anantapur, a short drive from Puttaparthi. We had not yet seen this college and I was most interested to do so. I also wanted to endow a scholarship for a girl as we had already done for a boy. I asked my husband to try to ask Baba for permission to accompany him on his forthcoming visit to the college. The very next day Baba stopped to speak to him as he sat with some of the other men on the verandah outside Baba's rooms. He took this opportunity to tell Baba of my request. He readily agreed, and promised to let us know when he would be going.

A few days later he told my husband that he would leave on the morning of January 30 and that we should be ready to accompany him. When this message was relayed to me I was especially pleased as that day would be our wedding anniversary. Once again we would be able to spend it with Baba.

The visit to the Girls' College was a very different experience from our more frequent informal contact with the students at the Boys' College next to Baba's house in Whitefield. Dr. Sam Sandweiss and his brother, also a doctor, and three other women were included in the group which accompanied Baba. On arrival, we were welcomed by the principal and the girls, all of whom were intensely excited over Baba's long awaited visit. They eagerly clustered at a discreet distance intent on obtaining his *darshan* at every possible opportunity, their eyes and faces shining with devotion. In their colorful *saris* they reminded me of bright hued butterflies seeking from Baba the nectar for which they thirsted.

He treated them very differently from the boys with whom he is informal and at times very playful. With the girls he was much more formal and reserved in his attitude, yet at the same time he gave the distinct impression that nothing about them escaped his notice. He seems to plumb the depths of everyone he meets and now appeared to know everything about each one at a glance.

We spent the day sitting in the large common room while Baba went about his many tasks, meetings and talks with the girls and teachers. He appeared at intervals to see if we were comfortable and to make sure that we were served cool drinks. Several of the older girls were detailed to show us around the college which had been swept and polished until everything shone in honor of Baba's visit. Some of the students served us lunch. Later, everyone gathered in the assembly hall for Baba's discourse. It was the highlight of the day and keenly anticipated by the entire audience, as was clearly apparent from the eager expressions on the faces of those assembled there. Dr. Sandweiss, author of the book *The Holy Man and the Psychiatrist*, the principal of the college, and several girls also spoke. We all joined in singing *bhajans* which Baba initiated by leading the first ones.

Many people wonder why Baba is starting colleges for girls since in India they rarely have an opportunity to use higher education in a job or profession, as they usually marry shortly after they graduate. But Baba sees education as extremely important for the young women who will become the mothers of future generations. He wants to prepare them to be better equipped to teach and guide their children wisely and in accordance with ancient Indian precepts. He feels that with the education they will receive at the colleges under his supervision they will also be more understanding wives to their husbands. He points out that the children of a nation are its future citizens so it is important that their mothers, who have the most effect on them during their formative years, should be given the kind of education which will fit them for such responsible roles. He foresees that when these children attain adulthood and infiltrate the many different organizations in their country, they will take with them their belief in the spiritual precepts they have learned, and in this way will raise the level of consciousness wherever they are.

As I looked around at all the young women gathered in the auditorium and observed the rapt expressions on their faces as they listened so intently to Baba's discourse, I was able to catch a minute glimpse of his plan for the future. Yes, these girls would be better mothers and more intelligent partners to their husbands, to whom they could impart their gentle influence to balance an excessively masculine approach. The children of such parents would undoubtedly become better future citizens.

We came away from that day's visit most impressed with all we had observed, and especially with the way Baba was quietly planning to bring about gradual changes in the Indian way of life. I was grateful to have been given the opportunity to gain such insight into his plans to lift his country and its people beyond the current rigid and narrow ways, yet at the same time to avert the danger of infection from the West with its overemphasis on materialism which, he warns, is fast becoming a major problem.

On the way back to Puttaparthi our taxi kept breaking down. The driver discovered a leak in the water tank, and repeatedly stopped every few miles along the way hoping to find water to replenish the fast diminishing supply. It was an even more nerve-racking drive than usual, and at best they are never exactly comfortable or without incident. We lagged farther and farther behind Baba and the others. When we finally came within sight of the familiar gates leading into the *ashram*, I discovered to my horror that I must have left behind the double case in which I carry two pairs of glasses. My heart sank as it was much too late to turn around and go back to retrieve them, especially in that taxi. One pair was for reading. Without them I would be unable to continue to write, as I am far-sighted. We decided to go directly to one of the offices in the *ashram* where there is a telephone, hoping it would still be open, so that we could call the college at Anantapur to ask if the case of glasses had been found. In India it is no easy matter to make a telephone call, even from a hotel in one of the big cities, let alone from an *ashram* in a small village. Fortunately, the office was still open and we were successful in finding someone to put through a call to the college. It was quickly verified that I had left the case there.

Our next problem was how to retrieve it. We had sent our driver with the malfunctioning taxi back to Bangalore to bring back another car in time to drive us back to Bangalore. We asked around the *ashram* and found another taxi driver who agreed to drive to Anantapur to pick up the glasses.

The next morning we were called to a farewell interview. When we arrived at the appointed time we found quite a number of other Westerners had also been called and were waiting to see Baba. As soon as he appeared he turned to ask when we were planning to leave. We explained that we had to wait for our driver to return with another taxi as the one he had been using was in need of repairs. We also told him that we would have to wait for yet another taxi to return from Anantapur with my glasses which I had left at the college. Baba was visibly shocked and reprimanded us sternly, saying, "Waste, waste. You should have asked one of the teachers to give the glasses to a bus driver to deliver to you." He elaborated at considerable length, ending with, "You could have had two new pairs of glasses made for far less than the cost of the taxi."

I was feeling more and more embarrassed and would have liked nothing better than to become invisible but since I could not hide from Baba, I would have to hear him out. Then without warning he swung around abruptly to face me, and wagging his forefinger like a school teacher, said with mock anger, "You are lazy." I promptly burst into tears. It was, of course, a release from the accumulated stress of the previous day's erratic drive culminating in the discovery that I had left behind my glasses. Baba's obvious displeasure at the waste of money and now his accusation of laziness were the final straw. I blurted out, "Oh Baba! No, not lazy! You yourself say I am a hard worker." When he saw my distress he smiled and with immense love and gentleness, like a mother comforting a troubled child, he almost crooned, "That was only my joke. Don't cry. You must have self-control." I quickly pulled myself together realizing that I had allowed myself to become weak and helpless.

He then went ahead with a group interview during which he commented on the work I do, the book I was writing, and repeated that I was a hard worker, all of which made me even more uncomfortable, especially in the presence of other people. He then mentioned quite casually that he wanted me to attend the summer course the next year and to give a lecture to all the students from the book I was writing. This announcement came like a bombshell and my reactions to it were acutely ambivalent. I was happy to have his approval of the work and to know that the book about it had his blessing. But the very thought of giving a lecture to hundreds of students and other people filled me with terror. It had always been hard for me to speak in public and I had so far successfully avoided speaking even at any of the Sai Baba centers. I knew that what Baba was now proposing would be an absolute impossibility. The only way it could be accomplished would be if he spoke through me, and I wasn't at all sure I could relax sufficiently for that to be possible. As usual with Baba, he uncovers whatever is most difficult for a person to do or to change. I realized that he had been purposely playing with me, slapping me down, and lifting me up again only to scare me to death. This was designed, I was sure, to shake me loose from my own ego with its many likes and dislikes. I was certainly shaken though far from being free of the problems he had lit up with his penetrating searchlight.

Meanwhile, the interview continued with a discussion of will. I got up enough courage to ask him how to differentiate between our own will, another person's, and God's. He smiled understandingly and said it was a very good question. He answered by saying that when we are in doubt as to whose will is in control in a particular situation, we should take no action until we could go alone to a quiet place, concentrate strongly on him and ask to be shown what to do. He promised that we would receive an answer within twenty minutes. Since then there have been innumerable times when I have been most grateful for this advice. When I can relax, genuinely surrender the whole question, and ask to be shown, I invariably receive a reply well within the twenty minutes.

In a private interview Baba elaborated on my work and casually remarked that I had written three-quarters of the book while with him. That later proved to be correct. However, that was only the very first rough draft, mostly in the form of separate groups of notes on the various sections. It would all need to be sorted and rearranged after we returned home.

Originally I had planned to have made simple xeroxed copies of the book for people with whom I worked to use as a reference when they practiced the various visualization techniques at home. It would also be useful as a textbook if I decided to teach the method at some future time. However, Baba insisted that it be made available to more people and should therefore be published. He cautioned that it should not be published in India where the paper and printing are not as good as in other countries. I asked him to help me to find the right publisher, which he smilingly assured me he would do.

I left the interview with very mixed feelings. I was deeply moved and grateful that Baba had given me so much encouragement about the work and the book, but the prospect of giving "a talk from the book," as he put it, at his summer course the following May, left me frozen with panic. Too many conflicting thoughts and feelings rendered me incapable of fully comprehending the deeper significance of all that Baba had been doing and saying to me during these past few weeks, and particularly at this last interview.

Now, from my present perspective, I am keenly aware of his motives in exposing several areas of my life which needed to be consciously examined and dealt with. My introverted way of life was a protective device to enable me to preserve my identity despite my mother's constant insistence that I fit her pattern, with which I complied only outwardly. As a result I did not pay enough attention to my contact with the outer world, and was often absent-minded and forgetful. On the one hand Baba's joke about my being lazy was correct. To pay too little attention to details is a type of laziness. However, the reverse side of the coin, which Baba also emphasized, is that I am a very hard worker. This is especially true with activities which I consider to be important or worthwhile, but I had always used my will to drive myself to work too hard. Neither of these two extremes of behavior represents a balanced way of life. The only solution to such a dilemma is to tune in constantly to the Baba within and ask to be shown how to bridge the two extremes. Only then could I relax and flow with the inner awareness of what to do, when, how and to what degree.

How deftly Baba had indicated the areas which needed to be brought into balance. At the same time, he had presented the perfect situation to prod me towards achieving it. The talk itself was not important. It was being used only as a means to spur me on to take the necessary steps in my daily life to find a middle way between the two extreme types of behavior, laziness and compulsion. But it took several years before I could see his point as clearly as I do now. I had to be willing to surrender the old ways, trust him to show me new ones, and accept whatever happened, even if it included making mistakes. How wise, patient and loving he was to give only barely enough of a hint to get me started, instead of telling me exactly what to do. He knew that would have prevented me from using my own muscles, both physical and mental, to take the many steps which would eventually lead to a more balanced way of life. Once more I saw him as the perfect Zen master.

Later that afternoon our driver returned with a different taxi assuring us that it would cause no trouble on the long rough drive back to Bangalore. The case containing my glasses also arrived in plenty of time for us to leave as planned.

The prospect of the forthcoming speech weighed heavily on me during the remainder of the year. Even at the time I realized only too well that Baba was purposely drawing my attention to a problem on which I needed to work. How could I be so presumptuous as to try to help other people to overcome their fears when the anticipation of giving a talk was now causing such terror in me? I had always vowed that I would never share any of the techniques I had received unless I first proved that they worked for me. So I must practice what I preach! I resolved to work on this fear immediately.

I soon discovered, however, as with many of the weaknesses Baba uncovers, that I could not plunge in and eradicate this one by pulling it out by the roots like a weed, merely because I had been made so clearly aware of the need to do so. Both from the inner teaching and from my own past experience, I knew that changing any habit, attitude, or negative emotion involves a process composed of many steps. Only rarely can it be accomplished in one big leap, though most people would prefer such a deceptively quick and easy method. I have often told those with whom I work that growth, healing, or any other basic change can only be achieved by first becoming conscious of the need to change and then by taking the necessary steps to bring it about. There is no magic wand which can be waved either by us or by someone else to effect the change. We can take the first step only from the point where we actually are in our development, and not from an imaginary place where we may mistakenly imagine or wish we were. We also need to be drastically honest, for only then can we move towards the goal of finally becoming one with the God we already are in reality. It is this step-by-step process which strengthens us spiritually, just as regular daily exercise strengthens our physical muscles. If Baba or anyone else did everything for us, it would rob us of the chance to become strong. Their muscles would be strengthened while our own would remain just as weak as before.

So, faced with this fear of speaking in public, I realized anew that I myself would have to take the necessary steps to overcome it. As with all problems and weaknesses, they remain a burden either because we have not yet found a method with which to eradicate them, or we have lacked the strength to do so. It was only too obvious to me that despite the work I had already done on fear, I had failed dismally to overcome it in this area. But what made me think that this time would be any different from past failures? However irrational it seemed, I was absolutely certain that there was a difference. Instead of initiating the process myself, Baba had deliberately brought the problem to my attention. Surely that must mean that he knew it was now the correct time for me to work on it. In that case there must be hope of success. Even so, I knew from experience that I could succeed only by constantly calling on Baba to connect me to my own inner Baba to assist me.

After our return home I continued to work on the book. It proved to be a much more arduous project than I had anticipated. I also continued to work with people on their problems. New techniques were frequently forthcoming. Consequently the scope of the work, and therefore of the book, was always expanding. But with Baba's help, by the time I was due to leave for the summer course, I had finished the first rough draft.

One day early in 1979 our daughter Lorna called excitedly to tell us that she was going to have another baby in autumn. I silently thanked Baba and asked for a healthy grandchild.

CHAPTER EIGHTEEN

BABA BELIEVES THAT the education now offered to students in India does not include a spiritual foundation. He decries the present tendency to copy Western methods, which stress materialism, in preference to ethical conduct and ideals. He feels strongly that education should encourage men and women to live lives of service to their country rather than strive only to achieve financial gain. The curriculum used at all the schools and colleges he has started includes Vedic teachings in addition to the standard academic subjects.

For several years he conducted a special summer course from mid-may to mid-June for selected boys and girls from all over India. His purpose was to expose them to a brief but intense glimpse of living close to him, as we had observed the boys at his college in Whitefield were privileged to do during the school year. The program was composed of daily lectures by well known authorities on various educational and philosophical subjects, with special stress on the Vedic writings. The students also engaged in a daily discipline of *seva*, or service, which included going to nearby villages to help the villagers to improve their lot. Both men and women students, often from well to do families, could be seen helping to dig wells where needed, sweeping the streets clean of age old accumulation of debris, assisting at clinics, and performing many other often menial tasks. Each evening they gathered in the auditorium to hear an inspirational discourse by Baba. Baba also invited some of his devotees, both Indian and foreign, to the daily lectures and to his evening discourses.

It so happened that it was not convenient for my husband to accompany me when it was time to leave for India. A legal issue had unexpectedly arisen which needed his immediate attention. So I left ahead of him and he planned to join me as soon as he could. I had received no further communication of any kind from either Baba or those responsible for arranging the summer program, but assumed that Baba still wished me to speak.

I arrived in Bangalore a few days before the start of the summer course. Baba had just returned from his annual visit to Bombay, where he usually goes in early May to celebrate the anniversary of the opening of Dharmakshetra. I went out to

Whitefield that afternoon for *darshan* and to be given a badge permitting me to attend both the daytime lectures and Baba's evening discourses.

I first went to the back gate, where we usually entered, but found it guarded, and I was refused admittance. I explained that on my last visit Baba had directed me to come to the summer course and that I needed to get a badge in order to attend. However, it seemed either that the men guarding the gate could not understand me, or that this was a test of my patience, faith and perseverance. I waited and waited, and finally caught sight of an American woman whom I knew. I managed to attract her attention and tell her of my dilemma. She quickly explained it to the gatekeeper and he then allowed me to enter. She told me that Baba was officiating at a wedding, as she escorted me to a secluded place to sit until he had finished, when I could go to the office to collect my badge.

As Baba was about to go outside to give *darshan*, he turned towards where I was sitting, and with a big smile of welcome asked, "How are you? How is your husband? In what place is he?" The last question seemed to indicate that he was asking about my absent flesh and blood husband and not the husband within. So I told him that he was still in California, but would be joining me later. He nodded approvingly and said, "I will see you," and continued on his way to *darshan*. I had no idea if he intended to see me on his way back, or if he meant that he would see me at some future time. Some Indian women, seeing my indecision, advised me to continue to wait there. Two hours later they came back to tell me that Baba had gone up to his room for the night, which was always the signal for guests to leave. By then it was too late to go to the office to get my badge. So ended my first frustrating day!

I returned the next morning and this time was allowed through the gate. Again, I tried to find out where I needed to go to pick up a badge. After several fruitless efforts I arrived at an office where I was told that Mrs. Ratan Lal would give one to me, but that she was out at that time. I would have to return the following day. The next day was the first day of the summer course, so I would be obliged to wait until the very last minute to be given my pass to the various events. Baba was certainly making sure that I would have to work hard to be more aggressive than I had ever been in my whole life and far more so than I cared to be. That inner husband to whom he had married me on our last anniversary was certainly being exercised in order to become a strong inner support for me. Undoubtedly an additional reason why I had come over alone this time was to be forced by circumstance to use both the masculine and feminine aspects of myself equally, in a balanced way, to achieve wholeness. It was perhaps another reason why Baba had asked me in what place my husband was, to emphasize the fact that my husband Sidney was not with me this time, so the inner one must act in his place.

Early the next morning I arrived at the gate once again. This time I was immediately admitted. I hurried over to Mrs. Ratan Lal's house. She is privileged to cook for Baba and take care of many of his daily needs. She greeted me warmly and we laughed over the frustrations which had prevented me from being given the badge earlier which we both realized was most significant. With that problem finally solved I could relax, assured of being admitted to the various functions for the next month.

I learned that neither men nor women were allowed in Baba's house, since the room in which they usually sat was being redecorated. Everyone attending the summer course joined the *darshan* lines with hundreds of other devotees each morning. I hurried over to take my place amongst the throngs of women already seated on the ground in neat lines, patiently waiting for Baba to appear.

The days from then on passed by swiftly. I drove out each morning for *darshan* and returned to the hotel for lunch, then out again for the afternoon lecture in the auditorium, followed by Baba's discourse and whatever entertainment he had arranged each evening. It was often very late before I returned to the hotel for dinner.

Sometimes, as Baba walked up and down the long *darshan* lines, he would give me a big smile, but not once did he indicate that he was ready to see me as he had promised that first day. There was never any mention by him or by anyone else of my giving a talk.

It was very interesting to see the hundreds of young girls and boys, from every part of India as well as from other countries, most of whom had traveled great distances to attend the course. Each evening, one boy and one girl presented summaries of the lectures given on the previous day. In addition a boy from the college in

Whitefield or a girl from the college at Anantapur gave a speech on a philosophical theme. Their talks were impressive and indicative of their genuine interest in this unique experience. They spoke so easily and confidently and without a trace of nervousness. I began to feel ashamed that I, who was old enough to be their grandmother, should be feeling so acutely apprehensive. But that only added to my discomfort.

The weather at this time of the year was not as pleasant as it is at our usual time in January. It was extremely hot, and the monsoon was just starting, making the air humid and heavy with the threat of thunderstorms which circled around and exploded every few days with torrential rain. Many times we were all drenched to the skin.

On some evenings Baba ordered the doors of the auditorium to be thrown wide open, and invited as many people as possible from the huge crowds assembled daily outside to come in to shelter from the rain. At such times there was a frantic surge as hundreds of wet, steaming bodies tried to squeeze into any available corner in the already densely packed hall. Such was their devotion and so intense their desire to catch a glimpse of Baba, and hopefully to hear his discourse, even if only via the loudspeakers setup outside in strategic places, that they had been willing to stand for hours in such inclement weather.

On the evenings when a storm broke, it was a strange sight to behold Baba calmly continuing to speak in his usual enthusiastic fashion while the thunder rolled and threatened to drown out his voice. At the same time flashes of lightning lit the eagerly upturned faces of the vast throng with an eerie light.

In order to be sure of getting into the hall, even those who had guest badges were obliged to arrive several hours early and sit outside the auditorium on the bare ground waiting for the doors to open. Because of the extreme heat and the daily possibility of rain, a makeshift canopy had been erected over a small area immediately outside the doors. It was made of heavy bamboo poles over which loosely woven mats had been laid to provide a meager protection from both the burning rays of the sun and the rain.

On Sunday evening, as I was sitting waiting, squeezed in with other women, a strong wind arose out of nowhere and blew one of the heavy bamboo poles off the flimsy canopy. On its way down to the ground it landed on my nose, knocking my glasses off onto the cement floor. My first thought was that I could easily have been knocked unconscious by such a severe blow. But to my complete amazement, as well as that of the women sitting near me, there was not even a scratch or mark of any kind on my nose or face and my glasses were not only intact but unscratched. None of us could believe it.

Another similar incident occurred a few days later. This was the first year I had brought a tape-recorder with me. I hoped to record Baba singing *bhajans* so that I could listen to his voice at home. I was therefore delighted to discover that at the end of his discourse Baba often finished the evening by singing a few *bhajans*. On one particular evening, just as he was about to leave the platform, we all stood up. In my hurry to rise to my feet, the tape-recorder which had been lying on my lap slipped and landed with a dull thud on top of the big toe of my right foot. The pain it caused was so sharp and sudden that I found it difficult not to cry out. A fleeting thought flashed across my mind that an injured toe would make the remainder of my stay extremely complicated, a thought I definitely did not want to entertain. Fortunately, I remembered to call silently on Baba to help, and found, to my surprise, that I was able to remain calm and impersonal, almost as if I were merely a spectator observing the situation instead of actually experiencing it.

I managed to walk out of the hall and into the waiting taxi with only slight discomfort. As soon as I was settled in the taxi I started to massage the hurt toe very gently, and at the same time I repeatedly called on Baba to heal it. An Indian devotee had asked for a lift back into town, so we talked about his many wonderful experiences with Baba over the years as we drove along. When I reached the hotel I was most surprised to find that the pain had left, and I could walk easily. On reaching my room I checked the toe to see if I should order ice to be brought up, but as I could detect no swelling or bruises I decided to go straight to bed. I slept peacefully and on awakening I again examined the toe. Surprisingly there was still no pain, no swelling or bruises.

That day I had to do several small errands in town before driving to Whitefield. These necessitated my walking short distances from one shop to another for about two hours, which would have been an impossibility with a sore toe. The morning went well, I found everything on my list, and suffered not even a twinge of pain in the process.

Looking back at the events immediately preceding the accident, I began to glimpse a pattern emerging. In his discourse, Baba had stressed the need to be above or apart from both happiness and sorrow. I recalled that for a split second my mind had recoiled at the thought of trying to move around in the crowd at the summer course with a hurt toe. But just as quickly I must have let go of that thought, called on Baba and given the problem over to him. I wondered if that was what he had meant in his talk. If so, how wonderful to have this demonstration of that truth so quickly and with such convincing results. Had I perhaps been given a glimpse of the possibility of preventing a problem by neither reacting nor becoming identified with it?

The only way such a thing would be possible would be to remember to call on Baba instantly, and then remain calm in the certainty that he would help. The secret is to remember, for we are all so forgetful.

I soon became aware that while I was in the immediate presence of Baba, it was much easier to maintain contact with the God-self within my own heart which he symbolizes in physical form. Because of this almost constant awareness, I found I could handle the heretofore hidden aspects of myself as they surfaced from the unconscious into the conscious level of my mind where they became recognizable. Admittedly, I did not particularly care for some of those aspects when they reared their heads, though I realized that I needed to see them clearly before I could let go of them or transmute them. Many other devotees have informed me that they too have observed this activity in themselves and in others. All agree that it is most disconcerting until it is understood that changes can be brought about only after the problem has been clearly seen.

Some devotees experience similar cleansing episodes in their physical bodies. Suddenly, for no apparent reason, they become very ill, often accompanied by a very high temperature which burns out the negativity as it emerges from the unconscious. Suffice it to say that around Baba's energy there is no knowing what will take place on the physical, mental, emotional, and spiritual planes.

A little less than halfway through the course my husband arrived, and shortly thereafter Baba called us to an interview. At last I would be able to give him the package of letters I had brought with me from other devotees. As usual, I also handed him one from each of our daughters. As soon as he took the one from Lorna, he quickly looked up and, with a happy smile said, "She is carrying another baby." He then added, "She wants a boy this time, doesn't she?" I replied that I didn't know if she had any preference, but he assured me that she did, which she later confirmed.

He then asked me about the book I was writing. I had brought the first draft with me and was delighted to hand it to him for his blessing. He placed it on his lap and turned over the pages, glancing at certain sections which caught his eye, and commenting as he did so. I asked if he would give me permission to add a chapter about him, since I had mentioned him and his teachings throughout the text. He shook his head and said, "No." then, after a short pause while he watched my reaction, he added, "Keep it separate. Write a whole book about me." I was stunned at the enormity of such a responsibility. He quickly sensed my concern and smilingly added, "I will help you."

I had brought with me a photograph taken by Janet Bock at the 1975 World Conference, of Baba looking down at me with a sweet smile on his face as I sat in the *darshan* lines. I asked if he would sign it and give me permission to include it in the book. He reacted strongly, objecting that the picture showed only the back of my head, and not my face. I told him I thought it was most appropriate, as the attention was on him and not on me, but he would not hear of it and insisted that I must have another one taken of the two of us side by side.

I had heard that he would be leaving for Puttaparthi as soon as the summer course ended, so I asked if he wished us to accompany him. He shook his head and told me that it was much too hot for me at that time of the year. He then assured us that he would see us again before we left and at that time he would make some more medicine to clear away the headaches which still bothered me.

A few days later I had an odd experience. On Sunday, *bhajans* were sung outside all day long by the crowds waiting for Baba to come out to give *darshan*. As I walked away after the morning *darshan*, I began to feel unaccountably ill and extremely depressed—so much so that I started bemoaning the fact that I must be getting too old for this hectic schedule. I simply could not stop complaining and became very angry. I joined by husband and as we were leaving to return to the hotel for lunch, we met some Western devotees whom we knew. They asked if I was ill, as I looked strange, so I recounted what had happened. One of the women, who knew I suffered from headaches and allergies, was convinced that the large bunches of incense sticks burning throughout the *bhajans* had caused me to feel sick. She went on to explain that a cheap brand containing strong chemicals is burned and could easily have caused an allergic reaction. I thanked her and sighed with relief at hearing the possible cause of the sudden storm which had overcome me, causing me to react so negatively.

After lunch I decided to lie down to rest before going back for Baba's discourse that evening. I took off my *sari* and lay down on the bed, which was covered with a creamy white bedspread. As I lay there I mentally apologized to Baba for my negative mood and my angry outburst. I also thanked him for sending the message via my friend to let me know what had triggered it. After a while I began to feel a little better, which I attributed to Baba's help and a direct result of baring my heart and asking forgiveness.

When it was time to get dressed again I noticed a bright red speck on the white bedspread. I leaned over to see what it was and to my utter astonishment saw a miniscule photograph of Baba's head and shoulders showing his black hair and just a touch of his red robe which had first attracted my attention. I was certain that it had not been there when I lay down, as it was too conspicuous for me to have missed. Where had it come from I do not know. It was as if Baba was showing me that he understood and accepted my apology.

Towards the end of the month's program Baba decided to move this herd of cattle from their stalls in the compound behind his house to the new *gokulam* built for them further away, in the village. On the day of the move the animals were all gaily decorated. Their horns had been painted, colorful coverings were thrown over their backs, and bells tinkled as they moved. They were then led off with great pomp and ceremony followed by a crowd of devotees. We went along and watched from a distance as Baba patted each animal and gave them bananas to eat as they were being led into their new quarters. It was an enchanting scene reminiscent of the Krishna Incarnation.

The next day, while I was sitting with several women outside Baba's house, my husband came running in search of me. As soon as he caught sight of me he hurried over and started to propel me ahead of him, explaining that Baba had called us to an interview.

It was a very windy day, so I hastily tried to straighten my *sari*, brushed back my hair, and generally tidy myself. As I hurried along I tugged and pulled at the *sari* to make sure I was properly covered, and pinned back strands of hair blown loose by the wind. As we breathlessly arrived, I burst into the room and almost knocked into Baba, who was standing just inside the door waiting for us, an amused smile on his face as if he had been watching our hurried approach. Across his outstretched arms lay a folded *sari*. I barely stopped in time to avoid colliding with Baba, much to his amusement. He handed me the *sari*, and explained that it should have been given to me the day before, as that was the correct time for the gift. But as the cows were being moved to the new *gokulam*, we were not in the house that day for me to receive it. I noticed that he was again stressing the importance of the right time. I knew there must be an intentional message for me to decipher, as I was sure he had no need to apologize for not giving it to me on the appropriate day. At the time I was so touched by his gift that I pushed the question into the back of my mind with a mental note to try to interpret it later.

I had heard that Baba sometimes gives *saris* to women who live in his compound to wear on special occasions and that he had sent some during the past few days for the final celebration at the termination of the summer course. As I did not live in the compound, it had not occurred to me that he would give one to me. I was, therefore, all the more surprised to receive one from his hand. I exclaimed, "Oh, thank you, Baba! How wonderful to have you give me a *sari*." He smiled like an indulgent mother giving her child an unexpected gift and delighting in her surprise. He cautioned me not to wear it the following morning, but to wait until the afternoon procession which would mark the last day of the summer course.

He continued with the interview by giving further encouragement and comments on the book, and my work. Then he turned and called out for Dr. Fanibunda to take a photograph as he had promised at our last interview. Dr. Fanibunda came running, and as he prepared to take the photograph Baba playfully cautioned him to make it a good one. My husband stepped forward to remove the visitor's badge from my *sari*, but I protested that I was proud to wear it. Baba overruled my objection by announcing, "She is always with me. She doesn't need a badge," which brought tears to my eyes, not from sadness, but from awe as I felt his over-whelming love flow out to me. In that brief moment, I was filled with the love I had always craved as a child. I felt totally accepted, just as I was, with all my faults, weaknesses and fears. So, with tears staining my face, Dr. Fanibunda took a photograph of me standing beside Baba, who had just filled my heart to overflowing. Then with a mischievous twinkle he said that when the time was right for me to make a speech, it would be a very good one.

Finally, after the long months of apprehension, and this past month of wondering if or when he would suddenly call on me to speak, he was now postponing the ordeal still further into the future. I had been given a reprieve, but I knew I would have to overcome the fear completely before I could give a speech which would satisfy Baba. That, I knew full well, would entail being so surrendered that he would be able to speak through me. Only he knew when I would be ready, and all I could do was to be willing when that time came.

Then, without any warning, he circled his right hand in the air and quickly gathered the *vibhuti* he had just materialized. He poured it into a piece of paper, handed it to me, saying that it was for my grandson. I must have looked a bit surprised until I realized that he must be referring to the unborn child Lorna was carrying. He watched my reaction, nodded his head and said, "Yes. Yes, that is correct," as he read my thoughts. Undoubtedly he could also foresee a time when it would be needed.

After the interview we returned to the hotel. On the way I had my first chance to look at the *sari* Baba had just given me, still neatly wrapped in a small bundle. It was so beautiful. The main part was of delicate flesh colored silk, and the borders were brilliant red encrusted with gold thread. It was a much brighter color than I would have chosen. I had to laugh as I realized that I could scarcely withdraw into the background attired in that gorgeous garment. Obviously, he had given me a color that he decided I needed.

As soon as we reached the hotel I quickly checked to see if I had a *choli* and petticoat to wear with it. It had loose threads left at each end which it is customary to have tied into little tassels to form a decorative fringe. I hurried to a *sari* shop in the lobby of the hotel to ask if they knew anyone who would have time to tie the knots by noon the following day. The young Indian girl to offered to do it herself. How very fortunate that with so little time it would be properly tied. The short time was probably another reason why Baba pointed out that it should have been given to me on the day before. We stopped by the shop the next day after morning *darshan*. The young girl had done a beautiful job and formed an intricate pattern with the knots instead of simply tying them. I was still a bit shy of the color and design. "Okay, Baba," I thought, "I will do my best, with your help, to live up to this brilliant costume. You certainly do make your point quite clear."

Imagine the scene later that afternoon, at the finale of the summer course. All those who had attended were assembled and waited quietly to join the procession when it started to rain so heavily that it had to be cancelled. Sheer confusion ensued in the dash for cars and taxis to drive the participants along the route instead! We barely managed to reach the hall in time for the evening events. Awards were given to outstanding students and various forms of entertainment, including musical groups, songs, and a play, were presented.

The next day was our last before returning home, so we went early to Baba's house. As he came down from his rooms and passed in front of me he handed me a large used envelope filled with packets of *vibhuti*. Earlier, he had asked if we would take some back with us to give to Jack Hislop who had been very ill. Naturally, I concluded that the package was for him, but Baba caught my thought and quickly turned back with a shake of his head and a big smile and said, "No, it is for your grandchildren."When I thanked him he jokingly mimicked my voice saying, "Thank you, Baba," and laughing gaily moved to the men's side of the room leaving us all amused at his antics. Later that afternoon he handed my husband a package of *vibhuti* for Jack Hislop.

It appeared that, having first tested me almost beyond endurance by keeping me guessing about giving a speech, he had then lavished love on me enough to fill the inner void. Yes, as he so often reminds us, he is the mother we never had who can and will give every one of us exactly what we need.

I left for home regenerated and with joy in my heart, but also with the awesome responsibility of writing a book about him and the prospect of having to give a talk whenever he would see fit to ask me.

Later that year, on November 3, Lorna gave birth to a beautiful little boy. I had told her about the *vibhuti* Baba had materialized for the baby long before he was born. For some strange reason she did not want to give it to him at birth, preferring to keep it for a future time when he might need it. As Baba had not specified when it should be given to the baby, Lorna's idea appeared to be a good one. I trusted that Baba would make known in some way when he should have it. Perhaps, I could ask him the next time we came. Meanwhile Lorna kept it safe in her wallet until a need for it arose.

CHAPTER NINETEEN

IN JANUARY 1980 we decided to go to the Galapagos Islands. One of our shared interests is the study of archaeology and related subjects. Though they are not of archaeological interest, these islands provide a most interesting link in the evolutionary chain of birds and reptiles. Since reading Darwin's fascinating account of his voyages and subsequent theories, we looked forward to seeing them.

We planned to end the trip in Bogota, Colombia, where we had hoped to go on a previous trip, but had been prevented from doing so by internal political problems at that time.

After an interesting tour of the islands, we arrived in Bogota. We were informed that as an election was due to take place the following day, all activity would cease and offices and shops would be closed to allow people to go to the polls. Our travel agent advised us to take a tour of the city as soon as possible that afternoon.

The tour ended with a visit to a shrine situated at the top of a small mountain. Our guide told us that this shrine contains a figure of Jesus Christ enclosed in a glass case. It is famous for the healings which have taken place for many years among the thousands of pilgrims who hoped to be cured of their various maladies. He added that we would be able to see the many discarded canes and crutches lined up along the walls where those who had received help had left them as testimony to their healings.

Sure enough, as we joined the procession slowly moving around the glass enclosure in which a most unusual and striking looking figure of Jesus reclined, we passed the rows of crutches leaning against a wall, literally covered with hundreds of plaques, each containing an expression of gratitude for a healing.

I felt a very powerful presence presiding over the whole place and decided to light a candle for each member of our family before leaving. As I lit each candle and stuck it into a holder, I silently called on the God-force immanent in all living things which emanates from yet transcends all the great teachers, healers and religious leaders, asking it to bless each one. As I performed this ritual, I remembered hearing Baba say, "There are many paths up the mountain, and all of them lead to God." I felt a strong sense of his presence as I recalled his words and a heightened awareness of the universality of all Truth. This "high" feeling remained with me as we made our way down the mountain in the cable car. From the cable car we had a wonderful view of the surrounding area and I noticed another mountain on the opposite side, on top of which could be seen a statue of the Virgin Mary. I asked our guide if he would drive us up to see it before returning to our hotel. His reaction to my innocent question was unexpectedly violent. He physically drew back at the suggestion and explained that it was so dangerous to go up there that there was not a single driver in the city who would be willing to take us. When I asked the reason he told us it was frequented by bands of ruffians and thieves who stopped all cars and molested and robbed the occupants. We were horrified to hear of such violence on the way to a holy shrine and decided not to tempt fate.

So our guide dropped us off at our hotel and we decided to take a short walk before dinner. We chose to walk along the main street to another hotel which had been pointed out to us on our city tour and was an easily recognizable landmark.

We were both in a relaxed mood with no deadline to meet, so we meandered around the lobby of the other hotel looking into shop windows. When we started to stroll back it was still daylight, but we saw very few pedestrians on the streets. All the signs were in Spanish, so I asked my husband to translate one on a building we were passing. As he did not recognize one of the words, he took out a pocket dictionary to look it up.

At that exact moment I felt a violent yank on my right arm as someone behind me tried to snatch my handbag which I was holding by its two handles. Quickly realizing what was happening, I immediately let go of it and yelled to Sidney, standing at my side. One of the handles must have caught on something, for the next moment I was violently thrown to the ground by my unseen assailant. I landed with a sharp thud on the hard cement pavement with my right arm, still pulled over to one side, underneath me. All the breath was knocked out of me and I could not speak.

A young American who had observed the whole scene as he was walking behind us, rushed up to help and took off after my attackers. My husband, hearing me scream that my bag had been snatched and not realizing that I was hurt, followed after him, and they both raced up a steep side street and were soon out of sight.

I immediately started to call on Baba over and over in a kind of chant, and tried to get up from where I was lying sprawled full length on the pavement. I was instantly aware that my right arm was broken, as I could feel the broken ends of the bone grating against each other. Somehow I managed to move up into a sitting position, and instinctively held my right arm tightly against my chest with my left hand.

A small crowd had quickly gathered around me as I sat on the pavement intoning Baba's name through chattering teeth as my entire body started to shake from the shock. They tried to ask me what had happened, but their meager English was as little help as my lack of Spanish. All I could do was point up the side street in the direction in which Sidney had disappeared, and say one Spanish word I could remember, *esposo* for husband. On looking back, I can laugh at the thought that they probably concluded that it was my husband who had assaulted me and then run off and left me there!

My assailants had a head start and were soon lost to sight amongst the houses and people on the streets, for they, of course, knew their way around. Finally Sidney and the young American gave up the chase and returned to find me sitting on the ground with a broken arm, the center of a crowd of strangers. Just as they reached me, a police car drove by. Catching sight of it, the young American dashed out into the street to stop it. When it haltingly came to a standstill, he explained to the driver in fluent Spanish that I was hurt and needed to be taken to a hospital for treatment. In a matter of seconds two strong policemen eased me up into the car. The young man gave them instructions to take us to a nearby hospital where he taught English to some of the doctors. He offered to accompany us and act as our interpreter.

The very thought of having to go to a hospital in a foreign country filled me with apprehension, so I redoubled my silent appeal to Baba to take over and stage manage the whole situation. If I had feared going to the hospital before I arrived, my fears were increased a hundredfold when I was taken to a huge bare room containing dozens of narrow benchlike wooden cots devoid of any covering, on which lay people in every imaginable condition. There was a screaming child, a woman blue from a heart attack, a man being catheterized to relieve a horribly swollen bladder, another man bleeding profusely from knife cuts and gashes all over his body, and many others, all equally distressed and expressing pain.

The whole room stank with the acrid smell of fear which I recognized from our experience in the hijacked plane. But this time it was intermingled with the stench of unwashed bodies, stale urine, various liniments, alcohol, and other strong smelling medications. I was afraid I was going to vomit and wanted desperately to escape, but realizing I couldn't, I held on to the picture of Baba on my *mangala sutra*, and immediately felt calmer.

It seemed like an eternity before a doctor was free to examine me. When at last he arrived and checked my arm he gave orders to have it X-rayed, but under the most primitive conditions imaginable. With a broken arm and badly wrenched shoulder I was faced with the ordeal of lying flat on a hard table, as there were no facilities for taking X-rays with the patient sitting upright. Even with Baba's help it was all I could do to stand the intense pain when I had to turn over from time to time and assume various positions for pictures to be taken from different angles. I continuously chanted Baba's name under my breath like a litany.

After a seemingly interminable wait the first X-rays were brought in. They showed that my upper arm was cleanly broken several inches below the shoulder. They indicated that my arm may have been pulled out of the socket when the thieves jerked it so violently in their effort to pull the bag free. The doctor explained, with the help of our kind interpreter, that if my arm was dislocated an operation would be necessary. I quailed at the very idea of such an ordeal under such gruesome and unhygienic conditions. However, the doctor ordered one more X-ray to be taken at a slightly different angle before he could make a decision. I was taken back again to the X-ray torture chamber. I continued to call desperately for Baba to help. It was the only way I could keep my faith that he would help in his own way and in his own time.

After another long wait the doctor came back with the new X-rays. He had a rather puzzled expression on his face, for they showed the arm solidly in place in the socket and only a small hairline fracture higher up on the bone above the main break. An operation would not be necessary. I breathed a huge sigh of relief and silently thanked Baba for the release from that dreaded ordeal.

I was next taken to another room where again we waited until an orthopaedic doctor arrived to put a cast on the broken arm. The X-rays had shown that the two pieces of broken bone were correctly aligned. This was a blessing, as it eliminated the need for them to be manually realigned. Apparently, my instinct to hold my arm so tightly against my side had kept the two parts from separating. The doctor produced a long elasticized bandage and bound it closely around the arm and body, so that the arm was held tightly against my chest. He explained to our interpreter that with an upper arm break a solid cast was not recommended as it would inhibit breathing to a dangerous degree. I soon discovered that even with the soft cast I could not breathe deeply, and had to be content to take short gasps of air to avoid the excruciating pain caused by any movement. Eventually we were free to return to the hotel which we had left so many hours earlier. However, because of the election, we were obliged to wait another hour before a taxi came to drive us there.

It was soon apparent that I could not lie down to sleep, but would have to sit in a chair propped up with pillows all night and hope in that way to get a little rest. All I really wanted was to go home as quickly as possible.

The next morning my husband tried to call the airline office to ask if there was an earlier flight we could take to avoid having to stay in Bogota for three more days, as originally planned. However, the operator told him that no one could travel out of the country during the election, and furthermore, all offices were closed for the same reason. The earliest flight was the one on which we were already booked. I dreaded the thought of having to remain in that city any longer, but when we finally left on the appointed day, and the plane put down in Mexico City for refueling, I was most grateful to have had to stay the extra time as it had allowed the bone to begin to set before it was jarred so badly as the plane landed both in Mexico City and again in Los Angeles, causing severe pain.

As soon as we arrived home we made an appointment to see an orthopedic doctor who had treated us before. We described the whole experience to him and, when he looked at the soft cast on my arm, he asked with obvious disbelief where it had been applied. He explained that it was a very new method of treating an upper arm fracture and had been invented by a doctor in the States. As far as he knew it was as yet unknown anywhere else. One explanation might be that an orthopedic doctor had been to Bogota on a teaching assignment after this method had been invented, and had demonstrated the application to the doctor who treated me. He repeatedly stressed how lucky I was to have found a doctor who knew how to apply it so expertly that he himself did not need to do anything further. He was also impressed that the two parts of the bone were so perfectly aligned, even after the two bumpy landings.

Again, as with the hijacking, I don't pretend to understand why this accident happened. But one thing of which I am absolutely certain is that Baba in India, as well as his counterpart within me, helped in every way possible just as soon as it happened. I also noticed that when I called on him, I seemed to be lifted to a level of consciousness where I still felt the pain yet was conscious of it as an onlooker rather than as the sufferer.

A few days after our return Sidney left for the office one morning but returned after only a few minutes, very upset. As he had driven away from the house he noticed that the ring Baba had materialized for him at our Vedic wedding ceremony was not in its usual place on his finger. He searched for it in vain, and later that day when he again returned home he literally ransacked the house, the luggage and his car, all without success. The ring was nowhere to be found.

I recalled an incident from a time when we were with Baba. A Norwegian devotee, who lived and worked in India, arrived hurriedly at Baba's house one day, visibly agitated. As soon as he saw Baba he confessed that he had lost the ring Baba had materialized for him. Baba appeared to be unusually disturbed by this news and, as he passed me on his way up to his rooms, he turned and said in an annoyed tone of voice, "Mistake. Mistake. He doubted Swami." As with all such remarks, I now realized that by directly addressing me as he passed Baba had intended me to take note of it for some future use or understanding. When Sidney lost his ring, the memory of Baba's remark came rushing back and so distressed me that I could not get it out of my mind. I kept wondering if the loss of Sidney's ring was due to a mistake. To put my mind at rest, I finally decided to cable Baba and, at the same time, ask him to help my broken arm. I sent the cable with a pre-paid return message, though I did not really expect a reply. I was certain that he already knew what had happened. Sending the cable helped me to let go of the nagging worry and surrender the whole problem to Baba.

To my surprise I received a reply cable from him. It read, "Don't worry about ring. Be happy. I will help you. Baba." I was vastly relieved. Baba must have known that at that particular time I really needed his reassurance. At other times he had withheld it, expecting me to deal with problems myself, without direct word from him. As long as the loss of the ring was not a mistake, I could stop worrying, and relax knowing that Baba was in charge.

Neither the pain nor the disability was removed, but I was given patience and strength to bear them. As he has so often promised, when we voluntarily come under his guidance he accelerates our negative *karmas* to the degree that we are able to endure such a cleansing, but he also helps to soften it as much as possible.

CHAPTER TWENTY

EARLY IN JUNE 1980 Lorna and Ed and their two children, Crystal Ann aged 3^1/$_2$ and Brian aged eight months, started out on a driving holiday to the Grand Canyon and other well known sights. They planned to return home via Oakland to spend a few days with our elder daughter Sheila.

Both Ed's mother, Shirley, and I had an uneasy feeling about the proposed trip. When she and I checked with one another later, we discovered that each of us had tried to dissuade them from leaving at that particular time. That in itself was most unusual, as we rarely give our children advice about anything unless they directly seek it.

Sidney retired from the practice of law on June first, and as my arm was almost mended by then, we decided to drive up into the mountains for a few days of rest and fresh air. As Lorna and her family had already left on their holiday, they did not know that we too would be away for part of the same time.

We planned to drive up to Mammoth Lakes and then on to Yosemite National Park where we had enjoyed many holidays with our two daughters during their childhood. Following our usual custom, we telephoned Sheila to tell her where we were going, though we had no definite reservations and could not give her a telephone number or address in case she needed to reach us.

The day after we arrived in Yosemite we went for a very long walk in the area of the Happy Isles. We were happily swinging along enjoying the beautiful scenery and fresh air when suddenly, and for no apparent reason, I felt completely drained of energy, so much so that I found it difficult to move one foot in front of the other. At the same time I felt overwhelmingly distressed and sad. Neither of us could imagine what had happened to create such a drastic change in so short a time. After I had rested for a while we slowly retraced our steps back towards the hotel, stopping every few yards for me to rest.

At one of these stops my husband happened to look over to the side of the narrow path along which we were walking and pointed out to me two of the tiniest baby animals I had ever seen. They were playing together in such a delightful way that we stopped to watch them. We assumed they must be baby chip-munks. They were all alone, yet were so fearless that they allowed me to touch them. Each one was no bigger than the end of one of my fingers. I very gently stroked their soft silky backs. As I did so I was literally flooded with a strangely profound feeling of love and compassion tinged with sadness for these tiny creatures who appeared to have become separated from their mother. The feeling was out of all proportion to the situation and I could not under-stand what was causing it. Stroking them seemed to restore some of my energy, and soon I was able to continue walking again. As we neared the gates leading out of the area, we encountered several people excitedly talking about some bears they had just seen. Sure enough, as we continued we saw two very young bear cubs cavort-ing playfully together. Again, I felt that same exaggerated concern and sadness that they were all alone, their mother nowhere to be seen. We sat on the side of the path to watch them play together, and again I seemed to derive energy from the scene. I was able to walk the rest of the way back to our cabin. We got back late in the afternoon, just in time to shower and dress for dinner.

I continued to feel very strange, almost dissociated, and decided to go to bed early that night hoping to sleep off whatever was disturbing me. I slept very fitfully and had just barely sunk into an exhausted sleep when the loud jarring ring of the telephone jolted us awake around two in the morning. As we both tried to grab the telephone, we heard the agonized voice of our elder daughter sounding tremendously relieved to have located us. She had been frantically trying to reach us for several hours with tele-phone calls to the various information centers around the valley.

Her shattering news was that Lorna and her family had been in a car accident the previous afternoon. Lorna had been driving out of Idaho Falls on their way down to stay with Sheila when the accident took place. They were all in a hospital up there. She told us they had all been injured, but that Lorna was so seriously hurt that she was not expected to live. My immediate response was "No! Baba will help her." Sheila told us that Ed had tried to tele-phone us as soon as he could, and when we did not answer he concluded we were out and continued to telephone at intervals. When he still received no answer, he managed to contact Sheila, and she immediately tried to locate us. I asked her if she knew the time of the accident, and when she told us it had happened in the late afternoon of the previous day, I immediately understood the reason for my strange weakness and depression.

Still only barely awake, we dressed as quickly as possible, threw our clothes into our luggage, loaded it into the car, and drove off as fast as possible for Sheila's house. While she was trying so desperately to reach us by telephone, she also checked all the possible flights from Oakland or San Francisco to Idaho Falls, and had already made reservations on the the first available flight. We drove out of the Yosemite Valley so blindly that we were stopped for speeding. I kept calling on Baba the whole way, and after what seemed like days rather than hours we finally pulled into Sheila's driveway. Meanwhile, she had done a truly fantastic job of organizing everything. She had telephoned the hospital and assured Ed that we were all on our way, and had also spoken to the doctor in charge who was not at all optimistic about Lorna's condition. The most serious injuries were to her head, and extreme brain damage was feared. My heart sank when I heard that, for Lorna had been trained to work with brain damaged children, and would therefore be more than ordinarily aware of the attendant problems. I continued to call inwardly to Baba to help as I was absolutely certain he could save her. I was also fully aware that he would do so only if he knew it was right, and would not interfere with her past *karmas*. Sheila told us that little Brian had a broken leg, and that both Ed and Crystal Ann were also injured, though not as seriously as Lorna.

I decided to cable Baba as I had done after the mugging, even though I was certain he already knew and had heard my call for help, as he had when we were hijacked. Again, it was great relief to have something specific to do.

The flight to Idaho Falls and our arrival at the hospital were like a nightmare, except that from this one there was no awakening to the realization that it was only a dream. We were hurriedly admitted even though it was long after visiting hours, which had worried me during the flight, as such seemingly trivial things are apt to do at such times. The four patients were all in different wings of the hospital, with Lorna isolated in the intensive care section. Where should I go first? I stood undecided in the middle of a corridor, asking within to be shown who needed me most, Lorna, Ed or one of the children? Now that we were actually there with them, and the long wait and feelings of restless frustration and helplessness were over, I was able to let go. From that moment on I literally felt Baba take over, and I became like a puppet or a sleepwalker gratefully moving under his guidance.

Suddenly I knew that I must run to Lorna first as she had sustained far more serious injuries than the others. Nevertheless, I was quite unprepared for the sight of our beloved daughter: a great angry looking gash over one temple, obviously in a deep coma and hooked up to various life sustaining systems ranged all around her bed. The sight almost broke my heart and I cried out Baba's name in pain. Again I felt him take over. I quickly kissed her wounded face, whispered in her ear that I was there with her, squeezed her hand, and promised to be back as soon as I had seen her children. A big tear slowly made its way down her cheek, giving me hope that she had heard me.

Next, I went to Brian, only eight months old and sure to be missing his mother acutely. Sheila joined me and we both entered the room where he was lying in a cot with weights attached to a traction apparatus. Unbelievably, he greeted us with his sunny smile. I would have given anything in the world to pick him up and hold him tight. I have never know such utter frustration as I felt when faced with that contraption which allowed no further contact than could be made by leaning over the side of his crib and barely managing to pat him. But he smiled and cooed in recognition, and help up his arms for me to pick him up, at which I had a difficult time not to break down and cry. He quickly earned the reputation and nickname of Angel Baby. I never once doubted that Baba was looking after him, and it was Brian who kept us all sane and hopeful with his smile and good nature.

Crystal Ann, on the other hand, had completely withdrawn, and had refused to eat, drink or speak until we arrived. As soon as she saw us she was able to break through the awful shock and let the tears flow. We were told that she had sustained a skull fracture, fortunately not nearly as severe as her mother's though enough to make her disorientated. Unlike the frustrating situation with Brian, I was able to take this terrified child in my arms and try to comfort her. She gradually responded and after a while was willing to take some nourishment. Then she began to talk in gasping sentences, accompanied by heaving sobs, asking why she couldn't see her Mommy, and telling me that she knew she was hurt and bleeding when she fell out of the car.

Then there was our dear son-in-law to visit, way off in the men's ward. He had the harrowing responsibility for his injured family in addition to his own injuries: several broken ribs and a punctured lung. What could we say to him to ease the dreadful fear and hurt so plainly visible in his grief stricken eyes? Only Baba with his infinite wisdom could know what was needed.

Sidney, Sheila and her fiancé Martin were a tremendous comfort and support tirelessly going from room to room to help in whatever way possible. Sheila also joined me in praying, singing, and chanting for Lorna's recovery. Thus began an endless stream of hours with little to differentiate between day and night, as we watched for any positive signs of a change in each of the patients. After our arrival Lorna rallied and was able to breathe without artificial aid and, though still in a coma, she seemed to hear us and tears would trickle from her eyes from time to time. At one point she took my hand in hers and placed it over her heart. Our hopes were raised. Baba must have heard the call for help, and was responding. I alternated between talking to her and singing *bhajans* all day and all night, encouraging, reassuring, and begging her to call on Baba to help her.

As soon as Ed was stronger, he and I shared a day and night vigil by Lorna's bed, singing, assuring her how much we all loved and needed her, and encouraging her to join us in our prayers for her healing. She seemed to hear and mutely responded. Ed's parents arrived with one of his aunts and a cousin, and later a very close friend of ours also joined us, adding her prayers. So from then on the children had their added love, comfort and reassurance to help them during this critical time.

One day I was faced with a very difficult decision. Crystal continued to beg to be allowed to see her mother until I began to wonder if perhaps I should consider taking her to her room. Maybe, if I took her just to the door and allowed her to peek in, it might satisfy her deep need and relieve her mind. I finally decided to take the chance. I carried her in my arms, holding her very tight and telling her that her Mommy was asleep, so she must be very quiet and not wake her as she needed to sleep to help her get well quickly. I stood inside the open door so that she could just see her mother lying on the bed. In a whisper, I gently explained that all the tubes were feeding her Mommy because she couldn't eat by herself since she was hurt. Crystal very carefully studied the scene from the door and mutely nodded her head as I described the various instruments to try to help her to understand instead of becoming frightened by them. After a few good minutes I asked her if she would like to blow her Mommy a goodnight kiss. She nodded her head eagerly as she did so, waved her hand and leaned forward in my arms to whisper, "I love you, Mommy. Please get better soon." She then willingly allowed me to carry her back to her room and was soon fast asleep. I knew I had taken a big chance and was greatly relieved when it appeared to have been successful. She now knew where her mother was, which seemed to create a very important bridge in her mind between the scene at the site of the accident and the present one at the hospital. From then on she was free to talk about her mother, and when she played with a toy telephone she pretended to call some of her friends to tell them that her Mommy was hurt and was sleeping.

As soon as Ed felt strong enough, he went to retrieve whatever could be salvaged from the wrecked car which had been moved to a used car yard in the town. It must have been a harrowing job to search for all those little things which had been left behind when the accident occurred, but he insisted on doing it himself. On his return he handed me a package of *vibhuti*. I immediately recognized it as the one Baba had materialized for Brian before he was born, when he had informed us that Lorna wanted a son. Lorna had kept it in her wallet and Ed had just found it when he rescued her handbag from the car. She had kept it for a time when Brian would most need it, which was right now. With tears of gratitude in my eyes I took it to the room where Brian was lying in the cot with his little legs held up in traction over his head. As he heard me enter he turned his head to see who was coming to see him, and greeted me with gurgles of delight, and his wonderful smile. I held up the packet, saying, "See what Baba has sent for you!" His face lit up as he tried to mouth Baba. Then he grabbed the packet out of my hand through the bars of the crib. He moved so fast that it startled me, and scattered the ash. I was afraid it was lost, but I managed to save most of it and quickly emptied it into his open mouth. He tried to help by rubbing it all over his face cooing delightedly at what he obviously thought was a lovely new game. It was not exactly the way I had envisioned giving it to him. I had only barely managed to deliver Baba's gift, and must trust him to do whatever was needed.

The prospects of Lorna's recovery were apparently improving, so Sidney decided to fly down to Sheila's house where we had left our car, and drive it from there to Los Angeles. It now began to look as if we might need to stay in Idaho Falls for quite some time to be near Lorna during the recovery period. Consequently, we would need more clothes than the few we had taken with us for the short holiday, so he planned to fly back with them as soon as possible.

Martin also had to return to work, so Sheila and I supported each other. We almost continuously prayed and meditated together and begged Baba to heal Lorna and pour his love and strength into us to enable us to fill the needs of each of the patients throughout each day and night.

One morning as we were seeking help in this way we were shown a vivid inner picture. It appeared that Lorna was with us on this inner level. We both jumped to the conclusion that she would join us in our work. We were surprised as she had always been a bit reluctant to accept it. We interpreted it to mean that with Baba's help she would recover, so certain were we that Baba would perform one of his miracles of healing and mend her broken body. At the time we desperately needed to believe it, for without that hope we could not have moved through the next few days attending to all that needed to be done.

Then quite suddenly there was an abrupt change in Lorna's condition, almost as if she had been making a supreme effort to rally but found the odds too heavily stacked against her, and chose to let go of her earthly shell.

Was it because she was so acutely aware of the dreadful effects of brain damage through her work with retarded children? Did she foresee for herself a life of uselessness and the awful prospect of being a burden to her family? I could almost sense when she made the decision to release from her damaged body, which was later confirmed when the instruments recorded brain death. We also learned that at about the same time the medication had been reduced as a precautionary measure, since it would have been dangerous to keep her on such a high dose for too long a time. We quickly put in a long-distance telephone call to Sidney. He flew back at once, and fortunately arrived just in time to say goodbye.

After the instruments had registered no activity in the brain for two days, we were asked to give our permission for her to be detached from the life-support system. That was the hardest decision we have ever had to make and would have been impossible had I not sensed that she was ready to go and that her wish must be respected.

Both families gathered in her room to send her on her way into the next phase of life surrounded by our love. We each spoke our farewells and gave her our blessing, while we watched the indicators on the various machines drop to zero after they were disconnected.

To the very end I had been so certain that Baba would save her. "Why did it end this way?" my mind questioned, while deep down in my heart I knew that despite all our hopes and prayers, it must be right. But it made no sense at the time.

Crystal Ann was sufficiently recovered to be released from the hospital, but Ed was still under observation and treatment for the lesion of his lung. Brian could not be moved until his leg was stable and a cast could be applied. So it was decided that Sidney and I and Ed's parents would all return home, and that Sidney would fly back up again as soon as Brian could be safely released when he would bring them all home. Meanwhile, Lorna's body would be kept on ice in the mortuary until Ed and the children could be moved, when it would be flown down with them on the same plane, and moved to the mortuary near where they lived. Martin had already left, and Sheila would also fly back home.

Before we left Ed brought up the subject of a funeral service and asked if we knew of a minister to officiate as neither he nor his family attended a church. Until then I had given absolutely no thought to a service. My first quick reaction was that we had all just participated in the only truly significant service at her bedside. My mind balked at the thought of any other. But I told Ed I would meditate on it and let him know what insights I received. Little did I anticipate the result of my request for guidance.

I was awakened the following morning from a deep sleep hearing Baba's voice clearly telling me that the only person who could conduct a service for a congregation consisting of people of so many different beliefs and religious affiliations was me. I was horrified and unwilling to consider such an idea. Then I began to think of all the friends and relatives of the two families who would attend, and realized what a mixture of beliefs and non-beliefs they represented. There would be Sidney and his family and many friends who are Jewish, Ed and his family whose background is

Protestant, some Catholics, new-born Christians, many Sai Baba devotees, devotees of Yogananda, meditators following many different paths, agnostics and atheists. Who could we find to address such a mixed gathering on Lorna's behalf? I was finally forced against my will to admit that Baba was right, and that I was the obvious person to take the responsibility for the service. But, could I manage it? Only with Baba's help would I even be willing to consider attempting it and then only with great trepidation. The more I thought about it the more I knew I must acquiesce. I told Sheila what had come to me, and she immediately reminded me that we could ask for instructions in a meditation. That helped me to resolve it, and I told Ed my decision. He asked if I really thought I could do it and, though I assured him that I would try, I was not at all sure I could actually do so.

Before we returned home Sidney insisted on taking me to see the car in which they were all driving at the time of the accident. At first I strenuously resisted. However, I am glad I reconsidered, for when I saw it I was absolutely amazed that any of them had escaped instant death. The whole driver's side was completely buckled, and the door wrenched open. No wonder poor Lorna was the most seriously injured. As she was driving at the time, she must have received the full impact of the crash. It was a veritable miracle that any of them survived it.

We were very worried that Ed might have been carrying an added burden of guilt, perhaps thinking that if he had been driving he might have been able to avoid the crash, being physically so much stronger. But he assured us that no one could have avoided such a freak accident. He explained that both he and Lorna had noticed the other car approaching from the opposite direction, traveling along the soft shoulder of the two-lane highway. They both thought it was strange and wondered if the driver was aware of it. Then, without any warning, just as the two cars were about to pass each other, the driver of the other car suddenly realized her mistake, and tried to correct it. But in order to lift her car back onto the road she had to drive it up over a rise of about six inches. As she tried to do so, her car hurtled up and straight into the side of Lorna's car, which was abreast of her's at the time. As Ed observed, no one could possibly have foreseen such a move, nor would anyone have been quick or strong enough to move the car out of the way in time.

I was strangely relieved to hear this account. It appeared more and more that it really had been her time to leave this world, even though it looked so wrong, not only for her to have to suffer so much, but to leave her family and the husband and children she loved so dearly, and who needed her love and care. At that time it was all far too incomprehensible to any of us, yet I still had the underlying sense that it was somehow inevitable and, in an odd way, right.

As soon as Ed called to report that Brian's leg was ready to have a cast applied, Sidney flew back to Idaho Falls on his sad mission to bring back the three remaining members of the little family who had set out so gaily on their holiday together. It was a sad and very different homecoming with Lorna's body traveling on the same plane.

The funeral service was arranged to take place as soon as possible after their return. Sheila and I asked in a reverie for Baba's inspiration and guidance in planning the service. To our immense gratitude the whole format flowed through as if he were dictating it, including two poems. Now I would have to trust him to help me conduct it without my emotions intruding too much.

At first it was decided not to have the children present, but Crystal Ann begged to be allowed to attend. So again, we all decided to take a chance and include them with all the members of the two families and the many friends who would gather to express their love for Lorna.

Brian of course, still had the heavy and awkward cast on his leg, so he had to be carried or held throughout the service, but there were many volunteers for that job. His sunny smile and Crystal's winsome and sad little face were a most important part of the service, as they helped us all to concentrate on these living symbols of Lorna's love instead of mourning her seemingly premature death.

With Baba's palpable presence and help, Sheila and I chanted the two poems which had been given in a reverie. Several friends, each representing a different belief system, spoke a few words about Lorna, each one stressing the love she had always so generously expressed. Sheila paid loving tribute to her sister in a most moving way despite her own suffering. Another friend sang an inspirational song as a finale to a most unorthodox service, but one which did indeed address all those present, coming as they did from such very different backgrounds and beliefs. Only Baba, who advocates the unity of people of all faiths, could have inspired such a service, and only Baba could have first initiated and then helped me to conduct it.

After the service many of the devotees who had attended accompanied us back to our house where we all sang *bhajans* together. I have never heard them sung with so much love nor could I have imagined a more fitting and truly beautiful finale to such an emotionally charged day. By singing praises to God we were able to express some of our pent up emotions and obtain some measure of peace. The room was filled with love and devotion.

Shortly afterwards, a lovely little poem came flowing through one day during meditation. I called it "The Gifts Lorna Left Us." Here it is:

We've lost our daughter as we knew her,
Though we know she's very much alive.
We miss her sorely, for we loved her
As we daily watched her grow and thrive.

She's given us gifts so very special
To fill the void her death has left.
And these are what we must remember
At times when we feel most bereft.

Her thoughtfulness will still be with us,
Reminder of her loving heart,
Her love of fun and family gatherings
In which she took an active part.

But most of all we want to thank her
For giving us a son in Ed,
For Crystal Ann and little Brian
Who beckon us to look ahead,

And help to nurture them, her treasures,
And give them all the love they need.
We thank you Lorna for these dear ones,
They're precious gifts we're all agreed.

We'll always love you dearest Lorna
And we all look forward to the day
When it is time for us to join you
And you'll be there to lead the way.

Not long after Lorna's death, Sheila came home for the weekend and, following our custom, she and I decided to work. As I sank into a relaxed state conducive to receiving impressions and instruction, with no warning whatsoever, Lorna burst in to my inner scene with such intensity that I felt she had physically entered the room with us. She appeared to be breathless and very excited, exactly as she often used to be. As she greeted me she called me by a pet name which I had not heard since the girls were very young, when they used to enjoy thinking of odd names to replace the usual Mom or Mommy. She was obviously in a hurry and indicated that she could not stay long this first time, only long enough to bring me a message. To say that I was unprepared for her message would be a complete understatement. She went on to say, "I had to come to tell you that God is the great big beating heart of the universe, and it's all love." No sooner had she delivered that deeply moving message that she hurriedly told us both that she loved us, said goodbye and withdrew to whatever sphere she now inhabits.

I need hardly mention that both Sheila and I were deeply affected by this unexpected happening—another of Baba's gifts, which reassured us that Lorna continued to live though hidden from our sight.

Much later, after the first horrible shock had worn off, I recalled something very strange. It appeared that a wise inner part of Lorna had led her to prepare ahead in such a way that she crowded an entire lifetime into those last five years of her life, almost as if she had known that her time was running out. I remember teasing her and urging her to slow down, assuring her that she had her whole life ahead of her in which to accomplish all she wanted for her family. But she was fiercely adamant, almost to the point of rebellion, and insisted on going ahead with all her plans. At some deep level of her being she must have known that she had only a short time to live and must make the most of it. I am now so thankful that she lived those years to the full and had extracted all she could from the experience of being a wife and mother.

A short time before the fateful holiday she did another strangely significant thing. For several years before she married she had owned two Siamese cats which she adored, and who also adored her and were her devoted companions. When she married and had children, their noses were so put out of joint that they withdrew and would have nothing to do with the children. It was also suspected that Brian might be allergic to them, so she knew she must find another home for them. She threw herself into the unwelcome task and spared no effort in searching for the right one. Even after they were safely and happily settled, she often called their new owners to be sure they were happy and not missing her too much.

She was so happy to be able to breast-feed Brian for the first few months, until it appeared that he might be allergic to her milk. She successfully helped him through the difficult period of trying to find a suitable formula. It was completed just before they all left on their last holiday, so Brian was spared the ordeal of having to make this adjustment suddenly and without the loving care of his mother. All these preparations made Ed's job a little easier when he was faced with the monumental task of trying to take care of the children "in the way she would have done," as he expressed it.

I wonder if perhaps she had finished whatever it was she needed to learn in this particular life, and that to remain here any longer was not necessary for her ultimate growth. Was that perhaps the reason she had unconsciously prepared ahead for her departure? I am now inclined to believe in such a possibility. However, at the time I was too numb from shock to do more than hope that Baba would have some comment on our next trip in November.

CHAPTER TWENTY-ONE

DURING THE WEEKS following Lorna's funeral we made every effort to see Ed and the children as often as possible. Ed needed time to recuperate from his injuries. He also felt very strongly that the children would feel more secure if he undertook their entire care for a while, since he was so familiar with their daily routine. He wanted above all else to try to rear them in the way he knew Lorna would have wished.

He often mentioned that while they were away on the holiday which ended so tragically, he and Lorna repeatedly commented on the fact that the four of them had been bonded together as a family unit even more closely than before. The photographs taken during the trip and salvaged from the wreck certainly confirmed this, and we are all grateful to have such glowing reminders of them as a happy family. Lorna had even managed to catch a quick flash of eight-month-old Brian, lying gurgling in his car crib, a contented smile on his face while they were driving.

At first Crystal was very pale and quiet and silently clung to us when we were together. Then I began to notice that she contrived to pull me into her room on some pretext. It became quite apparent that she had a specific reason, yet at first, as soon as we were there, she would grab my hand and drag me back out again. The same thing happened when they came to our house, until one day she pulled me into our bedroom and stood in front of me, her feet apart and firmly planted on the floor. For a split second I wondered what was going to happen. Suddenly she burst forth with, "Grandmother, it is all right to cry, isn't it?" Taken aback, I assured her that it was, indeed, all right, in fact, a very good thing to do. With that, she started to recount all the traumatic stages of the accident, describing them down to the minutest detail. This account was accompanied by dry racking sobs.

Such an unexpected outburst was at first so unnerving that I sent a silent appeal to Baba to give me the necessary wisdom and strength to help this poor little girl who so desperately needed to release the fear and sorrow bottled up inside her. She haltingly ended her account by almost defiantly declaring, "And I'll never, never see my Mommy ever again. She's in heaven with God and I don't have a Mommy any more."

Again, I mentally implored Baba to help me to know what to say. Immediately I felt a wave of cool, calm assurance surge up within me to replace the shocked horror I had been feeling all through the heartbreaking account of her loss and sorrow. Almost without my conscious participation words started to form in my mind and I heard myself telling her about all the people who loved her. First I mentioned Baba, then went on to her Daddy, both sets of grandparents, aunts and uncles, cousins, and friends. As I mentioned each one by name, she nodded her head in agreement and said through her sobs, "Yes, I know." I continued by telling her that many little girls and boys who still had their Mommy alive and with them were not as lucky as she was to have so many other people who loved her. Then I threw out my arms as far as possible to show her how much I loved her. She literally hurled herself into my arms sobbing uncontrollably. Her little body hit mine with such force that she knocked me backwards. We both landed in a heap on the floor, which struck her as being so funny that she wanted to repeat it. We did so, over and over again, until she was almost back to her normal self, giggling delightedly at how much she was loved—so much so that it knocked her over, as she herself expressed it, as soon as she got her breath and could talk about it.

From then on, each time we were together, either at her house or ours, she watched for an opportunity to get me away from the others so that we could repeat the whole scene over again, each time with a little less emotion and pain. Eventually she was able to tell the story almost matter-of-factly, without the terrible gasping sobs, but always ending on the floor helpless with giggles.

As the weeks passed I kept wondering how I should break the news of Lorna's death to my mother, who would be celebrating her 99th birthday in August. I even wondered if I should tell her at all, lest the shock hasten her demise. But she was always so happy to receive Lorna's chatty warm letters that she would certainly wonder why she did not receive them as usual. Finally, we decided that Sidney and I should fly to England to tell her in person instead of in a letter, hoping in that way to soften the news.

I told Crystal what we were going to do, as we did not want her to feel that we were deserting her. About a week before we were due to leave, we went through the usual ritual of "telling the story" with scarcely any emotion on her part this time. Then she announced, "It is okay for you to go to see Great Grandmother. I shall be all right now." I marvelled at the wisdom of this 3-year-old child who had initiated such a complete catharsis that she could allow us to leave with complete acceptance. I sincerely hope she will never have to be treated for repercussions later in life, resulting from that traumatic experience.

I would never have dared to initiate such a process in a child of her tender years. I am convinced that Baba must have brought it about in his inimitable way, and then not only spoke through me but gave me the necessary strength and assurance to help her through it to the final release which she so desperately needed.

As Brian was only eight months old at the time of the accident he was at the pre-verbal level. The hard cast on his leg made it difficult to pick him up and hug him, which I sensed he needed acutely. However, as soon as it was removed he initiated his own special way of replacing the love he so sorely missed from his adoring Mommy. Each time we saw them, as soon as he caught sight of me he would break into his beaming smile, hold up his little arms for me to pick him up, promptly wrap his arms and legs around me and cling like a little limpet. Sometimes he would stay in that position for as long as twenty minutes, heaving deep sighs every few minutes as if drinking in the mother love for which he hungered, and which he instinctively seemed to know he could get from me, his mother's mother. Sometimes while I held him in that tight, secure embrace, I would say under my breath "Lorna darling, I'll try my best to give your children the love you would have lavished upon them." On several occasions Brian lifted up his head from where it lay against my chest, and with a smile of delight, pointed over to a corner of the room, as if he had not only heard my thought but could see his mother.

We accompanied Ed when he took Brian to an orthopaedic specialist to check his leg. The doctor approved of the way the bone was knitting and told us that it was still too soon to determine what the outcome would be. In the case of a child of his age, it was impossible to predict whether the broken leg would eventually be shorter than the other one; stimulated to grow longer; or if they would both be the same length. Only in the latter case would he have no limp. As he explained these possibilities I felt a dart of fear flit across my mind, which I quickly asked Baba to erase. Then I left it all in his hands, though I still hoped Brian would not limp. I was to recall this fleeting moment when we saw Baba in India in November.

CHAPTER TWENTY-TWO

I HAD BEEN sorely tempted to fly straight over to see Baba after Lorna died but had resisted doing so for several reasons. The chief one was a reluctance to be away from the children, whom we felt needed our presence to reassure them that we, who were also dear to them, would be close and available when they most needed us. We would soon be leaving for the Third World Conference in November, in any case.

I was relieved when our departure date was set. I realized how very much I needed to be re-energized after, first, the mugging early in March, and then the tragic accident at the end of June.

Our son-in-law was doing a heroic job with the children, trying in every way possible to be both father and mother to them. He had recovered sufficiently from his injuries to return to work, having arranged with his mother to look after them during the day until he got home, when he again took over their care. He felt safer leaving them in the care of a member of the family. He had heard of so many cases of child abuse that he did not want to trust his precious children to a stranger. We too knew they were in good hands and felt free to leave with our minds at rest.

But shortly before we were due to leave a new shock appeared out of the blue. Our daughter Sheila was diagnosed as possibly having a serious lung problem. When she called to tell us my head reeled and my heart seemed almost to stop. Were both our daughters to be taken from us? We all discussed what should be done and decided that when we were with Baba we would try to ask him if he wished Sheila to fly over to see him after the Conference. If so, I could remain behind after Sidney returned and wait for her to join me there. We knew only too well that during the Conference Baba would be more than usually busy with a multitude of demands on his time. It had been very crowded at the last Conference in 1975, and would be even more so five years later, with so many more people having heard of him and his teachings.

In some ways I was torn between a pull to be with Sheila at this worrying time and the children who were barely adjusted to their loss, and my own need to see Baba. As if to answer my unspoken question, dear little Crystal announced one day, "It's okay for you to go away again, but only if you go to see Baba." I gratefully thanked Baba for confirmation from such an unexpected source.

On our arrival at Puttaparthi a few days before the Conference was due to start, we learned that we were to be housed in a new building. It was referred to as the round block due to its shape, built around a central court. The members of the Council and visiting directors all occupied rooms in the same building. We did not have to share our room with other devotees this time which, in the circumstances, was a relief as it would have added extra pressure.

Usually it is a pleasure to see so many familiar people. But this time it was somewhat of a strain. Many of them had either already heard about Lorna's death or had just been told and hurried over to offer their condolences. It was as if the scarcely healed wounds were being opened up again. To my consternation, during the *bhajan* singing on the first night, without any warning the flood gates burst wide open inside me, and the unshed tears started to flow. I tried desperately to stop them, but however hard I tried to control them, the flow would not stop and continued to the very end of the singing, when they suddenly stopped, leaving me with a feeling of relief. It suddenly became very clear to me that during the five days while Lorna's life seemed to hang on a thread I had been moved beyond my usual state to a different level of consciousness. I acted more like an automaton, doing and saying whatever was needed, but not of my own volition. During the months since then I had continued to feel as if I were living a different dimension from the one I had previously known. My whole body seemed to pulsate, and I had the odd but exhilarating sensation of being lived through and moved around like a puppet. When I became consciously aware of it, I fervently hoped I would continue forever to feel as disembodied and almost floating. But it slowly wore off and eventually I came down to earth again.

I also began to realize that in some strange fashion, Baba had lifted me beyond the ordinary human emotions, enabling me to accomplish all that needed to be done like a sleepwalker, only partially aware of what was happening. Hence, during all that time I had not been able to cry. It was not that I did not allow myself to do so, but rather that I had no need at a time when far too much else demanded my attention. As soon as I felt safe and secure in Baba's presence, I was free to let the pent up tears flow. A similar sudden flood occurred on one other occasion towards the end of our stay, also during *bhajans*, when we were all assembled in the auditorium and Baba was walking back and forth on the platform. Just as precipitously as before the tears started to flow in a steady stream while I sat on the floor in the middle of that huge crowd. I was intensely embarrassed, but again, there was absolutely nothing I could do to stop the flow, and it ceased as soon as the singing came to an end. Baba glanced down from time to time and, as our eyes met, I felt a surge of energy pour into me, which only increased the flow so I concluded that he was deliberately helping me to release the blocked emotion.

But I am getting ahead of the sequence of events. The day after we arrived, Baba stopped in front of me as I sat outside in the *darshan* lines. Bending down towards me he asked, "Why are you worrying?" and before I could tell him he supplied his own answer, saying gently in my ear, "Yes, I know. It is your daughter." I quickly explained, "Not my younger daughter, Baba, but the older one. She is now sick." He smiled sweetly, nodded his head and in a crooning voice whispered, "Yes, I will see you." With that reassurance he passed on his way down the long *darshan* lines. I really had not for a minute doubted that he already knew all about it, yet, to hear his words and receive his loving smile and promise of help enabled me to go through the conference with hope. I felt like a tired child who had come home and laid my burden in his capable hands. I could now relax and let him take over.

Later, when I had time to think about it, I felt awed that with all he had on his mind in the middle of this huge function he would take the time and interest to assuage the grief of one person in that vast crowd. I mentally multiplied the number to include the innumerable others to whom he reaches out daily, in the midst of all his other activities. Once more I was impressed by the magnitude of his activity, a physical impossibility for even the most evolved human being. This was further proof to me that he is indeed superhuman.

Like the previous conference in 1975, this too was an extraordinary experience. There were such huge crowds, yet everything flowed smoothly, as if on oiled wheels, with Baba at the hub arranging, coordinating, guiding and directing the many faceted scene. Added to the many meetings arranged for the various groups to discuss their work, there were colorful marches, daily displays of dancing and singing, and each evening Baba gave a discourse followed by performances by well known Indian artistes and musicians. The platform was freshly decorated each day by the boys from Baba's college at Whitefield. They painstakingly fashioned beautiful masterpieces of multicolored flower petals mounted on wooden scaffoldings. We were all impressed by the exquisite results of their labor of love.

The Conference culminated in the celebration of Baba's birthday. He donned his customary white robe, and consented to swing in the *jhoola* set up on the stage and gently pushed back and forth by some of the college boys. In this way the vast throng received his *darshan* on the auspicious occasion of his birthday. Also in honor of the day the women attached to the Western delegations were sent gold-trimmed silk *saris*, all the same design but each of a different color. With his usual thoughtfulness he gave gifts to his devotees instead of accepting gifts from them on his birthday.

Finally Baba summoned us to an interview. As usual when one is actually in his presence nothing else seems significant. Every thought fades away, leaving one's mind blank, making it extremely difficult to remember everything he says.

He quickly launched into the subject of Sheila's condition, confirming that she did have cancer and frowningly calling it black cancer. He repeated it several times when he saw that we were not quite sure what he said. I asked if we should cable her to come over to see him, but he shook his head and said, "No, not good to come now. Maybe later." Then he quickly assured us that he would help her, and waving his right hand in the familiar gesture, produced some *vibhuti*. He handed it to me together with a piece of paper and told me to wrap it carefully and to give it to her as soon as I reached home.

He then commented briefly on Lorna's death. He explained that the damage to her brain was so severe that it would have caused a great deal of confusion had she lived. He discussed the grandchildren and particularly asked about Brian who had not been born on our last visit. Almost nonchalantly he remarked that he would not limp. At first, we were not sure we had heard him correctly, and asked him to repeat it, which he did. Then I remembered what the orthopedic doctor had said about the three possibilities regarding the broken leg, that it might be shorter, longer, or the same length as the other.

I beamed at him in gratitude for setting our minds at rest on that score. He smiled and nodded understandingly, and once again we watched his right hand circle around in the air as we wondered what was about to come forth this time. Obviously enjoying our curiosity, he held out for me to see a beautiful little medallion fashioned from *panchaloha*. Embossed on one side was his head, and on the reverse was engraved an *Aum*. He told me to take it to Sheila, and until then to keep it in the *vibhuti* he had materialized for her earlier in the interview. I quickly unfolded the package, and he dropped it in, telling me to keep it all together until I gave it to her. She must them remove the medallion, hang it around her neck and eat the *vibhuti*. He reassured us that it would cure the cancer during the coming year. As I looked at the medallion I asked, "Oh Baba, she will love it! It is exactly what she herself would have chosen." He laughed and replied, "Yes, I know. She has always wanted one just like it."

After a few more personal discussions and enquiries about my work, my first book, and the book about him, I asked him when he wished us to return. He thought for a moment, and said, "In about a year," and commented that it was cooler in December and therefore more comfortable for me. Sidney asked if our usual time in January would be all right, and he replied that it was a good time too. We left his physical presence again filled with so much of his love to sustain us on our way home and throughout the year.

It was not until after we had left the interview and were sitting outside again, with the crowd of devotees, that I suddenly became aware that during most of the interview he had been lightly stroking my right arm and shoulder while he talked to us. He had not referred to the mugging which had happened earlier that year, and I had been far too involved with our two daughters to think of asking him about it, even though I had intended to. However, he obviously remembered it and used this unobtrusive way to accelerate the healing process. After his ministrations I observed an increased mobility in that arm, and a very noticeable reduction of pain when I moved it. Baba's gentle stroking finished the healing process.

As soon as the festivities were over and the crowd began to disperse, I felt impatient to go home and give Baba's medallion to Sheila. As it would be some time before we would se her, we sent her a cable to tell her that Baba was sending her a gift.

As soon as she set eyes on the medallion, she exclaimed that it was perfect and the only design she had seen that she really liked. I laughed and told her that that was exactly what I had said to Baba as soon as he materialized it, and he had replied that he knew it was what she had always wanted. When she first opened the package I noticed it contained less *vibhuti* than Baba had materialized, yet the package was still tightly closed. I can only assume that in some inexplicable way the medallion must have absorbed some of it. Since then I have heard other reports of a similar nature, where *vibhuti* was absorbed by a piece of jewelry materialized by Baba.

Sheila promptly swallowed what remained and took from her neck a locket containing a minute postage stamp picture of Baba. He had materialized four identical ones for each member of our family at an interview several years ago. She had worn hers constantly as a tangible connection to Baba, whom she had never met in person. Now he had made it possible for her to replace it with this beautiful new one materialized especially for her. She quickly removed the old locket from the chain, replaced it with the new medallion and fastened it around her neck, where it has remained ever since.

During the following year medical tests revealed a gradual improvement in her condition until she was pronounced free of the problem. In a more recent interview Baba told me that cancer is one disease which can be cured only by God's grace and with love.

CHAPTER TWENTY-THREE

EVER SINCE I first heard about Tibet I had always had an extremely strong desire to go there, though not for a moment had I imagined that would ever become possible. Because of its location it has always been inaccessible to outsiders, and since the Chinese occupation it has been closed even to visitors from Red China. In the early 1950s, when I was recovering some of my past lives, I had absolutely no expectation of going to any of the other countries where many of them seemed to have been led, least of all to Tibet.

Since that time my husband and I have traveled extensively and included many of the places where apparently I had lived before. Tibet was the only one I had not yet visited. So, when we heard that the Chinese were temporarily re-opening it to a number of travelers for short periods, I was excited at the possibility of a journey there. When we learned that certain groups were being granted permission to enter we arranged to join one of them. I was delighted at the prospect of a lifelong dream about to be fulfilled.

As we were not planning to go to Baba until January 1982, we decided to go to Tibet early in 1981. Lhasa could be reached by plane from Cheng-Du in Szechuan Province, so we would also be in China again. That too promised to be very interesting, as our first trip had preceded the death of Mao Tse Tung and we were curious to see what changes had since taken place.

However, the entire trip for me personally turned out to be a disaster, though it was also a learning experience. Most of our food was flown in to Lhasa from China, as the local supply is insufficient and not suited to the taste of foreigners. Rice was cooked fresh each day, but almost everything else was tinned. Many members of the group suffered from the extremely high altitude, and some had severe cases of mountain sickness. We were all cautioned to sleep with oxygen containers beside our pillows. I had very little problem with the altitude after an initial breathlessness, as I always feel particularly well in the mountains. However, I began to experience what I quickly recognized as a very violent allergic reaction to something. At first we were unable to determine the cause. One day we noticed that the tins of fruit and vegetables were imported from Japan, and were loaded with mono-sodium-glutamate, or

M.S.G., to which I have always been acutely allergic. As a result, for the eight days we were in Tibet I ate only white rice and a rice gruel. Oddly enough, that was all I had eaten in the past life as a monk, while immured in the cell. How strange that I should be forced to repeat it now . . .

The lack of food did not stop me from visiting the monasteries. I particularly wanted to visit the Potala, but was afraid that on such a meager diet I might not have enough strength to climb to the top. One of the guides, however, insisted on carrying me up on his back. He assured me that it would help to strengthen his muscles for his usual occupation as a guide to mountaineers. Whenever I felt weak I rubbed my forehead with the ring Baba had first materialized for me to heal the type of headache which originated in that life.

The weaker I became the more I looked forward to our return to China. I recalled that on our previous trip we had been served delicious food without M.S.G. However, I was headed for another unpleasant surprise when, on our return there, I developed the same allergic reactions. We learned later that the Japanese had saturated the Oriental markets with their innocent looking white "tasting powder." Not only in China but also in Hong Kong and Singapore I was faced with the same problem and, except for rice, found little I could eat.

I pleaded with Baba to help, as I became steadily weaker. But instead of improving, by the time we arrived in Singapore, I had developed a very high fever. Sidney called in a local doctor. He prescribed medicines and wanted to send me immediately to a hospital. We had reservations to leave for England the following day, so I decided not to follow his advice, as all I wanted at that moment was to be in the country of my birth to rest and recover.

That night when the fever was at its height I had a very strange experience. I am still not sure whether it was a dream or a hallucination. I felt as if I were lifted up and out of my body and into a wonderfully cool green place. Light as a feather, and free from all pain and discomfort, I floated freely. Into this idyllic scene appeared the figure of Krishna, playing his flute and dancing towards me. I remember being surprised at how very blue he looked, a dark midnight blue. The next moment he took me by the hand and began to whirl me around in a dizzyingly intricate dance which I was surprised to be able to follow. It was unbelievably exhilarating, and I felt I could continue dancing forever. But just as quickly as Krishna had appeared, a different very powerful figure arrived on the scene. I immediately recognized him as Christ. I was handed over to him to continue dancing. This dance, however, followed a very different tempo, slow and measured, like a minuet. It seemed to calm and center me after the wild twirling of the first dances. As it ended I reluctantly sank back down into my body. The fever had broken, but I was left utterly weak and exhausted and consumed with a desperate desire to leave for England. I was too weak to walk, so I had be taken to the plane in a wheelchair. But, my problems were not yet over. The wheelchair with me in it tipped over and fell on top of me as we were going up an escalator. I was afraid my back was injured and screamed to Baba to help me. The next thing I knew I was being lifted up as easily as if I were a rag doll in the strong arms of a tall and powerful young man. He must have seen what had happened and pushed his way back down the ascending escalator to reach me. He lifted me free of the overturned wheelchair, literally raced back up the escalator, jumped off and deposited me on a sofa in a waiting room, all so fast that I hardly had time to realize where I was. His accent sounded Scandinavian, but as soon as he was assured that I would be cared for by my husband and one of the attendants, he was off and away to catch his own plane. I regret that I did not have a chance to thank him adequately for rescuing me so swiftly. My back was excruciatingly painful, and one of my husband's ankles was hurt when the wheelchair overturned. We were both sorry sights when we boarded the plane for London.

As in the case of the hijacking I was able to receive the appropriate treatment for my back as soon as we reached England. The doctor who treats me at home had given me the name and address of an Indian doctor living in England, to give to an English friend who needed help. I happened to have his telephone number with me and rang him as soon as we arrived.

My husband's ankle was X-rayed revealing a fracture, so a cast was applied. When we eventually arrived back home it was discovered that I also had double pneumonia. As I had two other very strange accidents later that year, I began to wonder how much longer this series would continue, and what the reason might be. The same old familiar questions arose to haunt me. What was I doing wrong, or what was I omitting to do? I suspected they could all be due to accelerated burning up of past negative *karmas* and hoped to ask Baba about it at sometime. A few days after we returned I was putting away freshly laundered underwear in a drawer. As I sorted out the various items into piles, I heard an odd metallic clanking sound, rather like a coin dropping. Wondering what could have caused it, I scooped up all the pieces I had already laid in the drawer and out fell the ring Sidney had lost almost a year ago. I was almost certain it was the same one, but immediately called out to Sidney to come quickly. He confirmed that it was indeed the one he had thought lost. I had opened that particular drawer hundreds of times since the day it was lost. In addition, while packing for this recent trip to Tibet, I had emptied out everything to make it easier to see what I needed to take with me. So I was quite certain I would have seen it had it been there all those months. What had happened to it, and why it had so completely disappeared and reappeared, I do not understand. So far Baba has not solved that mystery for us. However, I did recall that at our last interview, when Sidney told him he had lost the ring, Baba said, "No, not lost. I will give it to you."

CHAPTER TWENTY-FOUR

TOWARDS THE END of 1981 we started planning to go to see Baba again. We felt it was very important to spend the holidays with Sheila, our son-in-law and the grandchildren, so we decided to leave as soon after Christmas as possible.

For some unknown reason I started to worry about the possibility that Baba might be away when we reached Bangalore. I was haunted by the recollection that he often goes to Madras to attend the Pongol festival sometime in January, as he had the first year we were there. I tried to ascertain the date of Pongol this year to avoid missing any time with Baba. But by the time we were ready to leave I still did not know.

Sure enough, as soon as we arrived in Bangalore, the first news we heard was that Baba was expected to leave for Madras to attend a special convention of Seva Dal workers. So my hunch that he would be going to Madras was correct, though the occasion was different from the one I had expected. There was nothing we could do at this late date, so I knew I must try to relax, leave everything in his hands and accept the consequences.

When we arrived at his house, we discovered that women were no longer permitted to sit in the front room. The women who lived in the house and elsewhere in the compound, together with the daily visitors, were relegated to an area behind a thick curtain, crowded together in a hot, dark, and airless space. Now, only men were allowed to sit in the outer room, so Sidney took his place as usual with the other men, while I tried to find a place in the crowded back room. As I entered it appeared to be already filled to overflowing, with closely packed women sitting on the floor. I later observed that in order to catch an occasional glimpse of Baba they all strove to secure a place in the front rows, as near the curtain as possible, hoping to peep through the openings at the center and sides whenever he passed by on the other side. This curtain was thick and opaque and hung across the room from wall to wall separating the area from the front verandah where the men were free to move about and walk outside in the fresh air while Baba was giving *darshan*.

I had hoped to have the time and opportunity to continue writing this book while with Baba. As I squeezed into a space barely large enough for me to sit, I reluctantly came to the conclusion that I would have to relinquish any thought of writing in such cramped conditions.

That first morning was sheer horror. Not only was it hot and airless in that dark room, but incense sticks were burning continuously. I found it difficult to breathe and thought my head must surely burst, it ached so badly. At one point Baba parted the curtain, took in the entire scene and chided the assembled women, asking how many eggs we had laid, indicating that we were lazy and sat around like broody hens sitting on eggs.

In the afternoon, on our return from lunch at the hotel, I decided to just sit outside the house in the open air. However, I soon discovered that the college boys were accustomed to congregate in that area, probably hoping to catch an occasional glimpse of Baba as he moved in and out of the house. I moved to another area, but as some of the women began to arrive they stopped to warn me that I could not stay there either. I kept moving farther away, and finally found a tree to the far right, quite separate from the boys' section, yet still close to the house. I could certainly breathe more easily and my headache began to abate, so I started to write. However, I felt vaguely uneasy about my decision and often gazed up at Baba's windows, mentally asking him to give me a sign to indicate whether he approved of my sitting outside in the fresh air writing his book, or whether I should sit inside with the other women.

After a while there was a veritable stampede as the boys started to race from all directions to positions immediately below the upper windows of the house. I looked up just in time to see Baba pull back the curtains and move his head from side to side to take in the whole scene below. So that was the reason the boys chose to cluster in that area! I quickly realized that Baba could not avoid seeing me and I felt very conspicuous. Ironically, I who have always tried to avoid attracting attention, was now literally asking for it! I mentally sent Baba a request to give some indication of where I should sit; and if inside the hot room, would he please help me to avoid developing a headache from the heat and incense fumes? Soon he was gone from the window and off on his afternoon rounds, so I concentrated on writing until it was time to leave for the day.

The next morning I decided to try sitting in the crowded room again, hoping that Baba had heard my plea for help. It seemed to be even hotter and more crowded and the incense was even more pungent and choking. But to my genuine surprise I found I could breathe, and managed to survive the three or four hours without a headache, thanks to Baba. I had my answer. From then on I would sit in the house unless he indicated otherwise.

The following morning my husband was able to give him a package of letters and papers he had brought with him, concerning the U.S. organization. Sidney told me later that Baba asked where I was and told him to tell me he would see me. Obviously that meant I should stay close by in the room where I was readily available whenever he chose to see us. I was relieved to know what to do, and silently thanked him for the message. From then on he gave me just barely sufficient indication of his wishes.

Very soon rumors started to circulate that he would leave shortly for Madras. My heart sank again at the thought of having to wait until he returned, for I knew that guests in his house should not try to follow him without his express invitation. His absence would cut down our time with him which was precisely why I had tried so hard to ascertain the date of Pongol. Finally, I decided to use it as a test to determine if I was able to surrender the whole situation to him, trust him to take care of it, and accept whatever transpired. To help me to remember to do so I chanted, as a *mantra* under my breath, "Surrender, trust and accept."

Sidney daily met Dr. Bhagavantam to discuss various matters pertaining to the U.S. organization. Baba joined them from time to time to comment and give suggestions, and finally decided that certain issues needed to be discussed with Indulal Shah, the head of the World Council, who lives in Bombay. Baba asked Sidney if we planned to stay long enough to accompany him to Madras and thence to Bombay where all the points could be discussed and a program worked out. Sidney said he would be most happy to follow that proposal. Baba then told him that he would be leaving shortly for Madras and that we should travel with him by plane. He added that our seats would be reserved and our tickets waiting at the airport as soon as the date was definitely decided. When I heard of the proposed plan I was thrilled. We had never had the privilege of flying with Baba, so it would be a new experience and, more important, it would allow us to spend all our time near him instead of having it curtailed while he went to Madras.

Soon we heard rumors that a *bundh*, or strike, of the airlines was imminent. I had heard that in past years whenever strikes

broke out they were usually accompanied by violence and loot-
ing. I also knew that many devotees would try to follow Baba to
Madras for more of his *darshan*. As Baba would be well aware of
this fact, he would probably either cancel or postpone his trip until
the strike ended and it was again safe to travel, rather than expose
his devotees to possible harm. The next news we heard was that an
official announcement had been made that only a one-day protest
strike would occur. It was due to take place on the very day Baba
and his party were to fly to Madras, so this plan would have to be
cancelled, since no planes would be taking off on the day of the
strike.

These many changes kept everyone on tenterhooks. Would
Baba go to Madras, or would his trip be cancelled? It proved to be
a practical lesson in non-attachment and patience. I wondered how
well I could really relax, and surrender, trust and accept whatever
eventually happened instead of remaining attached to what I
wanted. This seemed to be the main lesson this year. We would
all have to wait until we heard from Baba himself what he intended
to do.

A day or so later Baba called a young Western woman to an
interview and beckoned me to follow. His first question to me was
about Sheila's health. Fortunately, I had with me a letter from her
to give to him. As I handed it to him I thanked him for healing her
and told him how very grateful she was for his help. He weighed
her letter in his hand and then looked up with a big smile and said,
"Swami is very happy, very happy."

He spoke to the young woman for a while, and then suddenly
turned to me and announced, "My trip to Madras has been cancelled." I asked with obvious disappointment, "That means we
will not be traveling with you this time?" With a big smile at catching me reacting to a thwarted desire, he said, "Oh no, it is only
postponed," and laughed at the relief clearly visible on my face.

A couple of days later we were called to an interview with
Dr. Bhagavantam acting as interpreter. As soon as we had entered
the room and taken our seats on the floor at Baba's feet, he turned
to me and spoke in English. I thought he said, "And how was the
hijacking, Mrs. Krystal?" I decided I must not have heard him correctly since it had occurred eight years ago. So certain was I that I
had mistaken his words that I asked him to repeat the question.
He did so, but in a tone of voice which made it clear that I had

heard him correctly the first time. I was still at a loss to know how I should answer, but he did not wait for my reply. He quickly launched into a detailed description of the entire experience, including the way each of us reacted, even repeating word for word everything we had said to one another. It was exactly as if he had been on the plane with us all those years ago. It was impossible to believe such a feat; one that no ordinary human being could possibly accomplish. With obvious enjoyment at our amazement, he casually told Dr. Bhagavantam that the plane had been filled with his love. Then, turning back to me he asked, "Wasn't it, Mrs. Krystal?" He then assured us that it was his love that saved the plane and everyone in it. Thus, in the most matter-of-fact way, he corroborated what I thought had happened when I heard his voice inside my head telling me to send love to the hijackers, and I had replied that I would direct his love to them if he would pour it into me. As this memory flashed back into my mind, he smiled and nodding his head, said, "Yes, I heard you." So now, after eight years I knew without a doubt that I had not imagined it. I *had* heard him and his love *had* flowed through me to the hijackers, which he was now assuring me had indeed averted a disaster. With tears choking my voice, all I could say was, "Thank you, Baba, for the wonderful gift of saving us all and for now assuring me that it was true the way I experienced it."

He then went on to chide me gently for not always believing that he actually visited me in my dreams. I knew that by dreams he was also referring to the waking dreams or reveries in my work. I readily agreed with him that he was absolutely right, and admitted that I was afraid I might only be imagining that it was really he who appeared. He further reassured me on that point by saying, "No. Not your imagination. I really come. You must believe it. I am always with you when you work." Again, all I could do was thank him from my heart for setting my mind at rest and removing the fear that my inner experiences of him were merely wishful thinking on my part.

He then referred to the book about my work, and told me it would be published in England in May instead of September, the scheduled date. He then informed me that I would write three books. I asked if there was anything else he wished me to do, and with an indulgent laugh, he said, "You are doing quite sufficient," and after a significant pause, added, "for your age."

We had brought a large package of letters from devotees, many of whom were anxious about the various predictions of catastrophic earthquakes along the coast of California. I took this opportunity to ask Baba if they were true. He assured us that there would not be a cataclysm as in some predictions but many small quakes would occur and these would reduce the pressure which builds up within the earth. He added that one of the reasons he had incarnated at this time was to divert such calamities.

I then asked him about the series of traumas and accidents which had befallen me during the past few years. He nodded his head and said it was very hard, and repeated, "Very hard, very hard," with great compassion and sympathy. He then explained that they had provided a greater opportunity than a life as a *sadhaka* (a spiritual aspirant) to learn the lessons of patience, tolerance, forbearance and steadfastness.

I gathered from these remarks that instead of bemoaning our fate and complaining about our problems, as we are all so prone to do, he was suggesting that we ask ourselves what we could learn from them.

As usual, he inquired about the grandchildren and promised to make a medallion for our little grandson, Brian. He mentioned that he always grabs my locket, and should have one of his own. He then advised us on personal matters, and gave me directions on certain aspects of my work. He was the perfect combination of mother and father to both of us.

The next day I had a strange experience which I must preface with an earlier one for it to be understood. During the past few years my own reveries were becoming even more intense and meaningful. Many times Baba appeared on the inner levels to direct them and give some instruction. During one of these sessions, as soon as I had closed my eyes, he appeared before my inner gaze, and beckoned me to follow him. I felt exactly as if I were with him in India. He led me to the *darshan* lines at Puttaparthi, made a wide detour around the men's lines, and then began weaving in and out on the women's side. He hurried ahead, frequently looking back to make sure I was still following him, and beckoned me on with a wave of his hand. He finally stopped in front of an Indian woman across whose lap sprawled a grotesque looking boy about 10 years old. His head lolled uncontrollably from side to side, his legs were held stiff and straight out in front of him, and his arms flailed wildly over his head. I had seen such children brought by their parents for Baba's *darshan* in the desperate hope that a healing would result from the sight of Baba, that Baba might touch them, or better still, materialize special *vibhuti* to cure them. This woman was no exception. She was obviously full of hope. As soon as Baba stopped in front of her, her face lit up, her large pleading dark eyes overflowed with tears, and her whole body assumed a posture of desperate appeal for help. At that point Baba turned and asked if I wished him to heal this child. My heartfelt reply was, "Oh yes, of course, Baba." With that he turned around and, beckoning me to follow him once more, hurried off. This time we seemed to be moving effortlessly through the air at a tremendous speed until we landed in a strange place. It also appeared that we had moved back in time. He hurried along until we came to a scene in which two men were apparently meting out justice to various offenders who were brought before them. One of the men was obviously the judge and the other his assistant. With obvious relish the latter was noting down on a tablet what I presumed were the penalties. I could tell from the horrified reactions of the offenders that the punishments were far too severe to fit their crimes. Baba turned to make sure I had understood the implication of this scene. These two men had reincarnated, the harsh judge now imprisoned and tortured in the distorted and helpless body of the child in the care of his erstwhile assistant, now his mother. She was being given a chance to learn the compassion she had lacked as the judge's assistant by caring for her twisted and helpless child.

As soon as Baba saw that I understood, he took off again with me in tow, until we landed back in front of the mother and child. With a quizzical look at me, he turned and asked, "Do you still wish me to heal him?" My eyes filled with tears at his infinite wisdom, rather than for the plight of these two people. I sadly shook my head and said, "No, Baba. Not now." He nodded and smiled his approval that I had understood his point, that even he will not interfere with the working out of people's past *karmas*. To do so would steal from them an opportunity to learn from their past mistakes by compensatory suffering in the present life.

A sequel to this episode occurred the day after the interview. It happened to be a Sunday, a *bhajan* day. Sheila had asked me to look out for one of her friends who was planning to be there at that time. I decided to go out and sit in the *darshan* lines in the hope of meeting and introducing her to some of the other Western women. I looked around and asked if anyone had seen her. When no one responded I sat down to wait for Baba to appear for *darshan*. It was a most welcome change to be outside in the sun and fresh air with all the other devotees, feeling and seeing their eagerness to catch a glimpse of Baba. The air was electric with their deep emotion and anticipation as they craned their necks from time to time to see if his familiar form was visible emerging through the iron gates.

Soon he was drifting lightly over the ground, his feet seeming hardly to touch it. He made his way towards the nearest lines on the women's side, not far from where I was sitting, and slowly moved along taking letters from the many outstretched hands. Suddenly he stopped short, and I saw with a shock that he was standing directly in front of an Indian woman across whose lap sprawled a boy just like the one I had seen several months earlier in my reverie. I realized that I was being shown again that my inner experience had been a real one and not a figment of my imagination. After his brief stop, which had allowed me just enough time to recognize the scene, he moved on his way. Once more I was left marvelling at another instance of the inexplicable incidents which seem to happen around Baba and the enigmatic way his messages reach those for whom they are intended. So I hadn't imagined that strange inner experience. I felt a warm glow of gratitude at another corroboration.

A day or so later Baba sent word that he had decided to go by car to Madras the following day, but that we should take an early morning flight to arrive at the same time. We were also told that plane tickets were being held in our name and should be picked up before departure. When we arrived at the airport we went immediately to collect our tickets but were informed that none had been put aside for us. To add to our dismay we were also told that the plane was absolutely full. Again we were faced with a test of our trust and patience. After several futile inquiries and telephone calls, we were finally paged and informed that there were, indeed, two seats reserved for us. We hurriedly picked up our tickets and boarded the plane, just minutes before it was due to take off for Madras.

The hotel where we stayed was within easy walking distance of Sundaram, the Sai Baba center in Madras, similar to

Dharmakshetra in Bombay. We were happy to have the opportunity to compare the two centers. Both had been designed, with Baba's approval, by devotees in each city, yet they were quite different in style and setting.

We soon discovered that most of the activities, including *darshan*, took place at Sundaram, while the big meetings were held at a large hall at Abbotsbury, some distance away. On our first day it was a truly inspiring sight to behold the throngs of devotees streaming down the road leading to the center, all so eager to welcome Baba and receive his *darshan*.

For the next few days we could watch Baba moving among his devotees as their honored guest, attending the many and varied events at which he had been asked to preside. The devotion of all the men and women who had been instrumental in arranging them was most inspiring. No effort had been spared to welcome him into their midst for the Seva Dal Convention, whose activities were so close to his heart.

Baba gave daily *darshan* to the thousands who thronged into the area to catch sight of him. Yet with all this activity everything proceeded smoothly and without a hitch. A short while before an event was due to start chaos often reigned supreme only to be transformed into perfect order as the result he desired began to materialize within minutes of the designated time for the next event to begin.

When it was time for Baba to leave for Bombay we were again alerted to collect our plane tickets at the airport. This time there was no problem. The tickets were waiting for us at the desk with our seat numbers attached. We boarded the plane in plenty of time and as we took the seats assigned to us, I looked around and wondered where Baba would sit. Shortly before the plane was due to take off, he came up the steps accompanied by several of his college boys and some devotees. A wave of excitement swept through the plane as he was recognized in his familiar orange robe. To my immense surprise he slipped into the seat immediately in front of me, his hair only inches away from me when he was seated. What more could I have asked than to have his continuous *darshan* re-energizing and filling me with his love all the way to Bombay.

As soon as the plane had taken to the air and the seat belt signs had been turned off, we enjoyed the fascinating experience of watching people line up in the aisles as the news began to circulate that Sai Baba was on the plane. With hands held together in respect, they filed past him, their eyes seemingly glued to his face. Some of the braver ones reached across the student seated at his side in an effort to touch his feet, as he smiled and blessed each one. As I watched the stream pass by, I was amused and touched to notice that some people took advantage of this rare opportunity to walk past him more than once. I was impressed at the relaxed and serene way he smiled, spoke to some, greeted those he recognized, all with such good natured ease.

On arrival in Bombay we were again swept into all the many events arranged by the huge group of devotees in that city, headed by Mr. Indulal Shah. We had heard that he would shortly be celebrating his sixtieth birthday which we already knew to be a very important occasion in India. We were informed that Baba would preside at the celebration, so we were very happy to receive an invitation to attend, though at that time I had no idea how very significant it was going to be.

The service was very long, with chanting from the Vedas and many different offerings thrown into the fire. Mr. and Mrs. Shah performed the many symbolic acts associated with the special *puja*. As it was also a second wedding ceremony, Baba materialized a very beautiful ring for Mr. Shah, set with the nine precious stones representing the nine planets to ensure their protection. He materialized a *mangala sutra* for Mrs. Shah.

As soon as the service ended Baba delivered a discourse in which he outlined the path of *karma yoga*, the *yoga* of action. He started by defining a community as a grouping of people, and *seva* as service to the community performed by the individuals of which it is composed. But he cautioned that it is true *seva* only if performed with compassion, kindness and self-sacrifice. He pointed out that man has only the right to work to help him to purify his own awareness. But he does not have the right to ask for the fruits of that work. He assured his listeners that service to the community is the greatest form of *seva* and, as it can lead directly to liberation, there is no need for any other *sadhana*. However, he warned that such service is often accompanied by hardships, and gave as examples how Mohammed was driven away from Mecca for teaching devotion to God, and how Jesus was crucified for proclaiming that compassion is the true basis of life.

He also cautioned that if such service is done by a person who thinks *he* is doing it, than that is ego, which causes him to separate himself from enlightenment or self-realization. Only when the ego is removed can the divinity within shine and blossom. He illustrated this point by likening our hearts to the lake in which the reflection of the sun can be clearly seen only when the water is still and clear, and not covered over by a dense layer of plants, which symbolize attachment to worldly things and negative emotions such as envy, jealousy, greed and many others.

He repeatedly commended Mr. and Mrs. Shah for having followed the *karma yoga* path from ancient times and for continuing in this present life to be deeply committed in service to the Sai organization. He likened the *puja* that had just been performed to lighting a fire in an engine room. The union of the fire in Mr. Shah and the water in his wife produces the steam which enables the train, symbolizing the Sai organization, to proceed even faster and better than before. He said that this celebration was one of the reasons for his presence in Bombay on this occasion. So the ceremony which we had just witnessed was more than the personal *puja* for Mr. and Mrs. Shah on his sixtieth birthday. Baba seemed to be indicating that it was also a significant event for the whole organization.

He then outlined the steps through which we should all pass from birth until the age of sixty, when we should rededicate our lives to more intense service. By the age of seventy we should have eliminated the bad qualities and be looking forward to the enjoyment of divinity by exchanging the external look for the development of the inward look. In this way, by the age of eighty, we should set an example to others and continue to do so until a hundred years.

In other words, for the first fifty years we are involved in worldly matters. After that we should gradually detach ourselves and become submerged in the work of the community, but at the same time continue to fulfill all our responsibilities and duties to our descendants, as they arise. He illustrated his point by saying that although Mr. and Mrs. Shah had their own responsibilities, and in spite of the fact that Mrs. Shah's health had not been very satisfactory, they were detaching themselves from worldly pursuits and devoting their time and energy to the service of the community and the Sai organization. Because of such service they can truly be called *karma yogis*.

He then pointed out that all the Sai organizations were started in the city of Bombay. He reminded his listeners that in the Bhagavad-Gita Lord Krishna had said that he would come as a divine *Avatar* for the main purpose of establishing *dharma* at times when it had become weak due to untruth and injustice spreading throughout the world. However, he added, it is not necessary to read the entire seven hundred verses. In the very first verse the first word is *dharma* and the last word of the last verse is *mama*. The two together, *mama dharma*, mean "my duty" and, by extension, "I must do my duty." The verses in between contain the instructions to teach people how to perform their *dharma*.

He commended Mr. and Mrs. Shah not only for attending to their *dharma*, but also for not wanting this *shashtiabda puja*, which the other devotees had insisted on their having. He said that it was not only correct but the devotees' duty to insist on it, as it was a way to show their love and devotion in appreciation of the Shahs' selfless service.

He urged all those who attended to regard the offerings to the fire during the ceremony as reminders to redouble their efforts towards greater enthusiasm for service to the community. He encouraged all devotees to regard service to the community as more important than service to themselves. "Service is God and work is worship, which is the same as saying duty is God." He reminded everyone that Mr. Shah has repeatedly cautioned devotees to give up being lazy, and to take on service actively.

He ended on an emphatic note by saying, "Arise! Awake! Get to work!"

It had been a most inspiring experience which was to have more meaning for me as time went by, and I began to understand what Baba had meant by these words and how they could be applied in my own life.

As in Madras, we were privileged to be able to watch Baba in another new setting. We were invited to attend the many different events which gave us insight into the activities to which devotees all over India were so dedicated. Sidney worked with Mr. Shah and various other officers on matters concerning the U.S. organization. Baba sometimes sat in to listen and advise. We also saw how much Dharmakshetra had expanded since our very brief visit eight years earlier.

Baba granted us interviews in which he discussed my counseling work and the book I was writing about him. I handed him a stack of typewritten pages, representing the first part of the book. He held them on his lap. I asked if he had any suggestions or instructions. He replied that I would not need any, as he would show me how to proceed. He next asked what title I had chosen. I replied that I had tentatively selected "Surrender, Trust, and Accept." He frowned and said it was too long and that he would provide me with a more suitable one. I thanked him and waited for him to tell me what it was, but he moved on to other things.

Sidney showed him the ring which had been lost and found again and added that it had always pinched his finger which made it uncomfortable to wear. Baba asked him to hand it to him and, as he took it, asked Sidney if he wanted one with Shirdi or Sai. Sidney immediately responded, "Sai Baba, please," secretly hoping for one similar to the original one, though more comfortable. However, Baba decided otherwise, for after closing it in his hand and blowing three times on his closed fist, he showed us a very different one. It had a gold setting containing a brightly colored porcelain picture of Baba.

He then talked to us more about our personal lives, discussed our family, and poured out his love to us. I asked when he would like us to return. He replied, "In one year," and then added with a smile, "And bring the book with you." When Sidney mentioned that our anniversary would be the following day, he replied, "Yes, I know," and added, "The ring is a wedding ring. Be happy."

He stood up to indicate that the interview was about to end. Then he turned to me and told me to wait with the other visitors for him to bring me some *vibhuti*. We walked back down the long ramp to join the group waiting to be called for an interview. In a few minutes we could all see him emerge from one of the upper rooms carrying a large envelope into which he was busily stuffing packets of *vibhuti* which threatened to spill out as he walked. He continued to push them back in as he seemed to float rather than walk down the slope to where we all waited. Then, with a wide smile, he came up to me and as he handed me the envelope, said jokingly, "For my devotees and your patients." All I could think of was that he must have handled every package of *vibhuti* on his way down and that I must remember to tell the various people who would receive them that they had all been impregnated with his love and energy. Thus ended one more visit. It had been very different from any of the previous ones in many ways.

During this time of travel with Baba I gained a fresh perspective on his impact on people. I had been able to observe him with the many influential men who had been drawn to him and who gathered around him in a close group in each city. I began to see the groundwork he has been laying for his self-appointed task of first cleaning up his own back yard, as he expresses it, before journeying to other parts of the world at the urgent request of his many overseas devotees.

If he can secure the devoted cooperation of men of wealth and influence in India, he can more quickly bring about the transformation he has in mind for that country. He takes people as he finds them, good and not so good, knowing that as they participate in his plan to improve the standard of living of the masses, they too will benefit by such *seva,* or service. Slowly and imperceptibly it will make them less selfish and more compassionate as they become more involved. This aspect I would call the exoteric, or outer organizational, part of his mission.

The esoteric aspect involves far fewer people and includes individuals from all walks of life who have been searching for more meaning to life than they have been able to find in the material world. Some have undergone severe sorrows and hardships of a physical, emotional, mental or spiritual nature, but these very problems have forced them to seek further instead of plunging them into self-pity and despair. With these people Baba engages in a very different course of action. He hones away the outer superficiality to reveal the stark reality of their own indwelling God-self. This process, though subtle and hidden, is implemented as soon as an individual has willingly requested Baba's help to achieve self-development. In such cases he can be a relentless taskmaster, but only when invited to help, as he always honors our free will. Besides which, he never asks anyone to bear more than is possible at any time, though it sometimes seems as if one is pushed to the brink of endurance. This experience appears to be essential before most people are willing to surrender their ego-demands and ask to be shown the path towards union with the God-within. It is a matter of "Thy will, not mine," directed at the indwelling spark of the Divine which inhabits all living things.

CHAPTER TWENTY-FIVE

AFTER WE RETURNED home we began to hear about the proposed plans for the celebration of Baba's 60th birthday in November 1985. He emphatically stated that he does not want gifts. Instead he suggested that devotees follow a program for the next three years combining selfless service and a ceiling on desires. Thus he initiated a seemingly new plan of action in connection with what he knew would be worldwide preparations for the observance of this very special birthday. I purposely say "seemingly new," as it is really the same cause he has been enthusiastically encouraging from the very beginning of his mission—to raise the level of life, first in India, through reaffirmation of the ancient Vedic teachings, India's richest heritage. However, he knows only too well that any lasting changes cannot be brought about prematurely or forced on people. To be effective, change like all natural growth, is necessarily a slow and gradual process.

As I look back over the comparatively short time since we first journeyed to India to meet Sai Baba in person, I am aware of many subtle changes which have come about as a direct result of his patient yet concentrated effort to arouse his devotees to positive action in carrying out his plans. He never forces, but appears always to flow like a river making its way around boulders lying in its course, or gently but inexorably wearing down obstacles creating resistance to its flow. He never flouts tradition or custom, but effects imperceptible changes by his continued teaching that the power of love is the only effective force in overcoming resistance. He never loses a single opportunity to drive home his message with the utmost patience, so certain is he that it will eventually bear fruit.

So this apparently new thrust on his part is in direct line with his teachings. He is merely seizing this opportunity to accelerate his plans by using the desire of his thousands of devotees to honor him on the traditionally important occasion of his 60th birthday. Heretofore, he had made himself readily available to all who come to him in an ever increasing stream. They are from all walks of life, and from almost every country in the world. They include adherents of all the known basic belief systems, as well as a host of self-styled atheists and agnostics. They all bring to him their myriads of requests. For many years he has been granting their wishes like a wise and loving parent caring for his children. Interspersed among his countless activities he has woven into his discourses the basic tenets of his teachings, frequently illustrating them with enchanting little stories. But now a subtle change has taken place in his attitude as he starts to urge his devotees to redouble their efforts at *seva*.

He has always said he will give people what they want in the hope that at some point they will want what he has come to give them. Now he expects us to stop asking him for boons and be willing to ask him what he wants us to do in the world. He is stressing *seva*, or service, as more important than any of the other practices. He says, "*Seva* is more fruitful than the *japa, dhyana, yagna,* or *yoga* usually recommended to spiritual aspirants, for it serves two purposes, the extinction of the ego, and the attainment of *ananda*, or bliss."

This accelerated program will be the culmination of many years of gradual growth of the service organizations which have sprung up all over India. These units are now being exhorted to increase their determination, on an individual as well as a group level, to raise the standard of living of their less fortunate brothers and sisters, in the villages and in the cities where literally millions eke out a bare subsistence, begging by day, and sleeping on the streets at night.

He urges the rich to use their money in this way if they wish to gain his favor. He has often been criticized for gathering around him so many rich men. Surely, this is logical in view of the fact that they are the ones who are in a position to help in his vast scheme. First he wins their devotion and then, by repeated and firm encouragement, persuades them that the most direct way to his heart is by using their money and power to help those in need. He never tires of expounding his cause, fully aware that constant unwavering repetition is necessary to break through the thick overlay accumulated from years of habit and eventually to reach the hearts and consciences of the rich and powerful of every land. Like a fisherman, he has cast out his nets complete with lures and bait and is now ready to draw in his catch to help put his vast and far reaching scheme into action.

Anyone who has been to India will be acutely aware of the enormity of the task needing to be undertaken to change the present conditions existing in this huge country. It is predominantly rural, in sharp contrast to the few giant, sprawling and over-popu-lated cities. Such is the devotion Baba inspires in his followers that as soon as he made his desires known, thousands of members from the *seva* groups all over India went into the villages to help raise the standard of living of the inhabitants. When people are touched by Baba it invariably results in a drastic change of lifestyle and, for a few, complete devotion and service in some form.

So the theme was set for the period leading up to Baba's 60th birthday. The reaction was a concerted effort by each devotee to put a ceiling on his own desires by cutting down on waste, and devot-ing the resulting savings to make life more bearable for the thou-sands who endure a subhuman standard of living. In every speech Baba began to hammer home the need for everyone to prove that he or she is a true devotee, not just in name only, but what is more important, in action. He urged his listeners to prove their devo-tion by engaging in active *seva*, rather than going to seek his bless-ings for their own selfish ends.

And so his mission unfolds and he begins to reveal the extent of it. If it had been proposed any sooner it would merely have fallen on deaf ears or paralyzed his listeners by its vast scope. But patiently and perseveringly he has, little by little, inculcated in all who have been in the least receptive, the challenge of his mission. It will assuredly snowball and carry with it all who have become involved as its momentum accelerates.

This change of pace was first revealed in Baba's discourse fol-lowing Mr. Indulal Shah's 60th birthday celebration, which ended with the words, "Arise! Awake! Get to work!" I was as yet unaware of the deeper universal significance of that discourse while sitting on the hard floor tightly wedged in between the women who sur-rounded me. But now, in retrospect, I can see how he used the occa-sion of Mr. Shah's birthday to initiate the program with which he planned to mark his own celebration, three and a half years later.

On our last trip, when we had arrived in Bombay from Madras, Elsie Cowan had been waiting there for Baba. In the past she had often asked me to give a talk at her monthly meetings, but I had always refused. However, after Lorna's funeral, she firmly announced that she would never again accept a refusal from me to talk in public. So, while we were all with Baba in Bombay, she half jokingly told me that she would give me no choice as to whether I would speak, but would allow me to choose the time. Sure enough, after we had all returned home she telephoned one day to ask me to speak at her May meeting. I recognized that it was Baba's way of giving me another chance to overcome my fear and resistance, so I agreed.

As the time for the meeting approached I thought I had better decide what I wanted to say and make some notes to which I could refer while giving the talk. But I had not foreseen the problem I would encounter when I repeatedly needed to change my glasses, as I use one pair for distance vision and another for reading. It soon became both annoying and ridiculous to be constantly exchanging one pair for the other, in order to look at the audience and check my notes. I finally discarded the notes and with them any preconceived idea of what I would say. Almost automatically I continued to talk as I do when I am working with someone, by relaxing as much as possible, asking within for direction, and saying whatever comes into my mind. I have often been astonished at some of the things I say, yet have grown to trust this process since the results have been so positive. I had never yet put it to the test in a group, so I had no idea what would happen. To my amazement I found that it was not nearly such an ordeal as I had feared.

At the end of the meeting several people told me I had been speaking directly to them, as I had said exactly what they most needed to hear at that time. As they were all strangers to me I knew without a doubt that I could not possibly have known their needs, but Baba did. He must have spoken through me as I had requested. If I could really believe this, I would surely lose the deep-seated fear I had carried for so long. I knew that the core of the fear was that I might say something which was not really true, but ego-distorted, which could have a negative affect on the listeners. But Baba had helped me to see that it is just as unbalanced to bend over backwards in the opposite direction, as that leads to avoidance of taking the initiative and assuming responsibility. Only by tuning into his counterpart in my heart was I able to relax sufficiently to let him speak through me, and in that way bypass my ego. How gently Baba had urged but never coerced or pressured me. He waited for me to be ready and willing to take the next step.

During the summer of 1982 we spent six weeks in England, studying archaeology at one of the colleges of Oxford University. On one of the free weekends we attended a seminar on holistic healing under the sponsorship of the Wrekin Trust, an organization started by Sir George Trevelyan. In addition to being a most interesting experience, it included a pleasant surprise when we saw the first copies of my book among the others for sale at the seminar. It was published in May, just as Baba had predicted.

We also met Jean and Lucas Ralli, both active in the Sai organization in England. They invited us to spend a weekend with them in London. They asked if I would be willing to give a short talk about Baba to a group of devotees whom they had invited to meet us. I again felt the old familiar jab of fear, but quickly recalled the recent experience at Elsie's meeting, and knew I must again accept it as a further test of my faith. I explained to them that talking to groups had always been a problem for me, and that only very recently with Baba's help had I started to overcome it for the first time. They assured me that the small group of devotees whom they would be inviting would be most appreciative of anything I cared to share with them about my experiences with Baba. So, once again, I tried to relax and await whatever came into my head instead of saying what I thought they might want to hear. As before, the words formed and flowed out when I relaxed, and stuck in my throat when I started to worry, so I gradually gathered more courage. Just as with Elsie's group, some of the devotees told me later that I had said exactly what they most needed to hear at that particular time in their lives. It was obvious that I could not have known what they needed to hear, as they had all been strangers to me until then.

During our stay at Oxford I was able to fit into our very busy schedule some regular periods for writing this book. To my surprise, by the end of our stay, I had accumulated a pile of pages covered with my almost illegible writing. I mention this as a prelude to Baba's reaction at an interview the following year.

During the rest of that year more information arrived about the plans for Baba's 60th birthday. The organization in India proposed that small notebooks be made available for devotees to list ways in which they were successful in limiting their desires. It was also proposed that all the notebooks be collected and presented to Baba as a united birthday gift.

Jack Hislop knew about some of the methods I use in my work and wrote to ask if I would be willing to write an article on the ceiling on desires program for the U.S. Newsletter. Though at that time I had only a very slight idea of what Baba had in mind, I agreed to attempt this assignment. The Hislops left for India shortly thereafter. When the article was finished, I posted one copy to Jack at his Mexican address, and decided to take one with me to India, as we were planning to leave very shortly and might meet the Hislops there.

Just before we were due to leave we heard that Baba was traveling again to Madras and Bombay. We decided to leave as planned and to check with Indulal Shah in Bombay to ascertain Baba's plans and make our own accordingly. Mr. Shah told us that Baba was still in Madras but would be leaving any day for Bombay, and advised us to wait there for him. En route to India via Singapore I caught a severe cold or flu, so I was grateful to be able to rest until Baba arrived.

Baba welcomed us in his wonderfully warm and loving way, and asked us how long we planned to stay. When we told him, he asked us to accompany him when he returned to Whitefield and said he would arrange our flight and let us know when he would be leaving.

During the week we were in Bombay, we heard him give several discourses in which he enlarged on the ceiling on desires program. I soon realized that the article I had written at Jack Hislop's request was much too long and complicated. As usual with Baba, he kept his teaching so simple that it could be understood by everyone. The Hislops had left directly from Madras where they had gone with Baba. So I hurriedly wrote Jack a letter asking him to keep the article until I returned, as it would have to be rewritten.

When Baba was ready to return to Whitefield, he sent word that our plane tickets would be waiting for us at the airport. This time our seats were three rows behind him, so again we could watch as the long lines of passengers inched past him, all anxious to take advantage of this unexpected chance to obtain his *darshan*. Mrs. Ratan Lal was sitting directly across the aisle from him, and during the flight she came back to ask if I would like to change seats with her for a while. As I slipped into her vacated seat Baba leaned across and smilingly asked where my book was. Ironically enough, this was the only time I did not have it with me. It was safely packed in my luggage, as I had certainly not expected to have an opportunity to give it to him during the flight. But Baba enjoys catching people by surprise and laughed at his own joke. Then, in an exaggeratedly querulous voice, he asked, "And where is the book about me?" Now it was my turn to laugh at his playful attitude. He then asked about Sheila. I thanked him for healing her. When I told him that all the tests now showed she was free from the cancer, he smiled and nodded in agreement. Next he asked, "How are the grandchildren, the children of the daughter who died? Are they with their father?" He then asked about details of their daily lives just like an old family friend. I was deeply touched at his love and caring, but I knew without a doubt that he cares equally for everyone in the world.

That day after we arrived in Bangalore we were called to an interview. Indulal Shah's daughter and son-in-law were invited at the same time. Baba spoke to them at length in a language we did not understand. Then he turned his attention to us and immediately asked for a copy of my book, which I had taken care to bring with me this time. I handed it to him saying, "I give it back to you with all my love." Next he asked about the book about him, so I handed him a sheaf of loose pages on which I had written a section of it by hand the previous summer. As he held the stack on his lap and scrutinized the pages, he made a comical grimace and said, "What terrible writing. It looks like crow's feet scratches." We all laughed and as he joined in the merriment the loose pages started to slide off his lap. He bent over and scooped them up into a neat pile. In doing so he touched each page, so they were all filled with his energy exactly as the package of *vibhuti* had been impregnated with his power the last time we were with him.

It was not until I was writing about this interview that a much deeper meaning to his words was revealed to me. Quite suddenly I realized that the handwritten part of the manuscript I had handed to him contained accounts of the traumatic experiences which had happened over that difficult two-year period. Only then did I connect this remark about the "crow's feet scratches" with a reverie session with my daughter, Sheila, several years earlier which graphically illustrated his deeper meaning.

In the reverie I had felt I was walking on a tightrope with my arms held outstretched on either side for balance. As I carefully placed my feet alternately on the rope, a huge black bird like a crow appeared over to the left and attracted my attention. I was afraid from the way it looked that it was about to attack me, so I lunged to the left to push it away. As I did so, I lost my balance and fell to the ground. As soon as I got back up onto the tightrope, I noticed a beautiful white bird on my right. I was so attracted to it that I impulsively leaned over to take hold of it, and fell off again.

When I sought the meaning it became clear that the black bird symbolized all those things I did not want, or was afraid would happen, while the white bird represented all the things I did want and hoped for. By reacting to either one I lost my balance. I saw that the only way I could remain balanced was to resist the temptation to try to control either of the birds. So I started out again with arms outstretched, palms up, and allowed either bird to alight on my hands as and when they wished, and attempted to accept them both equally.

The part of the book I had handwritten at Oxford included the mugging, Lorna's death, Sheila's cancer, the escalator accident in Singapore, and several others. Like the black bird, these events were ones I would have preferred to push away, had that been possible. Instead, the crow's feet left scratches on the paper on which I wrote about them. Here was yet another example of the way Baba so often gives us a many-layered message in one simple sentence, like a Zen *koan* which we then have to solve ourselves. The process can take months and sometimes years, as in this case.

I recall another time when Baba told one of his little stories which also illustrated the message of the black and white birds. He started by saying, "You all walk on such bumpy roads. How can you have peace? When you get what you want you are so happy that you go up very high," illustrating it with his hand raised above his head. "But soon something will come along which does not please you and you go down very low," bringing his hand down to his feet. "See what a bumpy road you walk on. Be happy whatever happens and you will walk on an even path and find peace."

One of the miracles Baba has brought about in my life is a willingness to try to accept the black bird and to resist grabbing the white one. I hasten to say that it is far easier to write about it than to put into practice. However, once glimpsed it is a little easier to remember not to react with strong negative emotions when life presents us with some experience we simply do not want, or with too much excitement or pride when our most cherished dreams come true. Either extreme destroys the inner calm and throws us off balance.

Later in the same interview, he materialized some *vibhuti*, presumably to help with my heavy cold. Then, in his usual unexpected way he asked, "How is the ring?" I answered, "This one is fine," indicating the one he had given me during our very first interview, "but this one is still too big," as I pointed to the blue-green one he gave me to mark the second wedding ceremony six years ago. I showed him the gold guard that a jeweler had added to prevent it from slipping off my finger. He reached out his hand and asked me to give it to him, so I took it off and placed it in his outstretched hand. He examined it closely, and passed it to the other couple for their inspection. When they handed it back to him he held it in his right hand, closed it into a fist, and blew on it three times. I had heard that he sometimes changes the size of objects he materializes so I assumed that he would make it smaller so that it would fit without the guard. But when he opened his hand, there, lying on his palm was an entirely different ring. The setting was gold though different from the former one, and contained a large brilliant stone which looked like a many-faceted diamond. He laughed at my evident surprise and said, "A white stone this time." He first passed it to the other couple, and then slipped it on the third finger of my right hand on which he had placed the original one. As I thanked him, he looked at me inquiringly, so I said, "This one fits." He replied, "It is a perfect fit," and added, "I am always with you." At the time I was too overcome to catch the significance of this last remark. It was not until several days later that a deeper meaning was revealed. He then took the other couple into an inner room for a private interview. When they left, he beckoned us to join him for a private talk, in which he discussed more intimate details of our lives, our spiritual progress and my work.

After seeing Baba, we were going to England where I had been asked to give several talks and a weekend seminar on my work. It would be my first experience of sharing it with groups. To say that I was nervous would be an understatement, so I took the opportunity to ask Baba to help me. He raised his eyebrows and said, "But I have told you I am always with you." "Yes, I know, Baba, " I replied, "but I will be talking for a whole weekend." He countered with, "You talk all day everyday." I agreed and added, "But with only one person at a time." He laughed and said, "But one plus one plus one is one. All are one." Then with a beaming smile, like an indulgent parent he reassured me by saying, "Yes, I will help you."

Towards the end of the interview he mentioned the ceiling on desires program, and asked if I had brought the article I had written. When I told him it was in our room, he said he would devote another interview to that program the next day, and that I should bring the article with me.

Baba called us the next day, and asked Mr. Narasimhan to act as interpreter. One Indian and two Oriental ladies were included at the beginning. Baba spoke first to the Indian lady in her own language and completely took her by surprise by suddenly materializing a beautiful japamala of large lustrous pearls. As she tremblingly took it from his hands she wept with joy. He then spoke to each of the others, answering their pleas with loving concern. As soon as he had dismissed all three, he turned and beckoned us to move closer to where he sat until we were at his feet.

He then proceeded to enlarge on the ceiling on desires program beyond the brief outline he had given in his various public discourses in Bombay. He seemed to be directing his attention to me, and I remember wondering what the significance could be, as I knew it was not solely for my personal benefit. He explained that the object of the program was to encourage devotees to cut down on waste in four main categories of daily life, namely: money, food, time and energy. He promised that those who follow this routine will not only benefit themselves by reducing attachment to material things, as they placed a ceiling on their desire to possess them, but the resulting savings could then be used to help the less fortunate. Thus, the two programs, ceiling on desires and selfless service, can be worked on simultaneously for the benefit of all.

He illustrated his points in his usual simple yet effective way. First, he stated emphatically that there is far too much waste in the world. This is particularly true in the United States, while in other countries people are starving. He pointed out that in some respects the poor have an advantage over the rich. Their time and energy are devoted to staying alive. Therefore they have less temptation to be wasteful, self-indulgent or too attached to worldly possessions.

He mentioned that many Indian women have trunks and drawers full of unused or rarely worn saris. Since only a limited number can be worn during the week, the others are being wasted. Likewise, men should cut down on expensive habits such as card playing, gambling, drinking, and other pursuits that waste time, money and energy.

Another area of extravagance he referred to was the custom of giving elaborate and expensive dinners to entertain guests who could well afford to feed themselves. He advised that the money thus saved be used to feed the poor who have no one to care for them.

Next he referred to expensive travel as wasteful and suggested that a train could often be substituted for a plane. Hotels, too, need not be of the most expensive class, since they are generally used only for sleeping. However, he added with a twinkle, he was not recommending that people stay in rooms with cockroaches running around on the floor. He was obviously implying that very careful consideration should be given to all factors involved before making a choice, to avoid extremes.

His next statement really surprised me. Time, he said, is a commodity shared by everyone in the world in exactly the same amount. Everyone has at their disposal just twenty-four hours each day. I, for one, had never thought of it in that way until he pointed it out. He added that time wasted can never be retrieved; it is gone forever. He observed that most people waste a great deal of time every day in idle and meaningless pursuits which also distract them from following the path towards liberation. He listed such activities as attending unedifying films, reading trashy novels and magazines, drinking and gambling, and stressed that indulging in unnecessary chatter and gossip not only wastes time, but is the chief cause of wasted energy. He likened it to pouring water into a sieve. The valuable water is lost by being dispersed in all directions instead of channeled for use in a specific cause.

Lastly, he advised that indulging in such negative emotions as anger, greed, envy and jealousy uses up vast amounts of energy which could more profitably be used in positive ways. He referred to the common habit of making countless excuses for having too little time and energy to spare for regular meditation and, even more important, for service. With the proposed program and its clearly defined guidelines it should be possible to cut down on waste in all four areas and use the money, food, time, and energy thus saved to help some of the needy people in the world.

He then asked for the article I had written at Jack Hislop's request. He riffled through the pages and handed it to Mr. Narasimhan telling him to read it and give him a report. But now that Baba had personally outlined the program into four clearly

220 / Phyllis Krystal

defined parts, I was even more convinced that the article needed to be simplified. I only hoped that Jack had received my hasty note before he sent it in to the U.S. Newsletter.

Before we left his presence Baba asked how much longer we were planning to stay. When we told him he said that, in that case, there would be time for us to go with him to Puttaparthi and that he would let us know which day he would be leaving so that we could follow.

As I was thinking back over everything he had said in the interview to be sure I would remember it accurately, I was reminded of a very vivid dream of more than a year ago which now appeared even more significant. I had dreamed I was going to be married to Baba. I watched as he materialized a wedding ring for me in the form of a simple gold band studded with pieces of coral. As he handed it to me he looked very pointedly at me and said that it was very costly, as it contained precious stones. In the dream I was puzzled by this observation, as I knew that coral is not considered a precious stone, and nor is it very expensive. Baba seemed to read my thoughts and was very definite as he repeated his statement. He told me I could keep it but warned me not to wear it yet.

As soon as I awakened I immediately understood what he meant when I was reminded of a reverie I had many years ago. In that inner experience I seemed to be jumping back and forth between two very large mountains. When I landed on one I saw that it was composed of hard sharp rocks and crags which could cut and bruise me if I stayed too long. I quickly jumped back onto the other one only to discover that it was covered with deep snow into which I could sink and be smothered if I remained there. So back I jumped onto the craggy one, and alternated back and forth between them. I was shown that the craggy mountain symbolized the intellect and the snow covered one the emotions. I had been alternating between these two ways of functioning all my life. I was then directed to look down between the two mountains where I saw a third mountain which I had never suspected was there. It was not as high as the other two, and when I asked what it symbolized I received the answer that it was composed of the skeletons of all my released desires, either for things I wanted or the reverse, for things I did not want. I looked at it more carefully and was reminded of a coral reef composed of the skeletons of the tiny sea creatures known as coral polyps. It represented a state of knowing, neither solely feeling nor thinking, but the two blending. This mountain was beautifully green and dotted with thousands of lovely little wild flowers. As soon as I became willing to land on it instead of continuing to jump back and forth, it started to grow higher towards the sun and sky. I saw, as I let go of my desires, that it could eventually reach the sun, a symbol of the God force, with which I could merge and be released from the pull of all the pairs of opposites which keep us chained to the wheel of rebirth.

The dream of Baba giving me the coral-studded wedding band to mark my marriage to him must mean that when I finally release all my desires I would marry him or merge with him in my heart. Yes, the ring was certainly very costly, as each piece of coral represented a desire I needed to release. Releasing desires sounds so much easier than it really is! We all cling so tightly to what we think we need, and resist so strongly those things we fear may overtake us.

At this point, all I can say is that I am nowhere near ready to wear the ring and marry the Baba in my heart, nor have I any idea how long it will take to reach that desireless state where this inner marriage could take place. But the promise is enough to keep me working on it. If this applies to me it is also equally true for everyone who chooses the inner union rather than attachment to outer security symbols.

When we had first arrived in Whitefield we noticed that several other guests were suffering from an intestinal disturbance causing severe abdominal pain and diarrhoea. A day or two after Baba materialized the *vibhuti* for my cold and changed my ring, the cold vanished overnight, only to be replaced by acute cramps and diarrhoea. I tried Lomotil, garlic pills and other remedies I carried with me, but to no avail. The ailment continued unabated. Little did I know then that it would do so for a whole year and a month!

Baba left early one morning for Puttaparthi and left a message for us to follow. During the drive, I happened to look down at my hands lying in my lap, and was astonished to see Baba's image distinctly visible in the depth of the sparkling white stone in my new ring. I looked more closely to be sure I was not imagining it, but there was the shock of black hair, his profile and golden robe, all very clearly visible. I was fascinated. I had heard that devotees sometimes see his reflection in a ring he has materialized for them, but I had never yet seen it myself. Now here I was quite unexpectedly having the experience. When he gave it to me he had said, "I am always with you," as he so often assures us. But he must also have meant he was always with me in the heart of the stone as a constant reminder of that. I was deeply touched at another instance of his awareness of each one's needs. We all so often need to be reminded of his eternal presence within our hearts. The pain and distress of my physical complaint were forgotten, overshadowed by this new manifestation of Baba's mystery.

In 1980, during the World Conference, we became donors of a room for our use when we were in Puttaparthi. Other devotees would be permitted to use it the rest of the time. When we arrived it was already occupied by other guests, so they were asked to move to another room. When we moved in, I discovered to my dismay, that the Western style toilet was broken, and could not be flushed. In my unfortunate condition that was a shock, compounded by the information that the broken part was not available. It had been ordered several weeks ago but had not yet arrived. My heart sank. I would have to fill plastic buckets from the tap in the wall and flush it manually. Various people offered me medication to stop the diarrhoea but having always been allergic to many drugs and chemicals I hesitated to risk becoming even more ill, with the seminar in England only a little more than a week away.

The day we were due to leave we were called to a farewell interview. We were the only Westerners in a group of twenty or more Indians. After Baba had ushered us all in and we were seated on the floor, he smilingly greeted us and, looking at me, announced to the entire group, "Mrs. Krystal has a bad stomach, haven't you, Mrs. Krystal?" Naturally, all eyes turned to look at me, which was, of course, his intention. He wanted to break me of my longtime horror of being singled out which is also a form of ego. Resistance and the more easily recognizable aggression both stem from desire. To desire recognition or seek to avoid it are both attached to ego. Baba is indeed a hard taskmaster to those who have asked for his help in freeing themselves from ego and attachment to desires.

When it was our turn for a private interview I remembered to tell him that I had also been asked to give a talk to the therapists at an English holistic cancer society in addition to the weekend seminar. I asked if he had any message about cancer which I could share with them. He nodded and said very slowly and seriously, "Cancer can only be cured by the grace of God and by love." He then discussed the book about him, and said it should be published in England like the first one and also in California. At that time we had no plans to publish in California.

When we asked, as usual, when to return, he really took us by surprise this time saying, "Do not come back until the 60th birthday. Too expensive to come sooner. Go home, finish the book, have it published and bring it with you for a dedication ceremony."

He then listed all my physical problems, "stomach, back, feet, eyes, head," etc. and promised to help with everything. I asked if the stomach condition was *karmic* and if so, would he please use it to cleanse away the negative *karmas*. He laughed aloud, knowing that I did not realize what I was asking. Then he said, "Forget all past lives now. I will help you."

With that promise we left his physical presence for two and a half years. I felt a sharp pang of regret that we should not be returning each year as we had been in the habit of doing for the past ten years. I have often observed that Baba discourages his devotees from becoming attached to a routine, and says, "Learn to find your security in my insecurity." We must learn to flow and be willing to change direction without warning, as we were now being asked to do.

During the drive back to Bangalore, I thought of all he had said. One thing which occurred to me was that, when he referred to a trip to India as expensive, he probably meant physically rather than financially. It was true that I returned each time feeling sick and exhausted. As we grow older it becomes increasingly strenuous to travel and live in primitive conditions for any length of time. I also suspected that he had work for me to do, and I was soon to discover how right that proved to be.

The diarrhoea continued. With the seminars and other talks still ahead of me, despite Baba's promise of help, I continued to have intermittent pangs of apprehension. I knew from my talk to Elsie Cowan's group that it would be useless to try to prepare ahead, even in note form. I would simply have to relax and ask the Baba within me to show me whatever needed to be said, and say whatever came into my head. But above all I must remember his statement that a group "is composed of one plus one plus one, which adds up to one, as all are one." So that was exactly what I did during the seminar on the Friday evening, all day Saturday, and all day Sunday. To my relief it really worked. The subjects just seemed to present themselves and the correct sequence was indicated by the various questions asked by members of the group. Another big hurdle had been successfully overcome with Baba's help.

Several other single talks, including the one for the cancer therapists, and others to Sai Baba groups, all followed the same pattern. Whenever I began to feel nervous, I would silently ask Baba what needed to be said next and the flow of words would resume. I repeatedly thanked him for his help and for prodding me to take the necessary steps to overcome this lifelong fear.

It was not until I started to write about the seminars for this book that I remembered a dream I had had several years earlier. In it Baba was sitting up on the platform in the auditorium at Prasanthi Nilayam facing the thousands of devotees who filled it to overflowing. I was lying on a slab in front of him while he carefully removed everything from inside me leaving an empty shell. When he had finished he lifted me up and told me to talk. I could not believe he was serious and remonstrated with him, telling him I had no motor and therefore could not move, and like a clockwork toy I would have to be wound up. He leaned forward and gave me a push, and to my surprise I was able to walk and talk. Now I can see that what I had experienced in the dream actually did happen. I was able to lean back and ask Baba to speak through me during the seminars and other talks. His counterpart within each of us is the master puppeteer who waits patiently for us to be ready and willing to hand over the strings of our puppet selves and allow him to motivate us according to his superior knowledge of what we need.

Towards the end of our stay in England, four of Baba's students from the college at Whitefield arrived in London escorted by Mr. Srinivasan of Madras. Baba had sent them on a short tour of London, Paris, and Geneva ending up in Rome where they were met by Mr. Craxi, an Italian devotee. A hall was quickly found where devotees from all over England gathered to welcome Baba's emissaries. The boys' speeches, singing of *bhajans*, and obvious devotion to Baba and his mission and message to the world were an inspiration to everyone there. It was a wonderful way to end our stay in England.

CHAPTER TWENTY-SIX

WHEN WE ARRIVED home I was relieved to find that the article on the ceiling on desires program had been posted but had not yet been printed in the Newsletter. I was in time to retrieve it, and broke it up into separate installments to bring it into line with Baba's recent instructions.

During the interview on his ceiling on desires program I wondered why Baba was going into such detail. Then one day when I was asked to conduct a workshop on that program for the yearly Sai retreat in our area, my mind went back to our very first visit when Baba had materialized the moonstone ring. He had told me to rub it on my third eye to remove the cause of the headaches in the area brought over from the life as a Tibetan monk. Of course! Now I understood! In that life the monk had retired to a cell to concentrate on becoming detached from his desires. Release from desire must have been the lesson from that incarnation, but it was cut off by the premature death. Now I was being allowed to continue the task so abruptly interrupted, and in addition, share some of my insights with other devotees. Here again was another deeper meaning to Baba's words and actions than I had perceived when he gave me the ring. As soon as I had gained this clearer perspective, I was able to approach the talks and articles as a sacred duty which would also help me to work out old *karmas* and thus further my own spiritual development.

Meanwhile, the diarrhoea persisted. I consulted many doctors and had numerous tests for possible parasites, but none were detected. The condition remained a mystery, made even more puzzling by the fact that I lost no weight.

Not long after we returned home we heard that Baba had directed Mr. Antonio Craxi to organize a World Conference in Rome on October 30 and 31, 1983. The theme was to be "Unity is Divinity, Purity is Enlightenment." The conference had been preceded in the two previous years by a large *satsang*, or gathering or devotees, at the Craxis' spacious estate near Milan. These had been so successful that Baba chose to have the first public exposure of his world mission outside India take place in Rome, one of the most historic cities in the Western world. We decided to participate in it.

The conference was attended not only by hundreds of eagerly enthusiastic and dedicated Italians, but by representatives of the rapidly growing Sai family from thirty-four other countries. It was a most impressive sight to see each of their national flags hanging side by side along the front of the stage in the huge auditorium. The flags held out the promise of a new and very different league of nations, quietly coming into existence in a world weary of strife and turmoil.

Baba is the initiator of such gatherings, but he needs people as tools through whom to bring them to fruition. Antonio and Sylvie Craxi and their band of dedicated helpers worked tirelessly, harmoniously and self effacingly to carry out Baba's plan to make this first international symposium outside India a success in every sense of the word.

In Baba's inspiring message, read by Mr. Craxi, he stressed the fact that the divinity that pervades society can only be revealed through individuals who do not identify with their bodies, but know that their reality is the God which resides in each and every one of their hearts. As the symposium proceeded, as if on oiled wheels, the theme unfolded as a reality before our eyes. All those present, whether visitors or workers, concentrated on Baba, who was thus able to infuse and direct the whole gathering by working through his counterpart within each individual.

In his message, Baba quoted the ancient saying, "All roads lead to Rome." But he cautioned us that we had gathered in that historic city not to enjoy a Roman holiday for two days, or to make a few new acquaintances, but to derive inspiration from these new ideals about the human adventure.

All old cities throughout their long history have seen their share of violence and negativity, and Rome is no exception. It therefore seemed significant that the symposium was held at the time of All Souls Day when prayers are offered for the souls of all who have departed this physical plane.

Two dreams I had several months before the conference seem to have a direct relation to it. In the first dream I seemed to be floating in space looking down at the world. I was shocked and saddened to see so many areas where strife and warfare were erupting, creating dark clouds of hate and fear which blotted out the beautiful landscapes. As I looked around, off in the distance I became aware of a rainbow colored stream gently bubbling up and flowing in all directions like long ribbons of multicolored light. As I watched it expand I knew it was emanating from Prasanthi Nilayam, and that each color represented a positive emotion such as joy, love, hope and compassion—the opposites of fear, anger and hate which formed dark clouds throughout the earth's atmosphere.

The second dream came several weeks later. In it I saw Baba dancing as if on a dot, alternating as Nataraj and Krishna, his arms, legs, and head all moving to an inner hidden rhythm. It was an extraordinary spectacle, and as I watched fascinated and awestruck, I noticed wave after wave of rainbow colored light emanating from his body and flowing out in long ribbons all over India and out into the rest of the world. As I continued to watch I saw that these colored streamers encircled the dark patches I had seen in the previous dream, and gradually absorbed them, replacing them with the rainbow hued light. The tempo of the dance accelerated until a rainbow encircled the whole world.

I then recalled hearing how the late Joel Riordan announced skeptically, shortly after arriving on his first visit to Baba, that he would only believe that Baba was God if he could materialize a rainbow, as only God could make a rainbow. A few days later, Joel saw the perfect arc of a rainbow in the cloudless Indian sky. Baba asked him how he liked it.

A rainbow has always traditionally symbolized the hope of peace after a storm. In Rome we all experienced another of Baba's rainbows like a long tendril reaching from him in India and reflected in all our hearts. It reminds us of his promise to raise the consciousness not only of India but of the whole world. He is giving us hope and allowing all, who so choose, to seek his will rather than follow the dictates of the ego and to participate in this revolution. The transformation takes place not only on the level of society but on the individual level as well. The message for me in Rome was to let Baba dance his dance in each of our hearts. In so doing he can fill us with love, joy, and the hope of removing such negative emotions as anger, hate and fear, first in us and then in the world. In this way each of us can be like a ray of light helping to raise and lighten the atmosphere of the planet.

At about the same time as the announcement of the Rome Conference, Baba had given instructions for the American Sai centers to start organizing open public meetings to introduce him and his teachings to a larger audience. It was clear that he was getting ready to bring his message to the rest of the world. He has said that on his sixtieth birthday he will announce his special mission to bring balance into the world chaos fast accelerating everywhere.

One day, while in a reverie, I was given a most moving and revealing insight into the seriousness of the world situation. I had the distinct impression that Baba suddenly appeared in my inner scene and was beckoning me to follow him. He led me to a higher vantage point from which I had a clear view of the whole world spread out below. I heard his voice in my head saying, "Now I will show you the real heart bypass." I wondered what that could mean. He then pointed down to the earth and I saw superimposed over it, the outline of a huge human figure. It reminded me of the diagrams in books on *yoga* illustrating the locations on the human body of the seven *chakras*, each represented as a wheel of light. Baba indicated on this world sized body that there is very little connection between the heart *chakra* and the others. As he traced the pathways with his finger I could see very clearly that they were either partially blocked or closed off altogether. I began to understand what he meant, for the heart was indeed bypassed at the world level, preventing love from flowing out from its natural source, the heart. Love therefore has to be expressed through the head, throat, solar plexus or power center, or the lower centers, particularly the sexual one. I realized how true this was on an individual personal level. People think their love or fantasize about it, talk about it and say that they love, but often without real feeling. Some use so called love to control others, transfer it to material things, or confuse it with sexual desire.

Baba continued to show me that in past ages, when men periodically close off their hearts, engaged in wars and violence, the majority of the women continued to act out their role as the nurturing and loving members of society, thus preserving a partial balance. However, their true role became vitiated as they were relegated to a position of less value than men, who used them primarily to satisfy their physical desires. In recent years women have rebelled, but have often mistakenly chosen to mimic men in an effort to be their equals and in so doing have also cut off their own emotions. The result is the sorry plight of this loveless world, with all the attendant problems of violence, crime, incest and child abuse, addictions and promiscuity, and all the other miseries with which we are faced. So this is the mark of *Kali Yuga*.

"What can we do?" I asked. As if in answer I recalled that Baba has assured us that as in past years when the world was seriously out of balance, a divine *Avatar* has come forth to remedy the situation. How often has he declared that his mission is to bring about harmony in the entire world? "But what can we do?" I persisted. The answer was that the women of the world must be willing to lead the way by reconnecting themselves to their ancient heritage. They must be channels through whom the divine love can flow into the world to bring about a balance.

I was reminded of our experience of being hijacked and Baba's instruction to send love to the two hate filled men, and of his later assurance that the plane was saved by being filled with his love. We must all allow Baba to use us to fill the world with his love as he was able to save the planeload of people by using just one person.

In line with his various plans for bringing about balance and harmony in the world, Baba has also initiated a worldwide Education in Human Values Program to ensure that future generations will be trained to continue the work thus started. This program has developed out of the Bal Vikas course for children of devotees which for many years has provided instruction in right living as set forth in India's priceless heritage of ancient wisdom. This course was adapted and is now being taught in the Indian primary schools. Devotees in other countries are also starting to introduce it into their own schools to fill the need for moral education in addition to reviving and strengthening their own spiritual traditions.

CHAPTER TWENTY-SEVEN

WHEN I FIRST went to see Sai Baba I wondered if he was going to be my next teacher. The years since then have proved that he has taught me more than I could ever have hoped for or imagined. He has also corroborated, continued and augmented the teachings I had been receiving from the inner source of wisdom. His very presence in the world makes contact with that God part more tangible and therefore more available. It reminds me of the difference between turning on the radio or television at random, hoping to tune into the desired program, and knowing with certainty how to dial the correct channel.

However, I am acutely aware that this very personal account of my experience with Baba can reveal only a minute fraction of him and his power and love which are limitless. Nor can his entire reality be reduced to fit into his little physical body residing in India.

He says, "The *Avatar* has come as a man among men and moves among them as a friend, well wisher, kinsman, guide, teacher, healer and participant." But all the experiences of the countless thousands who have been touched by him in any or all those ways, if added together, would still not provide a complete or accurate picture of him.

He tells us that we cannot possibly understand him and that we should not even try. All that any of us can do is to be willing to let him reveal as much of himself as we are able to receive and absorb at any given time. In this book I have tried to show that step by step process in my life. But I hope that I have also made it clear that although I have tried to be as open as possible to receive his teachings, it has often taken me a very long time first to understand and accept them and then to endeavor to put them into practice in everyday life.

I continue to marvel at the patience, tolerance, forbearance, steadfastness and compassion he has shown at all times. I am certain that my experiences are not unique and are shared by thousands of other devotees. Yet, he never appears to be frustrated or impatient, like most parents with their children.

However, there is always a danger that such loving attention can be a serious pitfall if it has the effect of inflating a person's ego. What is more likely to make someone feel superior than to have a divine *avatar* speak to him, smile at him and materialize gifts for him? Yet Baba never tires of insisting that the innate God force is our only reality and to that extent we are all equal and one with it. Only our outer bodies and personalities are different. This is his primary message and everything he does or says to people is designed to make them consciously aware of this message. Since he knows exactly what will bring each one to this awareness that we all embody God, we need only to trust him to supply the means by which to shed the many thick layers composed of our desires which obscure the inner light.

His parting injunction to me at our first farewell interview still reverberates in my mind. I must remember that it is not necessary to go to India to see his little body. I must find him in my heart.

But how are we to put into practice? I was shown a simple method to use to develop awareness of the divine spark both within ourselves and others.

During a meditation Baba appeared and pointed to the heart of a person who seemed to become transparent as I watched. Clearly perceptible in the heart was a gold nugget. Baba indicated that everyone possesses this potential, but that as soon as a person comes under his influence or starts to follow a spiritual path the gold nugget becomes alive, like a glowing ember. We can use our own built in bellows to encourage it to burn more brightly by mentally directing each exhalation towards our heart. This will increase our capacity to reflect more light and will help us to see the potential light in everyone without exception.

The following verses flowed very quickly into my mind one day. They seem to me a fitting summation of Baba's message.

I love you all every single one
For deep within I see
Beneath the ego layers
Your own Divinity.

No one of you is special
Or more lovable to me
For each of you possesses
Your own Divinity.

So don't compete with others
To seek security

When my love you have already
From your own Divinity.

Direct my love to others
Who are blind and cannot see
The love they seek so desperately
Is their own Divinity.

For as you seek in everyone
The counterpart of me
You'll start to open up your hearts
To your own Divinity.

GLOSSARY

Abbreviations used:
Hin = Hindi
Pus =Pushtu
Skr = Sanskrit
Tam = Tamil
Tel = Telegu

A

abhishéka (Skr): anointing, inaugurating or consecrating by sprinkling water or other sacred substance.

ananda (Skr): happiness, joy; enjoyment, pleasure. Also "pure happiness," one of the three attributes of Brahman and/or atman.

Arjuna (Skr): lit. white, clear. Name of one of the five heroic Pandava brothers in the Mahabharata.

ashram(a) (Skr): a hermitage, the abode of ascetics. Popularly used to mean the establishment of and around a spiritual master/mistress where his/her disciples and devotees may gather and/or reside for spiritual inspiration and development.

atcha (Hin): (also acha, achha) good. A colloquial equivalent of well, very well, all right.

atma(n) (Skr): the self, the individual self, the abstract individual; divine essence in all beings; principle of life, the highest principle in life. The nearest Occidental equivalent is the Latin *auto*.

AUM (Skr): (sometimes Om, its written symbol is ॐ) the mystic monosyllable representing the Divine, said to be the sound of the Universe or cosmos, as also that of creation and divinity.

avatar(a) (Skr): lit. descent, entrance; incarnation and reincarnation. In this context always and exclusively used to express a divine incarnation.

B

Bhagavad-Gita (Skr): lit. God's song. Name given to the celebrated mystical poem (an episode given in the Mahabharata) in which Krishna expounds on dharma to explain Arjuna's dharma as a warrior to him as he reluctantly faces his enemies on the battlefield of Kurukshetra (sometimes referred to as Dharmakshetra).

bhajan (Skr): reverence, worship, adoration. Hence its later usage, in languages derived from Sanskrit, as the singing of and the songs of worship. Used as devotional songs throughout this work.

bhaktí (Skr): attachment or devotion, fondness for God; trust, homage, worship; piety; faith or love or devotion to a particular deity or guru. Most usually faith.

bhôga (Skr): enjoyment; consumption, consummation.

Brahma (Skr): lit. to go, to move. The creating deity of the Hindu Trinity of Brahma, Vishnu and Shiva.

Brahma(n) (Skr): the one self-existent Spirit, the Absolute. The impersonal spirit.

C

chakra (Skr): a circle; an astrological circle (zodiac); a mystical circle or diagram; a wheel. A term borrowed by Patanjali, as others, to describe the centers of energy in the human frame. Only this derived meaning is attached to it in this work.

chôli (Hin): bodice, brassière. Name given to the blouse worn under a sari.

D

darshan(a) (Skr): seeing, looking at; perception; view, doctrine, philosophical system. In this context always used to express the reverential and devotional seeing and gazing upon (as a blessing) of the Master.

dharma (Skr): that which is established and firm; law, statute, ordinance; usage, practice, prescribed conduct; duty; right, justice; virtue, morality, religion. Ethical precepts. Righteous divine order.

dhyana (Skr): meditation, thought, reflection, especially profound and abstract spiritual or religious meditation. Also attention and focus of attention. Here used solely as meditation in the Zen sense.

G

Gíta (Skr): song. The popular contraction for the Bhagavad-Gíta (which see).

gokulam (Skr): a family (herd) of cows, cattle. Hence a cow–house, stables; where cows are housed.

guna (Skr): a quality, peculiarity, attribute or property. Attributes of the five elements. The three attributes constituent in all beings, e.g. sattva, rajas and tamas (goodness, passion and inertia; or virtue, vice and ignorance).

guru (Skr): a spiritual parent or preceptor.

H

Hindi (Hin): language of northern India derived from Sanskrit, pre-eminently of the Gangetic Plain, also of neighboring regions, using the Devanagari script.

I

Idlí (Tam): a bread or bread roll made of rice flour in certain parts of southern India.

J

japa (Skr): to utter in a low voice, whisper, mutter, especially prayers or incantations, in a continuous and concentrated way.

japamala (Skr): a rosary used for counting muttered or inwardly expressed prayers, traditionally made of beads of a substance held to be auspicious and/or propitious.

jhoola (Hin): (also jhula) a swing, a hammock.

K

kaftan (Pus): a full length gown or robe with long sleeves worn by Afghan, Pathan and Central Asian women. Stylized summery version are widely available in southern Asian bazaars now.

Kali Yuga (Skr): the last of a cycle of four yugas (ages) after which a new cycle begins. The present is said to be in the Kali

Yuga. It is an age in which human negativity reaches a peak, giving rise to agitation in individual minds, collective unrest, conflicts, wars, extremes of materialism and frequent and widespread destruction.

karma(n) (Skr): act, action, performance, business; occupation, obligation; work, labor, activity (as opposed to inactivity); action as motion. The Occident uses it to signify only those acts leading to inevitable results, the certain consequences of acts in a previous life, as in the so called theory or law of karma—which is the meaning attached to it in this work.

karma yôga (Skr): performance of work or business, especially duties and acts of a religious nature. Also one of the four ways or paths of the yôga philosophy, that of realizing divinity through work and activity. (The other three are bhakti, jnana and raja yogas.)

karma yôgi (Skr): a follower of karma yôga. More generally one whose activity and work are both selfless and destined and intended to better the material and/or spiritual condition of others.

karmic (Skr): lit. engaged in action. In the West it is used in an adjectivial form for an act leading to consequences in another life, as also the effects of such an act in an anterior life in another body and identity.

Krishna (Skr): lit. black, dark, dark blue. Name of the 8th avatara of Vishnu.

kundalini (Skr): (from snake) word used to describe the latent energy or force in man said to be coiled in its quiescent form at the base of the spinal column, and rising along it to the extent that it is consciously developed and activated.

L

leela (Skr): (also líla) play, sport, amusement; mere appearance, semblance, pretence; grace, charm, loveliness. In this work, divine play, divine amusement, divine charm.

linga(m) (Skr): sign, token, badge, emblem, symbol; characteristic; an indication. Popularly, as in this work, used to denote a sphere (ovoid) symbolic of creation, customarily worshipped in relation to Shiva.

M

maha (Skr): great, greater.

Mahabharata (Skr): the great war of the Bharatas, or the narrative thereof. An epic work of about 216,000 lines said to have been composed and complied by the sage Vyasa.

Mahashivaratrí (Skr): lit. the night of Great Shiva. A winter festival of the Hindus celebrated at a particular new moon, when the mind is said to be the least agitated, facilitating conscious awareness of eternal truth.

mala (Skr): a wreath, garland; a string of beads, necklace, rosary.

mama (Skr): my, mine.

mandala (Skr): circular, round; anything round; the orbit of a heavenly body, the circle of influence of a state, king or other powerful entity; a division or book of the Rig Veda; tantric diagrams, usually circular, said to have or to generate mystic potency. C. G. Jung has taken the last usage, chiefly from Tibetan tantrism, and applied its sole meaning to the word, limiting its application to the present (psychoanalytic) understanding prevalent in the West, even popularly.

mandir (Skr): (also mandeer) temple.

mangala(m) (Skr): happiness, felicity, welfare; anything auspicious or intended to lead to felicity, e.g. a good omen, a prayer, or solemn ceremony on important occasions.

mangala sutra (Skr): lit. happy thread. The beaded thread given to the bride by the bridegroom symbolizing a happy union and worn by the wife until her husband's death. A Hindu custom.

mantra(m) (Skr): lit. instrument of thought. Speech, sacred text, a prayer or song of praise; a Vedic hymn or formula addressed to a personal deity or to the impersonal spirit. The utterance must be perfect, in rhythm, tone, pronunciation and attitude, in order to obtain the beneficent effects.

maya (Skr):   illusion, unreality; apparition. It is regarded in some Hindu philosophic systems as the source of the subjectively visible world.

N

namaskar(am) (Skr):   the gesture accompanying the oral greeting, namasté, made with both hands, palms together, held in front of one. Also a Hindi word.

O

OM: see AUM.

P

panchalôha (Skr):   lit. five metals. It is a metallic alloy made of five minerals said to be auspicious—copper, brass, tin, lead and iron; or gold, silver, copper, tin and lead.

pranayama (Skr):   a yogic exercise for controlling, circulating and regulating the breath undertaken only for spiritual aims and only at the guru's direction.

prasad (Skr):   lit. clearness, brightness, purity; calmness, tranquillity, serenity; graciousness, kindness, favor, aid; free gift. Food offered to a deity or the remnants of food left by a spiritual preceptor (as such, blessed food or gift is believed to confer the above qualities).

puja (Skr):   honor, worship, respect, reverence, veneration, homage to superiors or adoration of the gods. In Hindi, also the collection of objects of worship, as well as the ceremony or rite performed in worship.

R

rajas (Skr):   endowed with or influenced by the quality of passion, passionate. The 2nd or middle guna or constituent of Prakrití which activates and agitates a person's mind to the detriment of equanimity; in a thing it is heat, force.

Rama (Skr):   lit. pleasing, pleasant. Name of the 7th avatara of Vishnu.

S

sadhaka (Skr): effective, efficient, productive of (an aim); accomplishing, fulfilling, finishing, perfecting; an assistant; an adept, a skilful person; a worshipper. Used her to denote a pupil of spirituality.

sadhana (Skr): accomplishment, performance; the means of mastering, overpowering, subduing; any means of effecting or accomplishing (one's aim), any agent or instrument or implement or utensil or apparatus; an expedient, a requisite for. Finding out through the instrumentality of the mind or intellect, abstract instrumentality. Here used in this last sense for spiritual efforts, endeavors and disciplines.

sadhu (Skr): lit. straight, right; successful, effective. Therefore used as a noun to denote he/she who is as above, i.e. a holy man/woman, saint, sage, seer, hermit.

samadhi (Skr): putting together, joining or combining with; union; completion, conclusion. Intense application, fixing the mind on, concentration of the thoughts, profound or abstract meditation, the state reached thereby. Word used for the self–willed "death" of spiritually evolved masters. Also used for the monument, memorial or tomb of such an eminent personage.

samiti (Skr): (also samithi) an assembly, council; association, society for specific aim/s.

sankalpa (Skr): conception or idea or notion formed in the mind or heart, especially will, volition, purpose, definite intention or determination or decision; an act of will power.

Sanskrit (Skr): lit. completely formed, perfected; consecrated, hallowed; refined, polished. Name given to the classical language of the ancient Aryans for being and possessing all the above qualities; regarded as a sacred language as the major part, especially the sources, of Hindu scripture is written in it. Devanagari script.

sari (Hin): a 6- or 9-yard length of material worn by Indian (Hindu) women, originating in Dravidian India and adopted by a significant minority or women in other parts of India since the late 19th century.

sat (Skr):   being, existing; therefore lasting, enduring; good.

satsang (Skr):   intercourse or association with the good (sat = good; sang = company, group).

sattva (Skr):   being, existence, reality; true essence, nature, disposition of mind, character. Also the highest of the three gunas or constituents of Prakrití because it renders a person true, honest, wise; and a thing pure and clean.

satya (Skr):   (also sathya) true, real, actual, genuine, sincere, honest, truthful, faithful, pure, virtuous, good; valid.

satyam (Skr):   (also sathyam) truth, reality; virtuous act and effect; goodness; validity. That which is (without beginning or end), permanence.

seva (Skr):   service.

shastiabda (Skr):   lit. the 60–year cycle of Guru (Jupiter); hence a 60th anniversary of something good and/or elevating. In Hindi it is shashtiabdi.

Shiva (Skr):   lit. auspicious, propitious, benign, benevolent. The Auspicious One is the disintegrating or destroying and reproducing deity of the Hindu Trinity of Brahma, Vishnu and Shiva.

shrama (Skr):   fatigue, weariness, exhaustion of the body or mind (as a result of struggling). (So ashrama is a negation of sharama.)

siddhí (Skr):   accomplishment, performance, fulfilment, complete attainment. Hence popularly, especially outside India, a supernatural ability (attained through yôga or other spiritual effort), a yogic, spiritual or meditational attainment of a marvelous nature incomprehensible to physical science.

Shivaratrí (Skr):   lit. the night of Shiva. A popular contraction of Mahashivaratrí (which see).

stupa (Skr):   a round structure; sacred monument erected above or encircling a Buddhic relic. Popularly a dome shaped structure or rounded column associated with a god or gods or with religion and/or spirituality.

sutra (Skr): a thread, yarn, string, line, cord, wire. Fig. a scriptural theme, or scripture expounding a single line of thought, belief, discipline or prayer. Also a philosophical term for identical writings.

T

tamas (Skr): ignorant, inert, dull. The third and lowest guna or constituent of Prakrití which invests the mind with sloth keeping it in darkness; in things it is lifelessness.

tapas (Skr): lit. heat, warmth. Fig. the practice of austerities for spiritual aims. Colloquially used to denote any seemingly fruitless effort to reach a difficult (religious or spiritual) goal.

Télegu (Tel): (also Télugu) a principally Dravidian language influenced by Sanskritic forms spoken mainly in (Telengana) the state of Andhra Pradésh (therefore in Puttaparthi).

V

vibhutí (Skr): manifestation of might; great superhuman power. By extension that which is produced by or through such might or power. In this context, as popularly, sacred ash (in the specific context a miraculous result/effect of Sri Sathya Sai Baba's superhuman power).

vibhuti abhisheka (Skr): lit. anointing with the miraculous. In this context, the sacred ash (aptly, miraculously manifested) being sprinkled over an object of worship. Ordinarily, the term is used for the everyday sprinkling of puja idols with sacred ash (non-miraculously produced).

Vishnu (Skr): lit. all-pervader, the cosmic atom. The preserving and sustaining deity of the Hindu Trinity of Brahma, Vishnu and Shiva. As such, it is he who incarnates on earth when the balance of civilized ethos is weighed down by negativity.

Y

yagna (Skr): worship devotion, prayer, praise (of God); also act of worship or devotion, offering, oblation, sacrifice. In contemporary India, the word has taken on the added quality of pomp and circumstance in relation to the performance of the above acts.

yôga (Skr): the act of yoking, joining, attaching. Hence, name given to a system of developing the connection with the Divine, pre-eminently the system of Patanjali.

Yogi(n) (Skr): joined or connected with. Hence, a term for a man who has achieved union with the Divine. Popularly, any man who practices yoga and/or yogic postures. The feminine is yogini.

yuga (Skr): a period, age, or astronomical cycle; an age of the world. In this work the 2nd definition is preferred.

Phyllis Krystal is a psychotherapist. She was born in England but lives and works in California where she has developed her own techniques of psychotherapy. For over thirty years, she has been developing a counseling method using symbols and visualization techniques that help people detach from external authority figures and patterns in order to rely on their own Higher Consciousness as guide and teacher. To teach the method, Krystal gives lectures and seminars in the U. S., Europe, England, New Zealand, Tasmania, South America and Australia. She is a devotee of Sathya Sai Baba, A world-renowned avatar living in India whose teachings and personal influence have been an inspiration. She is author of *Cutting the Ties That Bind, Cutting More Ties That Bind, Cutting the Ties That Bind Workbook, Taming Our Monkey Mind* and *Reconnecting the Love Energy,* also published by Weiser.